W Vogdes

THE LIFE

OF

NATHANAEL GREENE,

MAJOR-GENERAL IN THE ARMY OF THE REVOLUTION.

EDITED BY

W. GILMORE SIMMS, Esq.,

AUTHOR OF "LIFE OF MARION," "CAPT. JOHN SMITH," ETC.

NEW YORK:

DERBY & JACKSON, 119 NASSAU ST.,

1859.

STEREOTYPED BY C. C. SAVAGE,
13 Chambers Street, N. Y.

ADVERTISEMENT.

In examining and revising for the publishers the manuscript of the present work, the editor has consulted nearly all the volumes which promised to have any bearing upon the subject. He has had before him the copious biographical sketches of Johnson, and the several volumes of Lee, Ramsay, Moultrie, Marshall, Tarleton, Graydon, and others, not forgetting the very graceful memoir of Greene, from the pen of his grandson, recently published in the collection of Sparks. In reference to the latter writer, he begs leave to express the hope that he will persevere in the intention of giving to the public a more elaborate performance on the same subject. There is much that is obscure in the history, much that is provocative of discussion, and needing to be discussed, which the narrow limits of a duodecimo must necessarily exclude. Who better prepared than himself to do justice to the great public services and private worth of his grandsire?

CONTENTS.

CHAPTER VII.

CHAPTER VIII.

CHAPTER IX.

CHAPTER X.

CHAPTER XI.

CHAPTER XII.

CHAPTER XIII.

CHAPTER XIV.

CHAPTER XV.

CHAPTER XVI.

CHAPTER XVII.

CHAPTER XVIII.

CHAPTER XIX.

CHAPTER XX.

CHAPTER XXI.

CHAPTER XXII.

CHAPTER XXIII.

CHAPTER XXIV.

CHAPTER XXV.

APPENDIX.

LIFE

OF

NATHANAEL GREENE.

CHAPTER I.

Introductory.—Family of Greene.—His Early Education.—Occupation.—Studies.—Intimacies.—Resolution and Strength of Character.

THE events which brought about the separation of the American colonies of Great Britain from the mother-country, have, somewhat improperly, we think, gone under the general name of revolution. We should prefer to substitute for this word, that of *transition*, as denoting a natural progress in history, rather than such an extreme and violent change as is implied by the term in most familiar use. To the thoughtful and philosophic mind there was nothing extreme or improbable — nothing which the political seer might not readily have foreseen — in the progress of opinion and necessity, in America, to that final action which severed the ungenial ligaments, which, from ties had grown into bonds, by which the colonies were united to the mother-country. Their growth and population, the gradually unfolding resources of their territories, the embarrassments which attended their political intercourse with Great Britain, the pecuniary exactions of the parent empire, and, above all, the humiliating character of the relation in which they stood to a country which claimed to govern them from abroad, and by those who were not indigenous to the soil—subjecting the native mind to a denial at once degrading to its character, and ruinous to the national interests—were sufficient reasons by which the separation could have been and was foreshown. The emancipation of the Americans from foreign rule, was the natural consequence of increasing numbers, and enlarged intelligence. The infant had grown into manhood. It was capable of going alone; and the impulse which sundered the leading-strings by which its movements were confined, was the fruit of a simple progress, step by step upward, to the possession and the exercise of a natural and inevitable strength. It was the great good fortune of the Americans that such was the case in their history—that there was no abrupt or premature outbreak which would have found them too weak for a struggle, which, under such a circumstance, would only have served to rivet their bands more firmly, and prolong the term of their endurance. This must have been the event had their history been that of a revolution—a change rather than a progress. But the progress found them prepared with all the necessary resources. Their numbers were not inadequate to the struggle; the intelligence of the people made the necessity for it a familiar and expanding thought; and, when, in course of time, they could evolve from their own ranks, statesmen and warriors who were capable of their government as an independent nation, it was permitted, as in the case of the Israelites—when they could boast of prophets, like Moses and Aaron, equal to any of the Egyptian magi—that they should be conducted out of bondage. When Virginia could produce such great men as Washington, Patrick Henry, and Jefferson; Massachusetts, Hancock and Adams; and

Carolina, her Marions, Moultries, and Rutledges—there was surely no proper necessity to look to a foreign country for the sage or soldier. It is the curious and conclusive fact in our history, at the beginning of the struggle for independence, that it found all the colonies in possession of some one or more remarkably endowed persons to whom the conduct of their affairs in council, and of their honor in the field, might be confided safely. Among the men thus constituting the moral stock of character with which the great national movement was begun, it is the boast of Rhode Island to have made one of the most valuable contributions, in the person of Nathanael Greene.

The family of Greene was English. It left the old for the new world somewhere in the seventeenth century, one branch of the family settling at Plymouth, whence it subsequently removed to Providence river; while the other established itself in the township of Warwick, upon lands procured from the Narraganset Indians. Here, upon the banks of the stream which still bears the aboriginal name of Potowhommett, Nathanael Greene, the third in descent from John, the original settler, built himself a mill and forge. The occupation of the blacksmith seems to have been in no wise detrimental to the social position of the family. They were among the first European settlers of the country; their career was marked by usefulness, and was not without its distinctions. John Greene, the founder of the family, was one of the colonists who appeared in the first permanent organization of the province under the charter of Charles the Second, and others of its members rose to offices of dignity and trust in the administration of the affairs of the colony. In new settlements, which suffer from a thousand influences of which a high condition of civilization affords no just idea, the distinguishing merit of the citizen must necessarily be his usefulness. He who, in such a condition of society, is prepared to meet and to overcome even its meanest necessities, is a benefactor, and in just degree with the importance of his service will be his social distinctions. Nathanael Greene, the sire, suffered accordingly no diminution of rank when he graced his arms with a sledge-hammer; and it is one of the honorable distinctions, in the descendant whose career is the subject of this volume, that he was duly taught to wield it also. The region in which this sway was maintained, on the waters of the Potowhommett, is still designated by filial pride, in connexion with this history; and the ancient mill itself, and the rude forge at which, father and son, the Greenes toiled, year by year, with praiseworthy perseverance, are still subjects of equal admiration and interest to all who delight in the upward rise of an ambition that founds its hopes entirely upon a compliance with the demands of duty. Here, too, stood the humble house of stone, a single story, in which Nathanael Greene, the subject of our memoir—the second of six sons by a second marriage—was born on the 27th of May, 1742. He was the fourth of eight sons whom the father raised to manhood. Of his infancy we know nothing. It was probably a somewhat cheerless one. His mother died when he was yet a child; and his father, as we may imagine, was something of a Spartan, in the guise of a quaker preacher. This venerable man is represented as filling the pulpit with rare ability; preaching with a force and eloquence, a simplicity and shrewdness, which continued to edify the meeting-house at East Greenwich for nearly forty years. The functions of a pastor, however earnestly prosecuted, found him in no degree forgetful of, or indifferent to, the domestic stewardship. His boys followed him at the forge and at the farm, and accompanied him to the place of prayer, with the most unvarying regularity. He was a rigid disciplinarian—an authority that never once suffered itself to be disputed, without testing the strength of the offender by the certainty of the punishment. Temperate and frugal himself, the training to which he subjected his boys—a training which was rather strict and rigid than severe—naturally produced similar habits among them; and they passed, by a natural progress, as they acquired strength for these several employments, through all the labors of the mill, the forge, and the farm, until they grew into athletic young men, healthy and vigorous of person, and calm and resolute of mind. In one respect, the education which Greene afforded to his sons was perhaps deficient. His own lessons had been simply religious. Of books, he knew none but the Bible, and regarded the sacred volume as superseding the necessity for every other. The humble elements of an English country-school, the lessons of which were sought only during the short, bleak days of winter, were not materially calculated to modify the effects of this education, which accordingly impressed itself upon the whole character and career of the subject of our memoir, in a manner which could not be mistaken. Hence the simplicity of his habits, the equable tone of his mind, his straightforwardness and integrity, the style in which he wrote, and the inflexibility of his purpose. These characteristics, however decidedly his own, were not entirely at variance with a mood which was gentle in its nature, and a disposition to society and its pleasantries. Young Greene was not indifferent to the sports of youth. The strictness of his training, in all probability increased their attractions in his eyes; and good limbs and an athletic constitution enabled him to excel in the usual amusements of a rustic life. He was chief among the actors in all rural sports; a leader among the revellers in all the wholesome and hearty enjoyments of the country; and quite an authority, at an early period, among his youthful associates,—proving clearly certain peculiar endowments in himself, which, by tacit consent, were admitted to have sway among their councils. Rustic superstition contributed to confirm this authority. His nativity was cast by a Doctor Spencer, who united the kindred professions of accoucheur and astrologer; and he predicted the future distinctions, disguised as usual in a happy generality, to which our hero was to attain. He was to be a mighty man in Israel.

The prediction promised to be verified. The deference which his young associates paid to his genius, extended to his stern and exemplary father. He was observed to yield to his wishes and opinions an attention which no other of the family could obtain. The natural ascendency of mind was felt in spite of the deficiencies of education. These deficiencies were of the extremest kind, and continued until our subject was fourteen years It was then that he formed an intimacy with a lad named Giles, a student of the university of Rhode Island, who spent his vacation at East Greenwich. This boy, who was probably only a clever sophomore, awakened in the mind of young Greene all its latent ambition. He made him a discontent, by showing him that there were other lessons which wisdom might teach, of importance to the career of man, beyond those, however valuable in themselves and vital, which took care of his spiritual interests. It was from this moment—and from the lesson so caught up—that Greene began to direct his attention to the acquisition of books. The shelves of his friends were ransacked with the view to the satiation of this newly-aroused appetite. The labors of his hands were voluntarily increased, that he might procure means to purchase the precious volumes which he could not otherwise obtain. His usual sports were foregone; the pleasures and toys of the child beguiled and satisfied him no longer; he was no more a boy, but a student, appropriating every moment of leisure—nay, without waiting for the moment of leisure—but beside the anchor forge, or the hopper of the mill, wherever the occupation would permit of the indulgence, he sat or stood, book in hand, dividing his time jealously between the toils of necessity and the object of the passionate desires of his mind.

This habit was not grateful to his father. He regarded it as a form of idleness, and perhaps, in some sort, as a profanity. Why should he want other books than the Bible? That had been enough for *him;* and the self-esteem which made so large an element in the father's character, naturally resented the enlarged appetites of the son, as so much presumption. But, as the boy conscientiously fulfilled all his duties—as neither indolence nor neglect of his tasks, nor slovenliness in their performance, could be charged upon him—the sire did not attempt to prevent him in the pursuit of his new enjoyments. Gradually, the old man became so far reconciled to the earnest and noble perseverance of the youth, as to consider the necessity of seeking for him a teacher of more capacity than had hitherto been thought sufficient for the purposes of education. He probably began to feel, in the influence which his son exercised upon himself and others, and in the extraordinary passion which he betrayed for books, that he was really destined to a career very superior to that of the village blacksmith. Lessons in Latin and mathematics, were obtained from a man named Maxwell, and young Greene soon formed a slight acquaintance with the ancients through one of their own tongues, and found himself most decidedly at home in the company of Euclid. Of geometry, in its application to navigation and surveying, he became a master; and his mind was now put doubly in possession of his materials, by being trained in their methodical management. Horace and Cesar were the favorites of his taste, and beguiled his imagination; while Euclid furnished the necessary exercise for his thoroughly-awakened and sharper intellect. Thus, toiling equally in mind and body—rising to the labors of the forge when necessary, and sinking at every opportunity into the well-worn seat beside it, where he had hurriedly laid down his book—he continued to increase his mental possessions, without forfeiting, as is so commonly the case, any of the vigorous muscle, or admirable health and strength of body, which the sports and labors of his youth had enabled him to acquire. His knowledge of books, speaking comparatively, had greatly increased in the brief period since he had made the acquaintance of the sophomore. An event was now to occur, which should contribute greatly to the proper direction of those aims, which, however profitable in their acquisitions, as compared with the past, were yet somewhat deficient in method, organization, and singleness of purpose. A happy accident was to order and direct the somewhat desultory course of study which he had hitherto pursued.

It was the custom of Greene, whenever his labors had afforded him the means to make any addition to his library, to visit Newport in search of a book. On these occasions, a little shallop, which was kept at the mills of Potowhommett, and sent periodically to Newport and other towns along the bay of Narraganset, with the manufactures of the mills, supplied the opportunity. Greene usually worked his passage when he visited the town, seeking a market for his wares, the product of his labors in his own time. It was on one of these voyages, made with this object, when he was about seventeen years old, that he hastened to a bookseller in

Newport, prepared to lay out his petty earnings for a book. But what book? His knowledge of literature was quite too limited to suggest to him the name of the volume which should be most acceptable; and when the bookseller naturally asked what book he wanted, he could only blush in his ignorance, and stand confused and silent before the inquirer. It happened that a third person was present on this occasion, and became interested in the ingenuous confusion of the boy. This was Dr. Stiles, then a clergyman, and subsequently well known as president of Yale college. He regarded Greene with eyes of curiosity; and, in his appearance—his simple garb, begrimed possibly by the labors of the forge, and whitened by the mill—he conceived instantly the struggle which was in progress, of a naturally strong and well-endowed mind, contending with equal ignorance and poverty. He engaged the boy in conversation, and his impressions were confirmed. The conclusion was, that Stiles took the boy to his house, counselled and encouraged him, became his ally in the pursuit of learning, and gave a proper direction to his tastes and studies. This help relieved him from all future embarrassment in seeking the means of knowledge. He had found something better than a teacher—he had found a guide; and it now became the important object with our hero to revisit Newport as frequently as possible. His process for the attainment of this object was quite characteristic. He made himself a skilful boatman. He studied the navigation of the river. He was finally promoted to be master of the shallop; and the bookseller of Newport found him frequently at his counter, gazing upon his shelves, with the look of one who asks himself, sighing secretly the while, "Shall I ever be the owner of such a treasure as this?" His private stock of books was certainly a small one We know that he possessed the

Logic of Watts, Locke's famous Essay, the able volume of Ferguson, on Civil Society, and a few other standard works, like these, of an educational character. That he spared no labor by which he might increase these treasures, may be inferred from the fact, that his heavy labors at the forge finally produced that lameness of the right foot which attended him through life; while, to enable himself to pass from the coarse work of the forge to the manufacture of those finer fabrics on which his own perquisites chiefly depended, he has been known to grind off the callosities from his hands at the grindstone, in order to give them the necessary pliancy and delicacy of touch; and this when he was studying logic and philosophy!

His visits to Stiles and Newport brought him to the knowledge of Lindley Murray. The latter was of a quaker family, as well as Greene, and was then on an excursion through the quaker settlements of the eastern colonies. A sympathy in their common objects of pursuit brought the two young men closely together; and Murray accompanied Greene to Potowhommett, where he so prevailed upon the father, that young Greene was permitted to return the visit the following winter to Murray in New York. The latter had been particularly well educated. His father, conscious of the unwise hostility or indifference of the quaker sect to all liberal studies, had done his best to make his son superior to all their prejudices. His acquisitions were naturally shared with Greene. We may be sure that the blacksmith and mill-boy, whom we have seen grinding down his fingers in order to acquire the means of knowledge, did not suffer the opportunity to escape for procuring it on more easy terms, and through the pleasant medium of friendship. It was while on this visit to New York that he gave a new proof of that decision of character, that forethought and superiority over his associates and education, which were the distinguishing traits of his character through life. The small-pock was prevailing with great severity in New York. Greene knew the superstitious dread which was entertained in regard to this disease; was aware of its real dangers; and felt the importance of passing the crisis, at a moment when his mind could contemplate it calmly, and when it could not interfere with any pressing employments. He availed himself of the opportunity, to become inoculated with it, and a blemish in one of his eyes, which did not, however, impair the sight, was the consequence. The present courage of the boy in this instance, saved him from all future apprehensions of a disease which continued to spread terror through the country.

CHAPTER II.

Youthful Habits.—Parental Discipline.—Progress from Books to Politics.—Military Studies and Marriage.

We have shown young Greene as a student. It will be admitted that the conditions of his career have been sufficiently arduous as well in letters as in war. But the mind most resolute on acquisition will yet need a respite from its toils. The body demands relief which no enthusiasm of the intellect will be able entirely to withhold, particularly in the case of one, whose physique, like that of Greene, is well developed, and whose temperament is sanguine. We have seen that his boyish habit, in the matter of sport, was quite unquakerish — that he loved, and usually led, in the recreations of his boyish mates. These early propensities did not desert him as he grew older, and in consequence of his newly-awakened passion for books. His character, though really sedate and temperate, was anything but morose. His tendencies were decidedly social. Though satisfied with a single meal per day, and indulging in no beverage more potent than a solitary cup of tea or coffee in the same space of time, yet there were some pleasures in which he was ever ready to indulge to a degree which was apparently inconsistent with his ordinary habits. Rising at the dawn of day, and laboring at forge or farm while the day lasted — and sometimes, at his own labors, to a late hour in the night — it would seem only reasonable to suppose that he was glad when he could retire to his couch, and that he slept soundly as soon as he touched the pillow. Such, for a time, was no doubt the opinion of his sober quaker father. But he was mistaken. Young Greene was at an age when the heart particularly needs society — when the instincts of the youth naturally incline to communion with the other sex, and when the impulses acknowledge few restraints of mind or body, of strength sufficient to keep them from the gratification of a favorite desire. Greene's quaker education might have inculcated a sufficient hostility to dancing, to keep him from the exercise, but that, in its indulgence, it conducted him to female society. At eighteen or twenty the desire for such communion must be acknowledged as sufficiently legitimate for youth. It is, indeed, one of the securities of virtue. But the father of Greene was a quaker and not a philosopher. He made no allowance for such an appetite, and the son was very soon persuaded that, if his passions were to be gratified in this respect, it could only be in the wholesome ignorance of his proceeding, in which he could keep the old gentleman. The household was a very sober one. At a certain hour doors and windows were to be closed and bolted, and all good boys were to be in bed. Young Green obeyed the requisition; but when the father was safe in the arms of sleep, and in full faith that all his family were similarly disposed of, he might be seen letting himself down from the eaves, and speeding away to the happy places where his young associates were busy in the rustic dance. Thus, night after night, in the depth of winter, would he speed away from the silent homestead, and mingle with the village revellers. His lameness was too slight to offer any serious obstacle to the inartificial movements of a country revel; and, in thus affording to his limbs and blood the exercises which his nature found equally agreeable and necessary, he did not forfeit in any degree, or impair the value, of his book acquisitions. On these occasions he gave a free loose to a temperament which was at once impulsive and amiable; and the usually sedate student, and laborious worker at hammer and hopper, proved as lighthearted as any of his neighbors. Before dawn, he was again at home, crowding with sleep the brief hours which were left him ere he should be summoned to his daily tasks. But there is a proverb that threatens the safety of any pitcher which goes too often to the well. Whether frequent escape had made young Greene careless, or whether he was betrayed by some hostile companion, it matters not; but the quaker sire had his suspicions awakened in regard to the practices of his són. To be told that the son whom he valued over all the rest, on whom he had bestowed the best education, and to whom he fondly looked as his successor on the floor of the meeting-house, was guilty of such a profanity as dancing implied, was to awaken all his indignation, and to render him equally śubtle and strict in his vigilance. He watched the movements of the youth, and was very soon in possession of the most ample proofs of the correctness of his suspicions.

Greene, as usual, had stolen forth from the house when it appeared to be wrapt in slumber. The occasion was one of particular attractions. There was a great ball in the neighborhood, to which he had been secretly invited. He danced till midnight, the gayest of the gay, little dreaming of any misadventure. But when he drew nigh the homestead, his keen eyes discovered the person of his father, paternally waiting, whip in hand, beneath the very window through which alone he could find entrance. There was no means of escaping him. The stern old quaker was one of that class of people who are apt to unite the word and blow together, the latter being quite likely to make itself felt before the other. In this emergency, conscious that there was no remedy against, or rescue from the rod, young Greene promptly conceived an idea which suggests a ready capacity for military resource. A pile of shingles lay at hand, and before he supposed his father to behold his approach, he insinuated beneath his jacket a sufficient number of thin layers of shingle to shield his back and shoulders from the thong. With this secret corslet he approached and received his punishment with the most exemplary fortitude. The old man laid on with the utmost unction, little dreaming of the secret cause of that hardy resignation with which the lad submitted to a punishment which was meant to be most exemplary.

It is doubtful if the father obtained more than a temporary triumph. Greene could still indulge in his recreations, as before, and without lessening his capacity for duty and acquisition. His sports were never of a kind to interfere with his proper performances. They were the result of a necessity, such as belongs to all healthful bodies, where the nervous energies demand various means and opportunities for exercise. His irregularities were never of an animal kind, though, in the case of a less justly-balanced mind, the ascetic philosophy and regimen of the old quaker might have made them so. His temperament remained the same, though his studies were resumed. His library was gradually enlarging. Swift and other writers of what has been—improperly perhaps—entitled the Augustan age of English literature, became his favorite studies; and, upon the clear, direct, and manly style of the first-named author, he endeavored to model his own. Nor did his mental desires limit themselves to literature only and philosophy. The possession of Blackstone and other legal writers—to the reading of which he was prompted by a law case of some difficulty which disturbed the repose of the family for some time, in consequence of the death of his two brothers by the first marriage — opened to him a very fair knowledge of the principles of English law, and prompted his frequent attendance at the neighboring courts, where he formed an acquaintance with judges and lawyers, and listened with delight to their conflicts. In all these modes was he preparing, unconsciously, for that career of usefulness and fame through which he was yet to pass, under the gradually-increasing discontents and troubles of the country. Here, too, he began, for the first time, to inform himself in politics. The village courthouse was the natural arena for those who loved to engage in political debate. Here it was, that young Greene began to study and to understand the true relations existing between the colonies and the mother-country. This was a new and grateful field for a mind rather strong and shrewd than fanciful or imaginative — of tendencies wholly practical — sedate as well as inquiring, and not easily led away from the true objects of study by any of its collateral topics. He came, by degrees, to be a politician as well as a lawyer.

His father, however much he might be disposed to regard his son as erring in his tastes, was far from being insensible to his acquisitions. Our hero naturally ascended to the second place to himself; and became, like himself, a strict disciplinarian in the household. His brothers were subjected to his authority; and the whole family prospered under this administration. Old Greene had not only become the sole proprietor of the Potowhommett mills, but had extended his domain by the purchase of another mill at Coventry. This was assigned to the management of our Nathanael. He was now in a measure his own master. His means were necessarily increased, and his library soon grew to a decent and well-chosen collection — large at that period — of nearly three hundred volumes. His active mind was not satisfied with the selfish concerns of the mill. He took part in the affairs of the community. Under his auspices the first public school was established in Coventry, and the eyes of his neighbors were already fixed upon him as one of those men, equally steadfast and intelligent, to whom they might properly turn in the moment of necessity or danger. He was now in his twenty-third year, with manners which were at once agreeable and dignified — intimate with most of the leading men of the neighborhood — on terms of familiar intercourse with the bench and bar of East Greenwich, the members of which were visiters at his father's house — and filled, in consequence of this position, with all the political excitements which naturally formed the habitual subject of discussion among such associates. To the examination of the great questions which now began to disturb the country, Greene bent all the energies of his mind. His quaker training was not permitted to defeat his present tendencies. It had not sufficed to restrain the courage and character of his ancestors, when they resisted the persecutions of the fanatical governor, Winthrop, of Massachusetts bay, when he declared war against the heretics, and sent his petty emissaries on a crusade after the sturdy quaker Gorton; and, if not sufficiently powerful to detain young Greene from the rustic revels of his neighbors, even when illustrated by the heavy arm and horsewhip of his father, it would scarcely prove sufficiently imposing to keep a nature, so equally firm and eager, from the assertion of an argument on which depended alike the principles and the safety of the country. The discussion of the stamp-act found him ready to engage in politics with a hearty interest, such as might well be assumed as fatal to his quakerism. In 1769, a king's cutter had been taken at Newport. Three years after witnessed the burning of the Gaspee, in Providence river.

Greene shared in the strong popular excitement on these occasions, and his expressions were of a nature which threatened to draw upon him the severities of government. But, escaping from this danger, he did not the less earnestly urge and maintain the sentiments which had provoked it; and, with that foresight which marked his character, he now began a series of studies still more at variance with the precepts of the quaker, and with due reference to the approaching necessities of the country. He added to his library several of the best military authors of the time, and attended the rude displays of the colonial militia, then in course of organization and discipline throughout the states. This last proceeding outraged all the proprieties of quakerism. He was cited before the fathers of the sanctuary for this errantry. A committee was appointed to sit upon his case; but he gave them no satisfaction. They were, however, unwilling to cut off the prodigal, and continued to visit and exhort him, until, in utter despair of his conversion from the errors of his ways, they read him, with a sad solemnity, out of their books of brotherhood. He still professed himself a quaker, and cherished great esteem of the sect, but his faith was one that claimed privileges for its own, and his respect for the brethren did not prevent him from denouncing many of its professors for their hypocrisy.

In 1770, Greene was elected to the general assembly of the colony. Such was his popularity, that, from this period, even after he took command of the army in the south, he continued to be chosen by his constituents. As a member of the legislature, without making any figure in debate, he commanded the respect of his associates for his integrity, his excellent and manly sense, and the general soundness of his judgment. He seldom spoke; but, when he did, it was always with effect, in a clear, dignified, and unembarrassed manner, which commanded the attention of the house. In cases of difficulty he was an understood authority. On committees of importance he was most usually employed. When envoys were sent to Connecticut to concert measures for public defence, he was one of the delegates; and here he had an opportunity of renewing his intimacy with his friend Stiles, who had become the president of Yale. Doubtless, his rank would have been distinguished as a politician, but that his peculiar talent preferred another field of distinction. It was in 1774 that he threw off quakerism entirely, in putting on the habiliments of the soldier. He enrolled himself as a member of a corps called the Kentish guards, contenting himself with being a private soldier, having failed to secure a lieutenancy. The Kentish guards were formed upon a favorite British model. The corps was composed of the most worthy of the neighboring yeomanry. In the war which followed, more than thirty of its members bore commissions. The time was pressing. Great Britain had thrown off the mask. Her determination was apparent: to coerce, rather than conciliate, the refractory colonies. The latter were equally ready to declare themselves. But the munitions of war were not to be had. Greene, in particular, had no firearms. They were not the usual furniture of a quaker family They could only be procured in Boston. It was necessary to go thither. An old claim upon one of his father's customers, in that place, was the pretext for his departure; and the externals of the quaker, the drab coat and the broad brim, suggested an adequate disguise for our adventurer in the prosecution of his real objects. At Boston, Greene first beheld a parade of regulars. The British troops were then in possession of that city. Little did they suspect the motives or character of the stranger youth, who looked so innocent in his quaker trim. Closely and earnestly did he watch their evolutions, and carefully did he treasure up in his memory the few hasty military lessons which he caught up from this survey. But he did not neglect the first object of his mission. He succeeded in buying a musket with all the necessary accoutrements; and, with the aid of a wagoner, who buried the treasure in a heap of straw at the bottom of his wagon, he contrived to smuggle it in safety beyond the garrison and guards of the enemy. He was successful in bringing with him to Coventry a treasure of still greater value, in a British deserter, an excellent drill-officer, to whom the Kentish guards were indebted for all that was valuable in their discipline. The success of this enterprise secured for young Greene no small eclât among his companions. The musket thus procured is still preserved in the family. One would suppose, from the summary which we have given of his employments, that they were sufficiently various and absorbing to satisfy the impulse and restlessness of any nature. But the enterprise which carried the young quaker abroad at midnight to the rustic *charivari*, in defiance of his father's discipline and horsewhip, had its special object, apart from the simple suggestions of a cheerful temperament seeking communion of its fellows. The same year which found Greene enrolled among the military, found him enrolled in the ranks of another order. In July, 1774, he became the husband of Catharine Littlefield, at whose house he had chiefly indulged in his propensity for dancing. She was an exceedingly engaging damsel, of good family, and but eighteen years of age. His position in life might now be supposed thoroughly established. It is scarcely possible that he should any longer apprehend further parental discipline, now that he was a politician, a husband, and a member of the Kentish guards. It is the responsibility, if anything, which makes the man. That Greene was sensible of this, is naturally to be inferred from the recognition of his claims by those around him. He was steadily rising in the estimation of his neighbors, and in the calm consciousness of his own claims, strength, and capacity.

CHAPTER III.

Battle of Lexington.—Rhode Island Army of Observation.—Greene its General.—Is made a Brigadier in the Continental Service.—Commands on Long Island.—Raised to the rank of Major-General.—Fort Lee.—Fort Washington.—Retreat through New Jersey.—Battles of Trenton and Princeton.

THE preliminaries of the conflict were all cleared away in the battle of Lexington. Those who still doubted of the struggle, hoping against hope, were silenced in the thunders of the strife on that occasion. This affair took place in the spring of 1775. With the first tidings of the battle, the drum of the Kentish guards beat to arms. Already they were on their march to Boston, when the orders of the governor of the province recalled them to their homes. The governor was a loyalist. It is curious that, with a knowledge of this fact, the whig officers of the guards should have obeyed him. They did so, and the troops returned, all but four of them, who, procuring horses, went at full speed as volunteers for Boston. Of these four, Greene was one; one of his companions was a brother; the remaining two were his most trusty friends. He arrived too late for service, but not for distinction. His resolute and independent proceeding opened the eyes of his comrades to his true claims. The people of Rhode Island were very soon afforded an opportunity of showing how gratefully his conduct on this occasion had impressed them. The assembly of the colony voted a force of sixteen hundred men, as an army of observation, to meet the approaching exigency. Its officers were to be appointed by the same body; and, with a common consent, Nathanael Greene was raised to its command with the rank of major-general. The preparations for war were immediate. In a few days the troops were raised, the organization begun, and Greene had exchanged the quiet of the domestic homestead for the busy strifes and anxieties of camp. He had been married scarce a year, and had just attained the age of thirty-three. His personal appearance at this period is described as singularly commanding and impressive. In height he was about five feet ten or eleven inches. His frame was athletic and symmetrical. His carriage was at once dignified, erect, and easy. His complexion was florid, and the general character of his face was that of manly beauty. His features were bold, without impairing their sweetness; nor did the blemish of the right eye from the small-pock materially diminish the keen and lively fire with which it sparkled, when in conversation, in unison with the other. The general expression of his features was that of a placid thoughtfulness, indicative of a mind rather contemplative than passionate. His movements were free and elastic, and his military carriage totally unimpaired by the slight obstruction in the motion of the right leg, which was due to his too severe, but self-imposed labors, in early life. His manners were calm and thoughtful, rising into cheerfulness when his mood was unimpressed by anxiety, and becoming even playful when the character of his associates, and the circumstances in which he stood, permitted him to cast aside the habitual sense of his responsibilities and duties. With a good heart, a mind subdued to its situation, a confidence in self which grew naturally, and by quiet degrees, with his acquisitions of knowledge and society, the deportment of Greene was usually graceful and impressive. With a rare pliancy and without effort, he could adapt nimself to the ircle in which he moved; and, whether serious or pleasant, could express himself with a facility which declared equally for the extent of his acquirements, his experience in the world, and the sound and excellent judgment which always informed his conversation.

It was in May, 1775, that Greene took command of the army of Rhode Island. Several of the officers under him became, like himself, distinguished in the war which followed. Among these was Christopher Greene, the hero of Red Bank, and General Varnum. The captain of the Kentish guards became a colonel in the new levies. It required but a very few days to render the command complete in point of numbers. The hardy yeomanry of Rhode Island turned out with a spirit which was unsurpassed by any of the colonies, and with which the zeal of very few could compare. Their training and organization were no such easy matter. Greene himself had nearly everything to learn; but he devoted himself with his usual industry and intelligence, and his acquisitions were extraordinary and rapid. His capacity for labor, the readiness with which he could bring mind and body to bear upon the necessity—all the fruit of his early habits of inquiry and toil—now stood him in admirable stead, and enabled him to compass, as by instinct, the knowledge which other men only acquire by the painful investigations and work of years. His mind was comparatively free to the one great duty which was before him. His father was no more; and his brothers, harmoniously working together, might safely be intrusted with the business—the mills and forges—which formed the common property of the family. It was his good fortune, no less than his genius, which rendered it so easy for him to address his toils so entirely to the interests of his country.

He soon qualified himself for the tasks which had

been confided to him. Early in June, we find him with his command engaged in the leaguer of Boston. The post assigned him, with his contingent, was Prospect hill; a conspicuous point, on which, in the event of an assault from the enemy, he would be particularly exposed. To discipline his troops for any event, and to prepare them particularly for this, employed his whole time and thought. When Washington took the command of the army, in July, the troops of Greene were pronounced "the best disciplined and appointed in the whole army." The Rhode Island blacksmith had not been hammering at them in vain.

The arrival of Washington was an event in the career of Greene. It afforded him one of the noblest acquisitions he had ever made—that of a friend, a model of the most perfect character that ever lived. The quick appreciative eye of the great Virginian discovered, in a moment, and distinguished by his favor and regard, the rare merits and talents of our subject. He at once took him into his confidence, and an intimacy grew up between them, almost from their first meeting, which was destined to ripen to a most perfect maturity, and to remain, without decay or rupture, to the last. It was Greene who, according to the usage of the time, welcomed Washington to the army in a public address. The quarters of the commander-in-chief at Cambridge were near the post which had been assigned to the Rhode Island contingent. The opportunities for communion between the two generals were accordingly very frequent, and their sympathies did not allow them to go unemployed.

The American army, soon after the arrival of Washington, was placed on the continental establishment. The effect of this arrangement was to reduce the rank of Greene from that of a major-general to that of a brigadier. This change, which was productive of much discontent with the other officers of the army whom it similarly affected, occasioned no complaint or repining with him. He modestly estimated his own claims as a military man, and cheerfully yielded to the arrangement which seemed to lessen their importance. His decision was probably influenced, in some degree, by his determination to devote himself to a military life; the change from the state to the national service being more than equal, in its advantages, to the loss of that rank which he held in the former. This descent in grade necessarily led to a change of his position in the siege of Boston. It brought him to the extreme left of the army, and in command of one of the brigades at Winter hill, the station nearest to the enemy. This station required constant vigilance, but afforded no sufficient employment for a mind so habitually active as that of Greene. The opportunities for distinction were very few during the campaign. The British showed but little disposition for active encounter, and they attempted no enterprises. The task of simply keeping them within their quarters was irksome only, as it required no military virtues higher than those of vigilance and patience. The spirit was scarcely more active among the Americans. A council of war did meditate an attempt on Boston, in the event of the ice in the bay of Charlestown becoming sufficiently firm to bear the army; and this resolve was of special disquiet to Greene, since it found him suffering severely from the jaundice. He trembled on his sick bed lest the attempt should be made without him. But his resolution was taken, under any circumstances. "Sick or well," said he, "I mean to be there." But the experiment was never made. Subsequently, when reparations were begun for making the attempt by water, Greene was assigned one of the two brigades, four thousand each, of picked men, who were designed for the service. But this purpose failed, also. A meditated assault of the British general, which might have afforded the Americans an opportunity for trying equally their courage and patriotism, was abandoned in consequence of a sudden tempest, and, hastily embarking his troops, he evacuated Boston for New York.

The leaguer thus undistinguished by active operations, would have been wholly without profit to our Rhode Island general, but that he employed the year of inactivity in unremitted labors to improve the drill and organization of his brigade, and to inform himself in every branch of the service. His correspondence, begun at this period and continued to the close of the war, is in proof of his industry, the clearness and coolness of his mind, his habits of patient investigation, and the eagerness with which he addressed his thoughts to all of the great interests which belonged to the present and future condition of the country. He was superior to those selfish prejudices which made the New England troops so unwilling to leave their own precincts. "I am as ready," said he, "to serve in Virginia as New England." The country was, in his eyes, a perfect whole; its commerce a common property; and its fortunes only secure in its continued and unselfish union. His opinions were largely national; his views liberal and expansive. As early as June, 1775, he declared for an entire separation from Great Britain, and urged a declaration of independence as absolutely essential, not only to the future prosperity of the country, but as the only process by which the present object, the support of the French nation, could possibly be secured. He had no hope of reconciliation with the mother-country, and his policy was against the measure. He argued on these topics with his usual earnestness and boldness; and his correspondence, embodying these and many other like opinions, on kindred subjects, written at intervals snatched from more arduous employments, and during great suffering and sickness, while before Boston, shows equally the indomitable energies of his mind, and the unselfishness of his patriotism. He counselled the inoculation of the army, while the British forces were suffering from small-pock in Boston; originated the hospital for the purpose at Coventry; and gave up his own house to the object. He urged the recognition of one commander over all the forces in America, to be sent wherever the service should require; the enrolment of a sufficient body of troops to be enlisted for the war; and many other measures of public policy; which, however much doubted and disputed in that day, are now the settled axioms of ours. His letters, in which all these propositions are discussed, are among the most valuable remains of our revolutionary correspondence.

The removal of the British troops from Boston to New York, necessarily led to the breaking up of the American camp at the former place. A portion of the enemy's force proceeded to Charleston, where they met with the memorable defeat at Fort Moultrie. Acting upon the presumption that New York was the object of the British commander, Washington ordered his troops in that direction. Greene's brigade was despatched to Long Island, where he arrived about the middle of April, and established his headquarters at Brooklyn. The division of the army posted on Long Island was placed under his command; while the remainder of the American troops were put in occupation of New York. The fleet of the enemy, after a long voyage, entered the Narrows late in June. Greene, whose command was that which was obviously destined for the first trial of strength with the assailants, devoted himself to such preparations as promised to render the issue honorable to himself and troops. But the British, for several weeks, lay in a singular state of inactivity at Staten island, and, in the meantime, Greene was brought to the verge of the grave by a bilious fever—the consequence of great exposure and extraordinary fatigue. It was while thus he lay, anxious and prostrated, the crisis barely passed in his disease, that he heard the cannon of the contending armies resounding in his ears. No situation could have been more humbling to the brave and ambitious spirit. "Gracious God!" he exclaimed, in his mental agony and disappointment, "to be confined at such a time!" He could scarcely lift his head from his pillow. The thought which added to his distress at this moment, arose from the recollection that he was the only general officer of the Americans who had made himself familiar with the scene of conflict. He it was who had explored highways and byways, marked equally the woods, traversed the passes, and established the redoubts and fortifications. He, only, knew where lay the greatest peril, which were the points most accessible, and how to provide against the exigency which might occur in each.

Terrible was the anxiety with which he listened, incapable, to the progress of the cannonade, and received, from time to time, the reports of the conflict. Bitter were the tears which he shed as he was told of the havoc made in Smallwood's division—his own favorite regiment; and long did he feel the sore of that first hurt to his pride and hope, in a career which, however noble throughout, and triumphant in the end, was destined to be particularly distinguished by reverses and disappointments. The command of his brigade had been confided, during his illness, to Major-General Sullivan. The attack of the British was made late in August, and was pressed with energy and skill. The affair is sufficiently well known. Sullivan and Stirling were assailed in front by a force strong enough to give them full employment, while another column of the enemy stealthily made their way along the south side of the island, and, turning the left wing of the Americans, gained their rear behind the range of hills that run from Brooklyn to Jamaica. The defence was creditable, but overborne by numbers. Stirling and Sullivan were both made prisoners; and the remnant of the American army was fortunate in making its retreat over East river, the evening of the day of the battle, before the British had any suspicion of their object.

Greene remounted his horse as soon as he dared venture from his bed. He was impatient to retrieve his position, and show himself in the front of danger. He had lost nothing in public opinion by his misfortune, but had rather gained, in the general conviction that had he been able to take the field the results must have been much more gratifying to the reputation and desires of the country. With the ability to reappear in the field, he rose to the higher rank of a major-general, and the resumption of his duties found them sufficiently arduous and important. The great point of public interest and anxiety was the city of New York. This was momently threatened by the British. Greene was among those who counselled against any effort to defend it. Washington went a step farther, and actually counselled that it should be burned; but the cause itself, of the American revolution, was quite too doubtful at this period to permit, or indeed to justify, Congress in a proceeding which seemed so desperate. Patriotism was somewhat deficient in the nerve for so bold a measure. Congress differed from both these counsellors; but, in willing otherwise, that body did not come to its decision with an energy sufficiently prompt and stern for the achievement of the best results. Halting between two opinions, even while the enemy was pressing his endeavors — reluctant to surrender the city without a struggle — and yet equally reluctant to peril the army in its maintenance — the result, as is usual in all such cases, was decidedly injurious to both objects. Nothing was done toward making a vigorous defence, and just as little toward putting the army in a position of security. Thus hesitating, when the evacuation of the city was finally resolved upon, it proved too late to prevent a heavy loss in stores and munitions of war, which were abandoned to the enemy. Pursued by the British with eagerness, a brief but brilliant stand was made at Harlem, in which Greene distinguished himself. It was his first battle, and he describes it as a severe one. He "fought hard" in it, and doubtlessly, at every angry stroke, found an emollient for that wounded self-esteem which still remembered his disappointment at Long Island. But the stand was made in vain. The army continued its retreat, and when Washington marched to White Plains he detached Greene to watch that portion of the enemy's forces which still occupied Staten island. The command of the American troops in New Jersey was assigned him, and his headquarters were at Fort Lee or at Bergen, as events required his presence at either place. The important object of his position was to keep open the communication with the main army, east of the Hudson, and secure for Washington a retreat, should circumstances make this necessary.

These duties were sufficiently heavy, with inadequate numbers, and inferior officers. Greene complains bitterly of both. His militia became insubordinate, and he was compelled, on one occasion to bring up his regulars to subdue their insolence. Washington, meanwhile, had been marching and countermarching to elude the manœvres of Howe, and to retard the progress of the enemy across the Jerseys. His army was growing hourly more feeble, and the troops were greatly dispirited. Short enlistments and an unwise deference to the requisitions of the militia, were rapidly reducing the chances of a successful struggle. The British, on the other hand, were exercising their best energies in the prosecution of the war. In possession of New York, their desire was naturally to penetrate the Jerseys, and concentrate their next regards upon Philadelphia. Their arms were pointed toward the position held by Greene. The garrison at Fort Washington was endangered. This post had been maintained as a check upon the navigation of the Hudson, but it was badly designed and quite inadequate for this object. The British shipping had already passed it with impunity, receiving and answering its cannonade, without detriment on either side. Useless for the leading purpose for which it had been held, it was proposed to abandon it. Such was Washington's opinion, differing from that of Greene, who urged the importance of the place in obstructing the enemy in a free communication with the country by way of Kingsbridge. He suggested other considerations for keeping it; but these, perhaps, would not have been conclusive, had not Congress by resolution, determined "on retaining it as long as possible." Under this resolution, Washington wrote to Greene to give the garrison every assistance in his power, coupled, however, with a discretionary power to withdraw the command should it be necessary. Greene preferred to maintain the post, which was in the keeping of Colonel Magaw, who had a force of two thousand men, chiefly drawn from Pennsylvania and Maryland. This body of troops was incorrectly supposed to be competent to its defence. When threatened, Greene added to the garrison a detachment of six hundred more. He himself was present with the garrison the evening before the place was assaulted, encouraging the troops by his presence and the officers by his councils. But the result showed the error of attempting the defence, particularly as the post could be commanded from contiguous heights, and as an overwhelming force could be readily concentrated upon it. The assault was made on the 16th of November. A severe conflict followed, in which, though successful in their objects, the British were very roughly handled. They lost eight hundred men under the unerring aim of the Maryland rifles. With anything like an equal number of troops, the defence must have been maintained triumphantly. But the numbers of Howe were as five to one, and his dispositions for the assault were made with masterly judgment. The garrison became prisoners-of-war. Greene suffered, for a time, from public opinion, which censured him for not abandoning the fort in season. We have shown his reasons for not doing so. They are such as would probably have influenced any officer who, like our subject, was new to military life, lacking experience, and necessarily influenced in his judgment by the opinions and wishes of his superiors. It is only that confidence which grows equally from indomitable will, and a veteran career, that can venture, in the face of authority, to assume the responsibility of independent action. Whatever reproaches may be urged against Greene, must be shared equally with Washington and Congress. The resolution of the latter stares him in the face, and, though allowed some discretion by the former, the importance of the post is yet dwelt upon as justifying every pains and expense in the endeavor to preserve it. It was for this reason that Greene, instead of withdrawing the garrison, added to its force when it was threatened by the enemy. It will be no disparagement to his ability, if we admit that he may have deceived himself as to the strength of the position, and its capacity for defence. He, himself, had but little training as an engineer, and in this branch of the service the American army, at the beginning of the revolution, and, indeed, throughout the progress of the war, was lamentably deficient. It was the consciousness of this deficiency, that led to the undue and improper elevation to command of so many European officers of small merit.

The fall of Fort Washington naturally led to a demonstration upon Fort Lee. Washington anticipated this attempt, and gave orders for the evacuation of the place; but the means of transportation could not be found in season, and the orders of Washington had scarcely been received before the British force, destined for the conquest of the fort, was seen crossing the Hudson. At the head of this force was Lord Cornwallis, with whom Greene was subsequently to come in conflict in frequent campaigns. With a strong body of British and Hessians, his aim was to cut off the retreat of the garrison, toward the Hackensack river. This was early on the morning of the 18th of November. Greene rose from his bed to the encounter. The space between himself and the river was four miles. Cornwallis was nearer the object by half the distance. Yet such was the rapidity and energy of the American general, that he contrived to throw himself in the path of the British, before the head of the river had been gained, and keep him at bay until Washington—to whom advice of the danger had been sent—could come up to his relief. Greene's conduct on this occasion was the subject of as much eulogy as, in the affair of Fort Washington, it had been of censure. Leaving the commander-in-chief to deal with Cornwallis, he hurried back to the fort, and conveyed the remains of the garrison in safety across the Hackensack.

The losses of the Americans, by the capture and abandonment of these forts, were particularly heavy. They left the army of Washington in a singularly feeble condition. The famous retreat through the Jerseys followed as a natural consequence of his diminished strength. With but three thousand men, the commander-in-chief sullenly yielded before his enemy, until he threw the Delaware between the pursuer and himself. This was, probably, the most melancholy period of doubt, humility, and apprehension, among the Americans, in the whole course of the revolutionary struggle. But it found Greene as firm and undespairing as Washington; ready for any sacrifice but that of popular liberty—prepared to retire to the wilderness rather than return to the domination of Great Britain. Their despondency was not irrational, nor of serious duration. It strengthened rather than impaired their resolution, and, deserving well of fortune, they were now destined to experience some gleams of sunshine through the cloud. Suddenly, at the moment of greatest seeming prostration, the columns of Washington were set in motion for the surprise of Trenton. This place was occupied by a force of fifteen hundred Hessians, under the command of Colonel Rahl. The surprise was eminently successful, and at once re-aroused the nation into hope and confidence. Crossing the Delaware on Christmas night, in a storm of wind and rain, a detachment of the American army made its way to the Jersey shore, and, by a forced march of nine miles, succeeded in a secret progress which left the British totally unapprized of their progress until they felt the shock of battle. A few minutes decided the affair, in the defeat and surrender of more than a thousand Hessians, considered among the best troops of the British army. This blow was followed up by the masterly manœuvre against Princeton, by which all the schemes of the enemy were defeated—his designs frustrated against Philadelphia, and his chain of posts temporarily broken up. In this brilliant *coup-de-main*, as in the affair of Trenton, Greene's credit was considerable. He was one of those by whom these enterprises were counselled, and, at Trenton, was intrusted with the command of the left wing, accompanied by Washington in person. It was this division which first reached the town, and, having seized upon the enemy's artillery, cut off their retreat to Princeton. The arrival of Sullivan with the right wing, secured the victory. The affair at Princeton was not less brilliant, and, next to the claim of Washington, as commander-in-chief, must be that of Greene, as his admirable and efficient second. In these two happy victories, achieved at a moment when all seemed desperate in the condition of the nation, the British were confounded, and the Americans proportionably inspirited at proofs in their officers, not only of a valor which could look coolly on the strife with the veterans of Europe, but of a skill in strategic warfare which could baffle their best plans, and put all their experience at fault. With these glorious events, closing the campaign of 1776, the army of the Americans, not exceeding three thousand men, retired into winter quarters, at Morristown, New Jersey.

CHAPTER IV.

The Army in Winter Quarters.—Greene sent on a Mission to Congress.—Explores the Highlands.—Manœuvres of the British.—Greene in Command of a Division.—Conspicuous in the Battle of Brandywine—and in that of Germantown.—Sent against Cornwallis.—Retires with the Army upon Valley Forge.

THE fact that the two armies had retired into winter quarters, did not imply inactivity on the part of either. The little force of Washington, scarcely more than three thousand men, regulars and militia, were kept sufficiently busy in watching that of the enemy, which numbered more than twenty thousand. It was in being able to keep in check such an overwhelming force that the great merit of Washington's generalship is to be found. The army of the British occupied a chain of posts from Brunswick, by Amboy, down Staten island, and thus kept up the communication with New York. It is not pretended that any vigilance or skill of the American general could have foiled the enterprise of such a force, but for the absence of that concentration, which the occupancy of such an extent of country must necessarily imply. The active incidents of the war were necessarily few, and of little importance, during the progress of the winter. Greene had his share of them, being stationed at Baskingridge with a separate division. A series of skirmishes, which annoyed rather than discomfited the enemy, was maintained during this period and served, in some degree, to improve the partisan capacity of the Americans. That Greene profited by these lessons, in full degree with any of his contemporaries, is the natural inference, equally from what we know of his past habits and his future career. The approach of a more active career was necessarily the result of the breaking up of winter.

The British plan of the campaign of 1777 promised to be sufficiently formidable. Their purpose was to get possession of the southern states, and cut them off from the support of the north. Philadelphia was still a first object. Burgoyne was to reduce the country lying along Lake Champlain and the river Hudson; while Clinton and Cornwallis, operating in Virginia and the remote south, were to destroy, in detail, the several members of the confederacy, wherever they were found most susceptible to injury.

To meet and counteract these preparations, Washington strove with all his powers for the reorganization of the army. But there was nothing encouraging in this progress. That Congress might be awakened to a proper sense of its dangers and duties, Greene was specially despatched to Philadelphia. This mission was intrusted to him, in consequence of the fact, now generally understood, that he was in the confidence of the commander-in-chief—a peculiar distinction, which had already begun to produce its natural effects of jealousy, suspicion, and reproach. We have every reason to believe that Greene executed this mission, which was one of considerable delicacy and difficulty, with a rare judgment and discretion. His own good sense and experience, not less than the detailed counsels of Washington, enabled him to set before Congress the exact conditions of affairs—the exigencies of the army and the country; the nature of the assistance and force required; how the approaching dangers were to be met; and how best the materials of the service were to be found and em ployed. His return to the army afforded him instant employment in another field. Foreseeing that the New York highlands were destined to become the theatre of the most interesting operations, he was despatched with General Knox to explore their passes; to prepare for their defence; for intercepting the progress of the enemy, and to oppose his advance, or embarrass his retreat, as the nature of the exigency might counsel.

To enable him to effect these objects, the militia of Connecticut and Massachusetts were placed at his service. To a certain extent these duties were performed as prescribed; but the more full development of the enemy's designs required the attention of Greene in another quarter. The advance of Burgoyne, from the north, was found to be simultaneous with a new effort of Howe to penetrate New Jersey; and, leaving the destinies of the former to other hands, the energies of the commander-in-chief were now addressed entirely to the progress of Sir William. His entreaties and expostulations, addressed to Congress, had not been successful in the reorganization of the army. He was scarcely better prepared, for the encounter of the enemy, at the close than at the opening of the winter. The dawn of spring, the season for active operations, found his regiments still lamentably deficient in numbers, and desponding from the peculiar pressure of casualties, such as sickness and small-pock, which continued to harass and to enfeeble them. But, inactivity in an army is perhaps its worst disease; and, with this knowledge, though still greatly inferior in force, with his men badly equipped and in great part undisciplined, Washington felt the necessity of motion. He resolved, accordingly, to throw himself in front of the enemy, as soon as he exhibited a design to cross the Jerseys. Toward the end of May, he broke up his camp at Morristown, and took up a position at Middlebrook, the natural advantages of which he diligently improved, rendering it a post of considerable security and strength. Howe was already in the field, and about the middle of June he marched out of Brunswick. Conscious of his own superiority, it was his policy to bring on an action with the American general; but the latter was quite too wary to be won by the arts of his rival, who, he knew, would never attempt to descend upon Philadelphia, leaving his enemy in the rear. Failing to provoke his opponent, Howe, after a sufficient demonstration, re-entered Brunswick, and commenced a retrograde movement, by way of Amboy, toward New York. It was then that Washington prepared to harass his retreating footsteps. The command of a strong detachment was assigned to Greene for this purpose. His orders were to follow close upon the track, to hang upon and annoy the rear of the British, and to embrace the first opportunity, upon the arrival of reinforcements, which were expected under Sullivan and Maxwell, to attack him with all his vigor. The design was only carried out in part. So far as it was possible for him to operate with the three brigades which he commanded, Greene's proceedings were all that could be expected or desired. But the anticipated reinforcements failed him. Sullivan did not reach the scene of interest in time to take a part in the performance, and the despatch to General Maxwell never reached him, having been probably cut off by the enemy. Greene followed upon the footsteps of the British rear, anxiously waiting the appearance of the expected regiments; but in vain. He pursued as far as Piscataway; but was compelled finally to submit to the mortifying events which enabled the British to reach Staten island in safety. His troops behaved with great intrepidity in several demonstrations upon the rear-guard of the enemy, but were quite too few to venture upon engaging it.

Sir William Howe, in retreating from before his enemy, was by no means prepared to abandon his object. He simply drew back, in order the more effectually to make his spring. That object was Philadelphia. But with great good fortune and skill, he contrived to keep the Americans in doubt as to his intentions. They knew that he was embarking his army in his fleet; but the destination of the fleet was the difficult question, which no clue in his possession could enable the American general to determine. To fly to the defence of Philadelphia, which Washington justly thought to be his real object, might be to leave to the enemy a country open to invasion; and the uncertainty of his designs was greatly increased by the length of time which, in consequence of baffling winds, the British were at sea. All doubts were finally dissipated by the appearance of the fleet off Elk river, in the Chesapeake. To meet him, and prevent his progress at every hazard, was now the necessity before the American general. Hastily assembling all his disposable forces, he advanced with the êlite of the army to the meeting with Howe. Greene was sent forward to reconnoitre and select a fit place for the encampment. He chose for this purpose the Cross-roads, about six miles from the enemy. This point was sufficiently near the hostile army for the purposes of skirmishing and conflict, and commanded, in the rear, an open country, from which supplies and succors could be drawn at any moment. But a council of war, in advance of Greene's report, decided upon another position, which he did not scruple to denounce as insusceptible of defence,—an opinion which was subsequently justified entirely by the progress of events.

The division that Greene commanded was composed

of the Virginia brigades of Muhlenberg and Weedon With this division Washington marched in person. The two armies came in sight of each other on the ridge that divides Christiana creek from the Elk river. The British were estimated at eighteen thousand; the force under Washington at fifteen thousand, but with only eleven thousand fit for duty. Howe manœuvred with a view to turn the right of Washington and cut off his communication with Philadelphia. To elude this design, the American general crossed the Brandywine creek, and throwing up some slight works at Chads-ford, on the east bank of the creek, he prepared to make a stand in this position. Howe, who was now quite anxious to measure swords with his wary adversary, advanced to the attack on the 11th of September. By a *ruse de guerre*, he obtained such an advantage over the Americans as to render the results of the day quite unsatisfactory to the latter. While a large portion of his army, under Knyphausen, engaged the Americans in front, another portion led by Cornwallis, secretly filed off upon their left, crossed the creek at another ford, which had been left undefended, and was rapidly gaining the American rear. It is said that Washington had foreseen this movement, and would have prepared against it, but for the fact that his mind had been held in suspense by contradictory intelligence. This may be so, but it neither excuses nor palliates the omission. Enough that, after a manly struggle with the foe in front, the necessity became apparent for providing against the enemy who had gained his rear. If Washington erred in any respect, in suffering this manœuvre to deceive him, he is admitted to have repaired his error by the readiness and skill with which he adapted his movements to the change of circumstances. The conflict had terminated in disappointment, if not defeat. It was now necessary, not only that Cornwallis should be arrested in his advance, but that Knyphausen should be kept in check. To leave him to cross the stream and fall upon the rear of the army, while it was engaged in the struggle with Cornwallis, would be a fatal error. Wayne was accordingly thrown, with his brigade, into the redoubt by which the ford was commanded; while Greene's division, consisting of the brigades of Weedon and Muhlenberg, was halted in the rear of Wayne, occupying such a position as would enable him to fly with equal readiness to the relief of either of the parties—that which remained at the ford, and that which went in pursuit of Howe and Cornwallis. The rest of the army, under the command of Sullivan, was hurried forward, with instructions to form and engage the main army of the British with all possible expedition. These orders were obeyed; but, in consequence of a miserable regard to etiquette, instead of forming and fighting as they arrived on the ground, General Sullivan and Lord Stirling stopped to do some very unnecessary counter-marching; and Cornwallis very judiciously seized the opportunity of turning upon his assailants, and charging the Americans while they were yet busy in forming their line of battle. Great was the confusion that ensued, followed by a complete rout. Washington hurried to the scene of action, but not in season to avert the disaster. Meanwhile, Knyphausen recommenced the battle at the ford, and Greene was preparing to advance to the help of Wayne, who was already in hot argument with him, when an order from the commander-in-chief summoned him to the support of the forces which had been led against Howe and Cornwallis. With such alacrity was this order obeyed, that the distance of four miles was traversed by Greene's division in forty-nine minutes He came in time to cover the retreat of the fugitives, and to arrest the fierce and bloody pursuit of the exulting enemy. It was a moment which needed all the cool and steadfast courage of a veteran soldier; and Greene never showed to greater advantage than in the steady front, and the firm, unembarrassed spirit, with which he encouraged his own troops, and encountered the British. While the brigade under Weedon was halted in such a position as to succor and sustain Wayne, should he be forced by the superior strength of Knyphausen, that under Muhlenberg, led by Greene in person, passing to Weedon's right, met the troops of Howe and Cornwallis upon the road. With a firmness and precision of movement, which compelled the admiration even of his foes, he opened for the reception of the American fugitives, and closed against their pursuers. A heavy fire from his field-pieces caused a temporary pause in the earnestness of the British assault, while, gradually incorporating the disordered battalions with his own, Greene slowly yielded to a pressure, which he might only retard, and not arrest. In this way he continued the combat—stubbornly fighting, sullenly retiring—until his retrograde movement brought him to a narrow defile through a thicket, where his quick eye readily saw that a stand might temporarily be made. Halting at this point, he hastily ordered his front for battle; upon which the British darted with flushed spirits, and a confidence that looked to this last struggle as putting a proper finish to the victory. They recoiled from the well-delivered fire which encountered them, and felt the necessity of a more deliberate demonstration if they calculated on success. The position taken was one which required time and industry before it could be turned. The Americans were now recovered from their panic. The steadfast courage of their leader had informed their own, and, fortunately, the shades of night graciously interposed for the safety of the weary squadrons. In this way, stubbornly fighting and sullenly retiring, with his face ever set against the enemy, and with steel and shot ready to confront him, Greene succeeded in saving the army from the complete disaster by which it had been threatened, and which, with a general of less coolness and nerve than himself, must have been inevitable.

Encouraged by the degree of success which he had obtained in this conflict, and dissatisfied that his victory had not been made complete by the entire capture of the American army, Sir William Howe prepared to renew the struggle. Nor was Washington entirely unwilling to gratify his desires; but, with a force inferior in numbers and dispirited by defeat, he required advantages in the issue, reconciling this inequality, such as his opponent did not seem willing to afford him. A few days brought the two armies once more within striking distance of each other; and they were mutually preparing for the encounter, when a violent storm temporarily prevented their purpose, and so damaged the arms and ammunition of the Americans, that Washington was compelled to decline fighting. The Americans retired upon Reading. The enemy continued his approach; and the public policy was supposed to require, as in the case of New York, that Philadelphia should be saved, if possible. But the desires of government, as in the instance just given, were not seconded by the adequate efforts. Greene was employed once more in the choice of a position for the army, which would enable it to fight or retreat at pleasure. He chose a region, mountainous and difficult of access, in the neighborhood of the Yellow Springs, from which the Americans might annoy and harass the enemy in partial encounters, or boldly endeavor to arrest its passage over the Schuylkill. A council of war again determined against this position preferring a series of manœuvres in the open field, and in the direct face of the enemy. The result was, that Washington found himself unequal to the encounter, and Philadelphia was yielded to the British general. He entered it in triumph on the 26th September; but it was an unfortunate acquisition. It became his Capua, and its loss in this way was of real service to the cause of America. Congress removed to Lancaster; their labors serving rather to establish a central point, upon which the several colonies could turn their eyes, than really to serve the cause with any efficient councils. In some respects their proceedings were greatly pernicious. Their resolution to defend Philadelphia, a place of no strength as a military position and of no importance to the integrity of the cause, may be described in this category. The control which they exercised over the army was commonly mischievous; particularly as they frequently offended that jealous sensibility with regard to rank which is so important to the self-respect of the soldier. Greene, Sullivan, and Knox, while the army lay at Middlebrook—under impressions of injustice arising from the supposed elevation of a foreigner, just arrived in the country, to a rank above them—declared themselves to Congress in such a manner as greatly to irritate that great council of the nation. But the lesson, if prematurely administered, was probably of some importance, in suggesting to the civil power a better regard to the necessary laws of rank, in military affairs, than it had been previously accustomed to display. Congress was very angry, on this occasion, with the general officers whom we have mentioned, as concerned in this "round robin." It called upon the offenders for an apology. But the spirits summoned by Glendower were not more ready with their answer; and the anger of the parties seemed to subside, without further demonstrations on either side, which should increase the provocation. Let us return to the rival armies.

The position taken by the British, after possession had been obtained of Philadelphia, was at the village of Germantown, within six miles of the former city. Here lay the main body of their army; but detachments of smaller portions were made, some having immediate charge of Philadelphia, while others were engaged in remote enterprises. The American army occupied a position about sixteen miles from Germantown. The troops, though recently mortified by defeat, were in good spirits. Their loss at Brandywine had been comparatively small; and as that had been the first occasion when the greater number of them had ever felt an enemy's fire, that they had been so little daunted by disaster, afforded every reason to hope better things from their future conduct. Washington determined to try their temper, and selected as the mark which he should first strike, the main body of the British at Germantown. His plan meditated a surprise, the post being without other bulwarks than the ordinary obstructions of house and fence, in a long and narrow village. In point of numbers, the two armies were nearly equal; the difference, however, was greatly in favor of the British as respects the equipments and quality of the soldiers. The Americans were mostly raw troops, half-clad, and miserably provided with weapons. The enemy were in excellent trim, with all necessary armaments and implements, veterans mostly from foreign service, and flushed with recent victory. To make a dash at them under such circumstances, argued a degree of rashness in the commander-in-chief which has not often been imputed to him. But something of audacity was essential to keep up the spirits of the nation, which had been greatly et down by the frequent facility of retreat which their army had shown on preceding occasions.

The order of battle in Washington's army assigned the right wing to Sullivan. This was attended by the commander-in-chief in person. The left was confided to Greene, and consisted of his own and Stevens's divisions, supported by M'Dougall's brigade. The army commenced its march on the night of the 3d of October. The attack was made at break of day on the morning of the fourth. The British, well posted, though unapprized of danger, were not unprepared for it. "Their line was divided nearly equally by the village, and from its right, strong detachments were posted, at intervals, as far as the *ridge* road." This road, which, at this point, approaches very near the Schuylkill, was guarded by the German chasseurs. "In advance of the village, on the Germantown road, was posted a battalion of light-infantry," and a little in their rear was the 40th regiment, under Colonel Musgrove. Advanced upon the limekiln road was the battalion of light-infantry; and on that of York, the Queen's rangers. Both roads were measurably watched by the 1st and 2d battalions of the Guards, which occupied prominent points between them. The British army, as may be seen from these statements, was judiciously ordered for defence against every point of attack. No precautions were spared, and the failure of the attempt of the Americans was probably due to the vigilance of his patrols.

The night was an obscure one, and the morning dawned imperceptibly in fog. The approach of the Americans was known to the British sufficiently long to afford them time for every preparation; but the former, prosecuting a midnight's march, in a darkness more than commonly dense, struggled on, without any apprehensions of an enemy forewarned and deliberately awaiting them. Their progress was a painful one, over fence and ditch, through bog and forest, seldom able, at any period, to distinguish objects in the gloom at an arrow-shot beyond them. The break of day scarcely aided their progress, though it found them near the scene of action. They were suddenly roused to a due sense of its approach, by a smart firing in the direction of the "*ridge*" road, which had been pursued by the American militia under General Armstrong. Believing this to be the quarter at which the assault of the Americans was to be seriously made, and that their appearance in front was only meant as a diversion — conscious, too, that this would have been the better policy of the assailants — the British commander strengthened his chasseurs by strong reinforcements. Unhappily, the militia afforded him but little occasion for these precautions. They scarcely looked the chasseurs in the face, and the latter proved quite equal to the defence against such customers. The reinforcements sent to this quarter by the British, were speedily withdrawn to the left wing, which they reached and strengthened at the critical moment. The action had begun at this quarter in the steady advance of the column under Sullivan. The battalion of British infantry, which this column first encountered, having delivered their fire, yielded before the bayonets of Conway's brigade. Striking into the Germantown road, Colonel Musgrove, with the 40th regiment, rushed forward to sustain them, and the battle raged warmly for a while, until the British, feeling now the whole pressure of Sullivan's arm upon them, again yielded before it. The scale was about to turn decidedly in favor of the Americans. They had forced their way into the village, and the squadrons which had been brought to encounter their advance, had twice proved inadequate to the purpose. But the brave Englishman, yielding slowly to the pressure which he could not oppose, was prepared to avail himself of every opportunity for showing front and offering resistance. At the head of the village, directly in the route to be pursued by the Americans, stood a strong mansion-house of stone. This afforded a means for arresting the assailants, of which Musgrove, with a quick military appreciation of its advantages, readily took possession. With five or six companies he quickly occupied its walls, while the rest of his division fell back upon the main body of the army. The fog lifted at this moment, and the advancing column of Sullivan found itself arrested by a murderous fire from the windows of the building occupied by Musgrove. Here, unhappily, with the view to the capture of the detachment by which it was occupied, the assailing division was halted for several precious minutes. Knox's artillery was opened upon the walls of stone, the unknown thickness of which gave no reason to doubt that a breach could be readily effected. But the delay being greater than had been expected, Washington, who rode up to note the effect of Knox's bullets, finally ordered the column to push forward, leaving a single regiment to observe and keep in check the temporary garrison. To avoid the fatal fire from the windows, the army inclined to the right and left, and pressed onward to the encounter with other and no less serious difficulties. "The left wing of the British army had advanced as the firing on the road commenced," and the whole line, extending from the Germantown to the Limekiln road, was drawn up so as to meet the attack of both the American columns. This required a new disposition of the troops, which lost still more of the valuable time. Posts and fences were to be torn away for the passage of troops, horses, and artillery, and before one portion of the army could do the work of pioneering, the other half had expended all its ammnnition.

Such was the fortune of the column under Sullivan. That under Greene was necessarily influenced and injuriously affected by the events which had taken place upon the right. It had reached the scene of action at the contemplated moment. Here it was encountered vigorously by the light-infantry of the British. This body of troops, however, was compelled to retreat, and continued to do so in good order, though pressed by the American light troops, and galled by their artillery. Through fog and darkness, with objects scarcely visible at thirty yards, the assailants felt their way with the bayonet, firing only when the flash from the British guns enabled them, with tolerable accuracy, to seek a mark. With the lifting of the darkness, at the dawn of day, the objects of search and assault were scarcely made more apparent. Reaching the ground directly east of the stone-house into which Musgrove had thrown himself, Greene's attention was drawn to the warm discharges of firearms which announced the conflict of the other column with the enemy. To halt, reconnoitre, and finally to display, for the struggle with him also, was the work of little time; but the progress of events, totally beyond Greene's knowledge, had rendered nugatory the previous arrangements for the battle. In the original disposition of the American forces, it was contemplated that Sullivan should meet and fight that part of the enemy's force which was encamped to the west of the village, and Greene that part which lay to the east." But the newly-formed front of the British, rendered a new organization necessary for Sullivan, and threw one half of his column on the same side of the village with Greene's. Here, expecting only to find an enemy, the rear line, composed of Stevens's division, in the obscurity of the morning, fired upon Wayne's division, which constituted Sullivan's left. The front, finding itself between two fires was thrown into confusion. Greene, meanwhile, whose division was on the left of the whole, pressing forward to feel the British, opened also upon the other column. A panic necessarily followed which was fatal to the order of Sullivan's division. They broke and yielded on each hand, in spite of all the efforts of their officers, leaving Greene's command to the encounter with the enemy, which, it is alleged, was never better sustained by the most determined veterans. It effected the service which had that day been assigned it; broke the British right, drove them at the point of the bayonet, and made a large number of prisoners—its very zeal proving fatal in the sequel, since, "by pressing forward in the pursuit, while Stevens was embarrassed and detained, its right flank became exposed; and two regiments on the left of the British line, not being confronted by any part of the American force, were at liberty to wheel upon the left of Sullivan." The battle, which had been almost won, was soon entirely lost. The confusion in the column of Sullivan was irretrievable. By this time, the light of day was sufficient to discover to Greene the danger which threatened his unsheltered flank. The rout which prevailed on his right, was sufficiently monitory, and, with a sullen anger, he gave orders for retreat from that field, which, but a little while before, he had fancied all his own. With practised troops, even then, the event of the day might have been retrieved; but with raw and inexperienced soldiers, the difficulties and dangers which menaced the retreat, presented to the minds of their leaders a more arduous and perilous duty than that through which they had already gone. Musgrove still occupied his fortress of stone; the British army had recovered from its surprise, and, with the light increasing and guiding their manœuvres, were pressing forward with the growing hope of converting a partial defeat into a com plete victory. To encourage them in this hope, Cornwallis, with a strong body of fresh troops, was pushing on from Philadelphia, having been aroused at the first sounds of the conflict. To retreat, under such circumstances, was a serious matter, and Greene devoted himself to the task of timing and regulating, with firmness and coolness, the retrograde movement which was now inevitable. To keep his men from panic or despondency —to retire sternly and sullenly, like the wounded wolf who turns momently to rend the incautious pursuer —to guard the rear with dogged watch and vigilance —were duties in the prosecution of which Greene pertinaciously exposed his person in a manner that showed equally his devotion to his troops and the deep mortification which he felt at being forced to forego a victory within his very grasp. The action had been a long and sharp one. It had lasted nearly two hours and a half. The lost in killed and wounded was nearly equal on both sides, each being seven or eight hundred. The Americans suffered the additional loss of four hundred prisoners in the surrender of Mathews's regiment. They brought off all their artillery. The pursuit was vigorously urged by the British, was continued for about five miles, and was marked by frequent conflict. Of this battle, Washington and Greene both concurred in the opinion which the former expressed in his letter to Congress, that "our troops retreated at the instant when victory was declaring in our favor." The British opinion was, that "in this action the Americans acted on the offensive, and, though repulsed with loss, showed themselves a formidable adversary, capable of charging with resolution, and retreating with order." Greene's enemies found several causes for censure in the part which he took in the affair; but his reputation has survived the assault, and the opinion of his more intelligent contemporaries, affirmed by the deliberate judgment of posterity, assigns to him the credit of a fair share of all that was meritorious in the action.

If the Americans did not succeed in the surprise and capture of the British at Germantown, they gave them, in the language of the provincials, "a mighty bad scare." It was not long that they remained in this position. They felt too sensibly the danger of a post which was so accessible to the assaults of a vigilant and enterprising enemy, and retired upon Philadelphia. Howe, meanwhile, directing all his efforts to opening a communication with his fleet, ordered a reinforcement from New York. With his eye keenly fixed on all his operations, Washington lay at Whitemarsh, but fifteen miles distant —not satisfied with the disappointment at Germantown— and eager, with better hopes, to try the experiment again. An opportunity was supposed to offer itself in a threatened descent of Cornwallis upon the Jerseys. With a force of three thousand men, he crossed from Chester to Billingsport. He had before him the twofold object of collecting supplies for the army, and of opening the navigation of the Delaware by the reduction of Fort Mercer —or Red Bank—a place already famous by its defence, under Colonel Greene, against Count Donop and his Hessians.

It was determined, on the part of the Americans, to despatch a force into the Jerseys, for the purpose of baffling the designs of Cornwallis; and General Greene was chosen to its command. He proceeded, with due diligence, upon his mission, but, before a junction could be formed of his own with the brigades of Huntingdon and Varnum, then in the Jerseys, the army under Cornwallis had been so greatly strengthened, by reinforcements from New York, as to render idle and improper any decisive demonstrations on the part of the Americans.

Greene, however, hung upon the left wing of the enemy, until recalled by Washington, who had reason to apprehend for the safety of the main army, in consequence of a movement of Cornwallis, which promised to unite the forces of the latter with those under Howe. Such a junction would have placed it in the power of the British general-in-chief to strike an effective blow at the American army, unless strengthened by the concentration of all their detachments. It was the last of November when Greene, with his column joined Washington at Whitemarsh. Here the army remained till the night of the 12th of December, certain movements of the British leading to apprehensions of an attack. But the storm passed over in cloud and murmur, and, content with a vigilant watch upon each other, the opposing armies tacitly agreed to forego more active enterprises for the season. The Americans went into winter quarters at Valley Forge, about sixteen miles from Philadelphia, while the British, within and about that city, after all their battles and successes, were content with just enough conquered territory to spread their blankets

upon

CHAPTER V.

Greene becomes Quartermaster-General.—The British evacuate Philadelphia.—Pursued by Washington.—The Battle of Monmouth.—The Conduct of Greene in that Battle.—Joins Sullivan in an Attempt on Newport.—Engages the British.—Retires before them on the Approach of Clinton.

WINTER quarters at Valley Forge, in the present condition of the American army, though promising respite from the active enterprises of war, contained no other promise. Repose, quiet, plenty—all of which seem ordinarily implied in such a withdrawal from the fields of war—were singularly wanting to our troops on this occasion. Without clothing or provisions—without order, method, or a proper officer to attend to the duty of providing the famished and harassed soldiers—Washington was compelled to issue orders to forage, as in an enemy's country. This painful duty was devolved on Greene. He naturally shrunk from a task so irksome; but the obligation of service was paramount to all others, and, however reluctantly, he complied with the requisition. He scoured the woods and meadows, and found spoil in plenty. The patriotism of the quakers contemplated no sacrifices; and the gold of Britain, which flowed abundantly in Philadelphia, possessed a value, in their eyes, very far superior to that which belonged to the depreciated currency of Congress. Their cattle and provisions, designed for those who could pay in the precious metals, were found concealed in swamp and thicket. Greene's scruples at appropriating them, if he had any, were removed by the orders of Congress—the resolves of which body rendered liable to impressment whatever was wanted for the army within seventy miles of the camp. However firmly, he performed his spiriting gently; with as much order and regard to the sensibilities of the sufferer, as were consistent with the character of the proceeding.

The manner in which he executed these duties—his known habits of method, systematic arrangement, and unwearying regard to the smallest details of business—suggested to Washington the importance to the army of employing him in the department of quartermaster-general. This office, one of the most vitally important to the successes and safety of an army, had hitherto been confided to incompetent persons, by whom it had either been grossly neglected or infamously mismanaged. Greene was, however, quite unwilling to accept this office. He disliked any appointment which required the keeping and expenditure of the public money; and was unwilling to forego any of the opportunities which might offer, of active performance in the regular line of the army. It was only at the earnest entreaty of Washington, who appealed to him to make the sacrifice, that he finally consented; stipulating, meanwhile, that he should not lose his right of command in action.

His acceptance of the office, at once relieved the commander-in-chief from most of his annoyances on the score which had hitherto distressed the army, and threatened its disbandment. The integrity of Greene, his precision, order, comprehensive grasp of details, and various resources, produced the happiest effects. Order sprang from chaos, light from darkness, and confidence, in the minds of the people, from doubt and apprehension. The whole course of his administration, in this new department, was such as to reflect the highest credit upon himself, and bring the most incalculable advantages to the service. But his couch was by no means spread with roses. This "hutting at Valley Forge" during the winter quarters of 1777, was neither a period of hope nor repose. It is true that the wives of both Washington and Greene were present in the camp; but the peace of Eden was not implied by the presence of woman in the garden. It was during this memorable winter that the intrigues which threatened to disturb the peace of the country, by the overthrow of Washington, became most active under the spells and machinations of Conway, Gates, Lee, and others. "Conway's cabal" is sufficiently known to history, to render it needless that we should do more than refer to it in this connexion. The intimacy of Greene with Washington, rendered it natural that he should share in all the odium and all the danger by which the commander-in-chief was assailed. He, indeed, was the frequent mark, on occasions, when Washington wâs the special victim; and, where the rank and station of the latter rendered him secure against the assailant, Greene was usually chosen as the substitute against whose bosom the shaft of malice might more surely tell. In other words, the blow was frequently made at Washington over the shoulders of the man who was his favorite; and the hostility thus exercised and tutored, continued to rage against him, long after it had despaired to do hurt to the more distinguished object of dislike. Undoubtedly, a great deal of this hostility was due to his individual claims and position. His integrity, which they could not shake; his alliance with Washington's cause, which they could not lessen or disturb; his prudence, which they failed to put at fault; his growing reputation, which they vainly endeavored to disparage, and which was calculated to compel the finger of public confidence to point to him as the only proper successor to Washington,—these were all qualities and circumstances which stimulated the rage of faction, and irritated the sore sensibilities of envy and self-esteem. That the conspiracy of which Washington and Greene were the destined victims, failed utterly of its intended objects, did not lessen the anxieties of the injured parties, or prevent that frequent grief and bitterness, which naturally flow tc the innocent from such a malicious warfare.

The season for active operations was now at hand, and Washington steadily addressed all his energies to the task of preparing his army for its duties. His winter quarters had not been consumed in idleness. With his men and officers, for the first time beneath his eye, he had employed the opportunity, which it afforded, of improving their common discipline. With his force gradually increasing in numbers, he might now reasonably calculate on a campaign, in which a modest confidence in his own resources might justify him in taking the initiate in enterprise. The capture of Burgoyne's army was an event which confirmed the revolution at home, and determined the doubts of those foreign nations who longed, but hesitated, to become allies of the rebellious colonies. These events led to auguries with regard to the forthcoming campaign, which naturally deepened the anxieties, while increasing the hopes, of the Americans. That Washington was in a condition to commence the campaign at all, was greatly due to the rare and valuable exertions of his newly-appointed quartermaster-general.

The British general Howe, meanwhile, had been superseded by Sir Henry Clinton. Intelligence, that a French fleet had sailed to intercept the British army in the Delaware, led to the evacuation of Philadelphia. With eleven thousand men, Clinton marched from that city, crossing the Delaware or the 18th of June, 1778.

His course was through the Jerseys. The aim of Washington was to thwart this progress, retard the march, destroy the enemy in detail, and, if no opportunity offered for less perilous enterprise, to bring on a general action. His force was nearly equal to that of the British, and he crossed into the Jerseys about the same moment. By the 22d of June, the whole of the Americans were on the eastern bank of the Delaware, and in a condition and position to offer the enemy battle. But, upon the policy of this proceeding, much discussion ensued among the American generals. Charles Lee, and most of the foreign officers—indeed, a majority of the board of war—were decidedly against fighting. Wayne and Cadwallader were as decidedly for the arbitrament of the sword, and their opinions were enforced by those of Greene, La Fayette, and Hamilton, who, without urging battle at all hazard, were disposed to follow up the enemy closely, protect the country from his ravages, and seize upon whatever chances might seem to promise a favorable issue for bringing on the final encounter. Lee, whose faith in British valor was only surpassed by his utter want of faith in the steadiness of the Americans, was opposed to any risks, however partial, which might result in conflict. Fortunately, Washington had been authorized by an express vote of Congress, which had been ascribed to the advice of Greene, to exercise his own discretion in regard to the decisions of his council. It was an advisory body, only, whose opinions he might follow, or not, under the guidance of his own judgment. The opinions of Greene and La Fayette determined his resolve against the suggestions of the majority. "You wish me to fight," said he; and the orders soon followed which led to the battle of Monmouth.

He had approached this place, following his enemy

with a close but watchful step, when he came to the conclusion that the moment for action had arrived. La Fayette, meanwhile, had been detached with a strong body of troops, instructed to hang upon the British rear, and, with discretion, to act, if circumstances should encourage him to do so. Other detachments, riflemen and militia, were in advance of him and on his flanks. To protect his enormous baggage-train from these parties, Clinton placed them under Knyphausen, with a very strong escort, while he united the rest of his force, in the rear to check the too close approach of the parties by which it was threatened. The interval between the force of Knyphausen, and that by which the rear was accompanied, suggested to Washington the idea of concentrating his assault upon the latter. It was advisable to hasten the attack, accordingly, before the enemy should reach the high-grouds of Middletown, about twelve miles distant, where he would be measurably safe. A strong detachment, under Lee, was sent forward to join Lafayette, with instructions to engage the enemy, and keep him employed until the rest of the forces could be brought up. Lee, ranking Lafayette, took the command, upon the junction of their separate detachments. In pursuance of orders, he proceeded to engage the enemy, but not seemingly with any desire to bring on the action in earnest. A very short trial of strength found him in full retreat—exhibiting a degree of misconduct which the world esteems to have been wilful, and to have been prompted by that incendiary spirit, engendered in the cabal of Conway, the object of which was to baffle the enterprises of Washington, lose him the confidence of the country, and thrust him from the eminent position which he enjoyed. In this purpose, however, Lee only wrecked himself. He was already retiring from the field of Monmouth, when Greene, in command of the right wing, approached the scene of action. He had been ordered to a particular position in the rear of the enemy's left, but the change of circumstances, which followed upon the hasty flight of Lee, forced upon him the necessity of using his own discretion in the choice of another position; and here it was, according to the common opinion, that he rendered the most signal service in checking and repelling the pursuit of the British, which must otherwise have proved irresistible. Washington, on first meeting with Lee in full retreat, indignantly reproached him with his conduct, and commanded him to face about and engage his pursuers at all hazards, while he brought up the main body of the army to his support. Aided by a sharp fire from the artillery of the first line, Lee was enabled to obey these orders. He turned about in good earnest, and, after a spirited but not prolonged conflict, he retired in good order from the field. It was during this conflict that Greene appeared with his column. A movement of the enemy which threatened Washington's right, caused him to order Greene to file off from the road to Monmouth, and, while the residue of the army pushed directly forward, to win his way into the wood in the rear of the courthouse. He was already on his route, in obedience to his orders, when, foreseeing, from the flight of Lee, that Washington must now be exposed to the whole weight of the enemy's attack, he suddenly resolved to adapt his own progress to the altered circumstances of the field. He did so, and took an advantageous position near the British left. This movement, as he had foreseen, diverted their attention from the fire of the American army to his own division. A most furious attack followed, but was encountered by a cool determination which showed the value of the winter discipline which the army had undergone at Valley Forge. The artillery of Greene's division was in the charge of General Knox, and, well posted upon a commanding situation, poured in a most destructive fire upon the assailants. Seconded by the infantry, who steadily held their ground, and gave volley upon volley from their small-arms, with equal rapidity of fire and excellence of aim, the advance of the enemy was checked. Repeated efforts of the British serve only to renew their disappointments and increase their losses. Their shattered battalions, which had been greatly thinned by the murderous volleys, were at length withdrawn from the field, and were finally driven back, under the united advance of Greene's and Wayne's infantry, with great loss, to the position which they first occupied when Lee began the attack. Reconnoitred in this position, with all their strength concentrated for its defence, Washington perceived the fruitlessness of any renewal of the assault. The American army retired accordingly, and slept upon their arms that night, Greene, like his commander, taking his repose, without couch or pillow, on the naked ground, and with no other shelter than a tree, beneath the broad canopy of heaven. Nor was this shelter sought, or this repose found, until the wounded had been placed in due keeping, and every soldier who had fought in his division had been solaced with the best food that the camp supplied. With the dawn of morning the enemy was gone. They had halted only long enough for a slight rest and refreshment, and then silently stole away, wi[illegible] such rapidity, as, when their retreat was made known, put them beyond the chances of pursuit. If the Americans did not win a victory at Monmouth, they acquired many advantages from the combat. Their conduct betrayed the effects of discipline and service — showed large improvements in both respects, and led to larger hopes and expectations from their continued exercise Lee's disobedience of orders, assuming a discretion which the result did not justify, was probably the true reason why a complete victory had not been obtained; yet, if Lee lost the victory by his disobedience, it is quite as certain that Greene's departure from orders, insured the final safety of the army, after the first disaster had endangered it. His quickness, the excellence of his judgment in the choice of a new position in the moment of exigency, and the firmness with which he maintained it, greatly contributed to raise his reputation.

The cloud of war continued to pass to the northward. Clinton reached New York in security, while Washington inclined to the left, in order to defend the Jerseys, and secure the passes of the Highlands. The American forces were now in a condition to attempt offensive operations. Their conduct at Monmouth had inspirited the hopes of the people, and the arrival of a French fleet, under D'Estaign, which was decidedly superior to that of the British, encouraged to the boldest enterprises. An attack, of the combined troops of France and America, was planned against the British forces in Rhode Island. They had held the town of Newport, since the fall of 1776, and Clinton, on his retreat from Philadelphia, had increased the strength of his arms in that quarter, and abundantly supplied them with all the munitions of war. To be in train for making an attempt on this position, Washington, on the first advices of a French fleet to be expected, detached Sullivan to Rhode Island with a small army of observation, and with a power to make requisitions upon the neighboring militia. When the French fleet did arrive, after a grievous season of delay, Lafayette was sent, with a reinforcement, to join Sullivan. Greene soon followed, and from him, though serving under Sullivan, the largest expectations were formed. He, himself, was anxious for service in his native state; and he gladly yielded the duties of the quartermaster-general's department, for those of more conspicuous performance in the field. His arrival was welcomed with delight, volunteers crowded to his standard, and the utmost confidence of the result prevailed equally among the people and the troops. On the 8th of August, the French fleet entered Narraganset bay, under a heavy fire from the British batteries, which they quickly passed. Preparations for the attempt on Newport were then begun. A plan of attack was arranged for the next day, but was delayed till the 10th, "in consequence of the non-arrival of certain troops of Massachusetts and New Hampshire." Meanwhile, Pigot, who commanded the British, became alarmed for his outer line and withdrew the troops from it within the lines by which the town was immediately defended, thus abandoning without a blow, at least two thirds of the island. With the discovery of this proceeding, Sullivan instantly crossed, with his whole force, to the island, and occupied the lines which had been abandoned by the enemy. This movement gave serious offence to Count D'Estaign, a captain who stood very much on etiquette. The next day, instead of being employed in action, was consumed in discussion; and while D'Estaign was proving himself a very prince of punctilio, a new party appeared in the field, to engage in the dispute after another fashion. This was Lord Howe, in command of the British fleet. It was still in the power of the allied forces to have captured Newport. The fate of the British garrison was inevitable. The French fleet lay in a position of complete security, and the only hope of the wily British admiral, was in beguiling his conceited adversary from the game which was certain, to the doubtful issue of a sea-fight. Melancholy to say, he was successful in his object. The French count, who had been captious in asserting his supposed authority and resenting fancied slights from the first moment that he showed himself in the country, held it a point of honor to accept the challenge of the British fleet, in advance of all other considerations. He was thus carried out to sea, several days' sail, manœuvring to get the weather-gage, and finally losing the very object of his quest, in a furious gale, which separated the rival fleets, and scattered them over the ocean.

Left thus to their own resources, the situation of the Americans became embarrassing, if not full of danger. There were but eight thousand men fit for duty, and more than half of these were militia. The British were nearly the same number, well chosen, under excellent discipline, and protected by the most admirable works of art. To carry the place by storm was out of the question. To maintain themselves against the enemy, when any amount of reinforcements could be brought in twenty-four hours from New York, was not possible; yet, to abandon an enterprise which had been undertaken under such encouraging auspices, and when they might hourly look for the reappearance of the French fleet, was a resolution which the American general was exceedingly loath to adopt. Thus undecided, an attempt was made to operate by leaguer; but, before ground could be broken, a storm of the greatest violence arose, which, for three days, raged with a fury such as marks only the terrible hurricanes of the lower latitudes. The operations of the army were suspended; their tents, tools, and provisions, destroyed; ammunition and arms made unfit for service; and the hearts of the soldiery, already daunted by the disappearance of their allies upon whom they had counted so confidently, were oppressed by the most gloomy auguries. Ten days of painful suspense followed, in which the Americans lay before the garrison of the enemy, divided between hope and apprehension, and distressed by the most humiliating incertitude. Fortunately, during this period, though Clinton was making his preparations for the relief of the place, no enterprises were attempted by the British which could increase their perils. At length, the French fleet reappeared, and bore in toward the land. But the storm had made itself felt among their shattered frigates. Full of confidence, and sanguine now of success from the co-operation of their allies, the Americans prepared to prosecute the assault on Newport. But, what was their discomfiture when apprized by D'Estaign that he was no longer in a situation to afford them any assistance. He was compelled to go to Boston to refit. It was all-important to the American general to effect a change in this resolution. Greene and Lafayette were accordingly despatched to the fleet to confer with the French commander. It was in vain that they argued and entreated. The co-operation of two days only was implored; and Greene pledged himself that, under cover of the guns from the shipping, he would plant himself firmly within the lines of the enemy. But the French count was inflexible. We have already seen that he had his weaknesses. The miserable regard to etiquette which had prompted him to forego the game within his grasp, for that which might, and did, elude it, was in proof, to a certain degree, of his incompetence for such a trust as that which had been confided to him. For his farther conduct, there is some excuse. He was unpopular with his officers; and the council of war, which had been called to decide upon the arguments and entreaties of the American general, sufficed to show to Greene the progress of such a spirit of discontent and disaffection on board the French fleet, as might well render its admiral reluctant to engage in any enterprises of great responsibility. It does not concern us to inquire the causes of D'Estaign's unpopularity with his officers. Enough that it served to deprive the Americans of all the anticipated succor from their allies

Great was the mortification and indignation of Greene, when compelled to carry back to the camp the final refusal of the French admiral. There, it produced nothing but dismay. Another effort was made to stay the departure of the fleet; or, at least, to secure the co-operation of the land forces. But it proved equally ineffectual with the former. D'Estaign pursued his voyage to Boston; and, to increase the fears and dangers of the Americans, it was now understood that Clinton was rapidly approaching from New York. These tidings completed their panic and disappointment. The militia could no longer be detained. That very night, they deserted in such numbers, that, with the morning, Sullivan found his force reduced from eight to five thousand men.

The situation of the army had now become sufficiently perilous; and, in silence and darkness, on the night of the 28th of August, the camp was broken up; the whole American force retreating to the shelter of a couple of redoubts, which had been raised on the north end of the island. Their departure was discovered with the dawn, and a pursuit was instantly commenced by the British in two strong columns. Greene, with the gallant regiments of Colonels Livingston and Laurens, covered the retreating movement; and, under their steady valor and admirable order, the whole army reached its point of destination, and was at once drawn up in order of battle. They had scarcely put themselves in trim for fighting, when a brisk fire from the enemy announced their close approach. Under the belief that they had pressed forward in detached bodies, which might be cut off separately, Greene was for marching out to meet them promptly, and before the several divisions could arrive to the support of each other; but this counsel was rejected as too full of peril. The troops were held on the defensive, only. Greene commanded on the right, and, from a redoubt in his front, a cannonading was maintained throughout the day upon the enemy. This was warmly answered from an opposite hill, of which the British had possession. At two in the afternoon, they made an attempt to turn the American right, and concentrated on this point all the effective force which could be brought to operate. Reinforcements were soon ordered to this point, and the engagement that followed was equally prolonged and desperate. Here, Greene was in immediate command. His force was doubled by that of the assailants, but his troops were among the best in the army, and now amply declared, by their cool and steady valor, the admirable training which they had received at Valley Forge. He was not less fortunate in his officers. They sustained the unequal conflict with a spirit worthy of the most stubborn veterans; and the enemy was finally repulsed with great slaughter—repulsed, rather than defeated. The British were picked soldiers, also; and they retired, in good order, to the hill from which they had descended to the attack. The engagement was a partial one. It relieved the Americans from present pressure, but did not extricate them from their difficulties. Though not conclusive, it did honor to the American arms, and was particularly gratifying, in its results, to Greene, who was fighting in sight of his birthplace. Hundreds of the militia, who emptied their guns from walls and fences, were nerved to the most desperate exertions, as they felt that they fought beneath the eye of one of their own kindred. Greene, himself, felt how many eyes of kindred—how many dear friends and old associates—were watching anxiously the behavior of their former comrade. There was one, dearer than all in his sight, who, sitting by their own lonely hearthstone, could hear the deep and hollow reverberation of every shot, in the long and heavy cannonade that day. The battle was resumed, at long shot, with the next. But, "though most vigorously pursued and repeatedly attacked," was the language of the very enemies of Greene, "yet, in every quarter where an opening was made, he took his measures so well, and had chosen his posts so judiciously, that, although much honor was claimed and deserved on both sides, he gained the north end of the island without sustaining any considerable loss." He barely saved his distance in doing so. Another day, and the Americans would have been totally cut off by the overwhelming force, with which, the very night of his departure, Sir Henry Clinton appeared on the ground. He found the nest still warm. The Americans had crossed to the main in security; and their assailants, warned by the sharpness and loss of the previous encounter, were not sufficiently desperate to pursue them.

CHAPTER VI.

Greene defends Sullivan for the Affair in Rhode Island.—Difficulties with Congress in regard to the Duties of Quartermaster-General.—Anecdote of his Brother.—Resigns from his Office, and offends Congress.—Debates in that Body.—Greene commands at the Battle of Springfield.

THE failure of this expedition, on the part of the Americans, from whom so much had been expected, occasioned deep mortification, and a wide excitement. Blame fell heavily upon the officers in command of the expedition, and Greene naturally came in for his share of the reproach. A visit to the abode of his father, which he took occasion to make about this time, was chiefly employed in preparing an elaborate exposition of the true causes of the failure of the enterprise, in an energetic defence of Sullivan. This paper appears in the form of a letter, in which a frank and generous ardor speaks unreservedly the opinions of a mind secure in its position, and governed by the most uncalculating rectitude. His visit to his birthplace was thus employed in a manner which was quite inconsistent with the opportunity afforded him and the objects by which he was surrounded. In the homestead of his youth, with the old familiar faces in his sight, one would naturally seek escape from the thoughts of strife and the recollections of war. Greene had now been more than three years away from his home. He had only once passed through it, in all this time, while hurrying from the siege of Boston to the defence of Long Island. During this period, change had necessarily been at work. The administration of his affairs had been confided to others. The family estate had been divided, he simply assenting to all that had been done, and taking and receiving, without inquiry, the portion which had been allotted him. A few days only were stolen for his delay at Coventry, when he hurried on to Boston, where he was called by his duties as quartermaster-general. Here he strove, and not unsuccessfully, to conciliate Count D'Estaign, whom his former deportment had greatly prepossessed in his favor. This labor of love was equally politic and amiable. It was one evil result of the failure of the expedition against Newport, that it prompted the American officers to such an expression of their indignation, at the conduct of the French, as must have greatly vexed the self-esteem and increased the soreness of the latter. Sullivan, himself, had expressed himself in language of a character which was likely to be greatly offensive to the government of France. To soften the offence, and mollify the feelings which it might produce, was equally the care of Washington and Greene. An opportunity occurred to the latter, in which his prompt decision was of the last importance in preventing new cause of provocation. It was desirable that Congress should be put in possession of all the facts relating to the expedition against Newport, through some confidential agent, having authority to speak, and without resorting to any means, such as a court of inquiry, which would give publicity to the particulars obtained. Greene was sent by Washington for the purpose of making these revelations. He repaired to Philadelphia, and, by a unanimous vote of Congress, was invited to a seat on the floor, and shown to a chair beside the president. Henry Laurens at this time occupied the chair; and, but a few moments had elapsed, after Greene had taken his seat, when a communication from the governor of Rhode Island was announced, and an order passed that it should be read. Conceiving, instantly, the character of the document, and that it embodied the same feeling and sentiments with those of Sullivan and others, which had already given so much offence, Greene seized the moment, while the clerk was unsealing the envelope, to convey to the president a slip of paper, on which he had written, ' For God's sake, do not let that paper be read until you have looked it over." His suspicion was instantly adopted by the president, who, in a whisper, arrested the progress of the clerk. A call for the order of the day, judiciously interposed at this moment, diverted attention from the governor's despatch, which, in fact, embodied a remonstrance against the conduct of D'Estaign, such as could not but have painfully outraged the French minister, who, with his suite, D'Estaign himself, and other distinguished persons of his nation, was, at that very moment, in the gallery. It is difficult to say what might have been the degree of mischief done, had not the happy tact of the Rhode Island blacksmith interposed for its prevention. Greene, in fact, was quite as much a politician as a general.

The year 1778 terminated without affording any opportunity of distinction to our subject, except in his capacity of quartermaster-general. With the departure of Sullivan from Rhode Island, the British army under Clinton returned to New York. Their enterprises were no longer of a character to merit the attention of the historian. They degenerated into predatory expeditions only, in which recklessness rather than courage, crime rather than combat, were the distinguishing features. The details of this career, as it nowhere involves the progress of Greene, will not require more of our notice. The campaign of 1779 opened with characteristics not much more reputable. Indeed, all things tended to show that the British army, hopeless of making any decided impression in a region where the nature of the climate and the characteristics of the country offered few opportunities of successful enterprise, and where the absence of available wealth among the people, held forth as few inducements to it, had really relinquished all hopes of effecting a conquest of the states north of the Chesapeake. Their eyes were now naturally turned upon the southern states, where a more scattered population, and, in some places, greater opulence, promised a more easy progress and more abundant spoils. The northern armies, on both sides, were now chiefly employed in watching each other, seizing upon small lapses of conduct, and engaging in enterprises, which afforded employment rather than results. The British government, during this campaign, appeared scarcely sensible of the necessity of making adequate efforts to reduce the colonies, strengthened as they were by foreign alliance; and was, in fact, too busily employed upon the ocean and abroad, to concentrate her resources upon this object. The Americans, on the other hand, were, in a large degree, enfeebled by this very alliance, and attached so much importance to what was to be done for them by France, that, in the northern states, at least, they were scarcely disposed to do anything for themselves. New England, in particular, from the moment of the withdrawal of the enemy from her own coasts and cities, and the appearance of the foreign auxiliaries in the country, regarded the contest with an apathy and indifference strangely in conflict with her previous activity and warmth.

To a certain extent, as a natural consequence of the inactivity of the British, this apathy prevailed in all the colonies. It did not, however, prevent the growth of jealousies and dissensions, such as ordinarily flow from the selfish hopes of partisans, and the diseased ambition of distinguished men. Assuming the war as really at an end,—calculating largely upon the simple effect of the alliance with France as conclusive to this effect,—not regarding how much more naturally such an alliance would provoke the worst passions of the British, rather than their fears, and bring down upon the colonies the whole volume of that long-nursed national prejudice and hostility which had been engendered between the two great nations by the protracted strifes of centuries, the Americans yielded themselves up to those domestic struggles for power and place, which, but for their premature assumption of safety, would never, perhaps, have been allowed to discredit their honorable achievements. Congress was the theatre for these dissensions. It was rapidly growing into disrepute among the people. The states had their own discontents and strifes, and no longer felt disposed to comply with the federal requisitions. The army, badly clothed and fed, and impatient of the neglect which answered its complaints and expostulations—worn out with the drudgery of the war, without being enlivened with the excitements of battle—was daily sinking in repute and lessening in numbers. The system by which it was to be sustained, that of depending upon the states for the maintenance of quotas, instead of resorting to regular enlistments, was one of fatal errors, against which the intelligent officers of the army were remonstrating always, and constantly in vain. Public credit, a subject equally important, needing even more fostering, was rapidly undergoing destruction in the equally unwise system of resorting to expedients, instead of, at once, honestly and frankly declaring a necessity, and boldly advancing to contend with it. In this condition of things, nothing was done toward the promotion of the cause of independence; nothing, certainly, was gained for its popularity; and, in all probability, a great deal already gained was forfeited. The year 1779 was marked by nothing in the councils of the nation, and as little in the business of the field, which could confer credit upon the revolution, or render its progress permanent. No general action occurred to call Greene away from the bureau of the quartermaster-general, in which, by the way, he endured as much toil, and enjoyed as few consolations, as could have been found under any fortunes, directly in the pathway of a powerful enemy.

The ambitious strifes and dissensions in Congress did not, of course, suffer him, or his administration of affairs, to escape severe and unfriendly comment. If the members of that great national council could not perform themselves, they had sufficient leisure for prompt judgment on the performances of others. The departments of the quartermaster and commissary were subjects of particular inquiry, and the most unfounded complaints were put in circulation against the mode in which their duties were administered. There is a vicious appetite in man, that makes it rather grateful to him to listen to the story of his neighbor's shame; and the ear which hearkens only to a conjecture and a suspicion of misconduct, is very apt, in the next moment, to find for it a tongue of evil, which soon converts it to a tale of crime. Greene suffered from these suspicions. Secure in the favorable opinion of Washington, and in the approving voice of his own conscience, though stung and mortified to the quick by indirect imputations which he could not condescend to combat, he was only persuaded to retain his office in consideration of the difficulties by which it was environed, and of the vital importance, to the cause, of its energetic administration. But rumors, equally of his incompetence, and against his honesty, continued to circulate. They, at length, reached the ears of his kindred, and occasioned an interesting and touching incident, which reflects honorably on the character of that training by which the venerable old quaker, his sire, had striven to inform the sensibilities of his children, with an appetite as eager for virtuous name, as for popular renown. The report which disparaged the honest fame of our subject, at length, reached one of his brothers in Rhode Island. Greene's quarters, at this time, were near Morristown. The parties were separated by a space of nearly two hundred miles; yet, the moment that the brother heard the humiliating story, he took horse and hurried to the army. Greene's cordial reception of his guest met with no answering sympathy. The brother, before he opened his heart to the embrace which it yet solicited, was first to learn that he dealt with an honest man. He demanded a private interview, which was at once vouchsafed him. "I am come, brother," he said, in a voice nearly choked by emotion, "to inform you that you are charged with improper conduct in your office. Are you innocent?" With an affectionate smile, a calm voice, clear countenance, and a hand pressed upon his heart, Greene answered, instantly, "I am!" The assurance was satisfactory. The brother knew, from the experience of long and trusting years, what degree of confidence could be yielded to such an assurance. It was then that he embraced him, and, happy and relieved, he departed as suddenly as he came. He had but one object in the interview, and, the single interrogation answered, he had no other motive for delay.

But the communication sunk deeply into the heart of Greene. He had met the inquiry of his brother with a smile. With clear and unembarrassed brow and eye, he had answered the painful question; but he did not the less suffer from the cruel wound which it inflicted, and he resolved, as soon as possible, to break away from the shackles of an office, equally responsible and burdensome, in which he had toiled without regard to selfish considerations — in spite of them indeed — and had reaped reproach and suspicions, instead of gratitude. Fortunately for the fame of Greene, calumny itself, with all its agents, was not able to oppose the unquestionable evidence which his friends could produce, in favor of the administration of his department, and in proof of his own integrity. Congress, after an inquiry, passed a resolution, declaring its confidence in his ability and integrity. Greene was sufficiently soothed by this resolution to listen to the entreaties of the commander-in-chief, and of the army, that he would not relinquish the department he had so ably managed. But calumny was not so easily silenced: the creature was very soon, again, at her dirty work. A remnant of the old faction of Conway, no longer able to hurt Washington, were always eager to wreak their malice upon Greene. To such a degree did they carry this malice, that it was even designed, if possible, to deprive him of his command in the line. But their most obvious game was to impeach his integrity. He was supposed, or asserted, to have made a fortune by his office; while, in truth, he was about to retire from it something poorer than when he entered it. It had been to him, indeed, like that supper of the Barmecides, in the Arabian tale, in which, without a single dish before him, he was required to fancy that he enjoyed the most delicious variety. A resolution from the treasury board required a statement of his accounts. For this performance, but twenty-seven days were allowed him. He expostulated against the unreasonable and oppressive requisition, demonstrating the moral and physical impossibility of traversing such a wide and various field of investigation in such a space of time. An additional month was grudgingly allowed him, while a committee was appointed to inquire into the condition of his department. The investigation resulted in his triumph. The members of this committee, to borrow the language of one of them, "entered upon the investigation with the strongest prejudices, and closed it with a unanimous conviction of his ability, fidelity, and zeal." Here, then, was a favorable opportunity for Greene to withdraw from the ungracious service in which he was engaged, and resume his station in the line, which he had always greatly preferred; but Washington was unwilling to lose him, in a capacity in which he could render services of so much importance; and a scheme for the regulation of the department was drawn up by the commander-in chief, in conjunction with a committee of Congress, which Greene entirely approved of, and which he professed himself willing to administer, without other pay than that which accrued to him from his commission as major-general. But Congress, with its numerous amendments, so mutilated the plan submitted by Washington through its own committee, as to depart from all its most essential particulars. Under these circumstances, Greene no longer hesitated to make his escape from an office, in which he had neither enjoyed repose, nor realized profit. There was no sufficient motive to remain in a department which subjected him to equal annoyance and mortification. His preference was wholly given to active duties in the line; and indeed, as we remember, he had stipulated for the privilege of resuming his military rank and duties whenever a general engagement was anticipated. Thus feeling and desiring, it was with a sentiment of relief and pride that he covered his resignation to Congress, of the office of quartermaster-general, requesting that body to appoint his successor without loss of time. He declared his own resolution no longer to officiate in the office, except so far as was necessary to close up his accounts, and to set fairly in operation the new system, as adopted, for the future government of the department.

This letter, so proud in tone and so peremptory in requisition, gave great offence to Congress, and was instantly seized upon, as so much capital for hostile declamation, on the part of his own and the enemies of Washington. One member immediately rose, and proposed that he be dismissed from the service altogether. He had warm and powerful friends in the house, who combated this attack. A keen and exciting discussion followed, which ended in referring the letter of Greene to a committee. The report of this committee embodied the hostile sentiment, and concluded with a resolve, that "the resignation of Nathanael Greene be accepted, and that he be informed that Congress have no farther use for his services." This report proves something more than hostility to Greene. It proves that the party against Washington was in the ascendency in Congress. But neither his nor Greene's friends, in that body, were prepared to suffer the question to go by default. For ten days, the report was under consideration; and, during the greater part of this time, was the subject of fierce discussion. Still, Congress was exacting, and the supposed offender incorrigibly firm. He better knew his grounds of security than did his enemies. The discussion was not confined to Congress. The people and the army partook of the excitement, and Greene felt sure of a verdict of acquittal and approval at their hands, if he might look in no higher quarter. His cause, indeed, was that of the army. They needed no arguments, in his behalf, more satisfactory than their better care and provision, their increased comforts and resources, during his administration, than they had ever enjoyed when Mifflin, the leader, in Congress, of the opposition against him, had occupied the very office in which Greene had superseded him. But the excitement gradually subsided. Warned by the threatening aspect of the army, exhorted by the letters of Washington himself, and recovering, by delay, a better tone and temper than had lately impressed their deliberations, Congress gradually cooled off; and, when the vote was finally taken, his resignation as quartermaster-general was accepted, as tendered, without any farther allusions to his commission in the line.

In the former capacity, Greene was succeeded by Colonel Pickering; but for two months he still continued to execute the duties of the office, and prepare it for his successor. He had borne the heavy burthen for nearly three years, and had placed the department in very good condition, all circumstances considered. His successor, though of unquestionable ability and integrity, was not so fortunate. The department suffered in his hands; and six months' experiments were sufficient to satisfy the worst enemies of Greene, as well as his best friends, how much injury had been done to the country by the captious and cruel interference which had driven him from duties he was so peculiarly calculated to fulfil.

The hostility against our subject began to subside the moment he was relieved from the office which he had only continued to hold by the persuasions of others, and against his own desires. He gladly resumed his duties in the line. We have noted his military career to the close of the campaign in Rhode Island. A brief summary of events, in the history of the war, is perhaps necessary for the purpose of preserving the continuity of our narrative. Withdrawing his troops from Rhode Island, somewhere in the autumn of 1779, Sir Henry Clinton proceeded, with all despatch, to New York, where he apprehended the arrival of D'Estaign, with his fleet once more refitted, and prepared for some leading enterprise. The French commander was now operating with Lincoln against Savannah, which was in possession of the British. With the fall of Savannah, which was confi dently anticipated, D'Estaign was to unite with the commander-in-chief in an attempt upon New York. But Savannah did not fall. Admirably defended by the British, the united forces of the French and Americans recoiled, with terrible loss, from its batteries, which the injudicious indulgence and overweening confidence of D'Estaign, in his own strength, had given the enemy sufficient time to perfect. This defeat was one of the disasters which contributed to the final conquest of South Carolina, the troops of which state suffered severely at Savannah. Disgraced and mortified, D'Estaign, instead of moving upon New York, sailed for the West Indies, while the arrival of a strong British fleet under Arbuthnot, enabled Clinton to operate offensively, and to concentrate all his energies for the prosecution of a design, long entertained, and twice already defeated, upon Charleston and the southern states. It was in December, 1779, that the British general sailed from New York, with the best part of his army, on his expedition against Charleston, leaving behind him a force under Generals Knyphausen and Patterson, which was deemed quite equal to the duty of keeping at bay the skeleton regiments under Washington. Had the New England troops been only half as numerous in the field as they have ever been on paper, New York must have fallen; but the American army under the commander-in-chief, was really less in numbers than the garrison in that city. It will not concern us to pursue the career of Clinton in the south. Suffice it, that Charleston was taken, and the British general returned to New York on the 17th of June, 1780. During his absence, his substitutes were busy in enterprises rather petty — and perhaps profitable — than brilliant; acquiring reputation as successful marauders, rather than daring conquerers. With the return of Clinton, preparations were made for something more serious on the part of the British; and the American general was kept on the *qui vive*, uncertain where to look for the approaching danger. Anxious for the safety of his garrison on the North river, Washington left Greene, with two brigades of continentals and the Jersey militia, at Springfield, in New Jersey; while he, himself, moving slowly but steadily for the north, prepared to take command at West Point. The movements of the British general seemed to menace this region. His complete command of the New York waters, naturally indicated West Point as accessible to enterprise; and this citadel of the nation, which held its armories and magazines, and constituted the key to a wide and important interior, compelled Washington to anticipate every danger by which it might be threatened, and to make its safety conspicuous in his regards over almost every other consideration. But he had not proceeded a dozen miles from Morristown, on his march for the north, when, on the 23d of June, the heads of the British columns were advanced from Elizabethtown in the direction of Springfield. It was here that a considerable supply of military stores and munitions of war had been deposited; and the force of the British, now moving on this quarter, consisting of five thousand men, a large body of cavalry, and fifteen or twenty pieces of artillery, commanded by Clinton in person, was quite too large to leave it doubtful that his demonstration was a serious one. Washington was soon advised, by express from Greene, of the threatened danger to his post, while the latter prepared with all his energies to meet the emergency. This was the first occasion in which he was in possession of an independent command; and he soon satisfied all parties of his admirable capacity to enjoy it. No movement of the enemy had been taken without his knowledge, and with the first show of danger, the commander-in-chief was apprized of its approach. To do much with small means is one of the highest proofs of excellence in any sort of performance. It is, perhaps, one of the most admirable tests of a genius for the military. Greene's force was an humble one, and it was employed in detail to guard numerous passes. To draw together his detached bodies, was the first necessity, and to economize time in doing so, was a part of this necessity. To hasten the remote detachments to a point of rendezvous, and to order the several bodies, more within his control, to advance and retard the progress of the enemy, were simultaneous, and the work of an instant.

About eight miles from Elizabeth point the village of Springfield lies, upon the western bank of the Rahway, a little stream formed by the confluence of two other and smaller streams. A range of hills formed the background, and was the position, naturally a strong one, which the American army occupied. The village was accessible by two roads from Elizabethtown, one running through Springfield, the other north of it. The usual facilities for crossing the Rahway and its branches, by fords and bridges, were present, and rendered the stream itself no sort of obstacle to an enemy's approach. To guard these bridges, three in number, and to cover the two great routes which led to them, were the only means of protecting the village; but this required such an extensive front as was scarcely within the compass of Greene's numbers to exhibit. His proper policy, therefore, was to push forward select bodies to check the advance of the British columns separately, as they approached on the different roads, while, from his position on the heights, he could extend succor to either of these bodies, as they separately seemed to require it. Colonel Dayton was advanced, accordingly, to skirmish with the left column of the enemy, while Major Lee, afterward famous as the leader of the partisan legion, with his dragoons and a small force of infantry, was despatched to perform the same duty against their right. The whole force of Greene was but thirteen hundred men, and of these, three hundred were militia. He disposed these, as we have seen, to the best advantage, to economize their strength, and gain time; and he had no reason to complain of the manner in which the skirmishing forces under Lee and Dayton performed the tasks assigned them. They made a spirited resistance to the enemy's approach, and offered all the opposition that squadrons so inferior could make; but without being able to prevent the junction of the assailing columns, which at length united upon the main road, and made their appearance almost as soon as Greene's troops, on the right bank of the Rahway, were drawn out to receive them. His artillery was posted behind the bridges by which the principal stream was crossed; that of the enemy was in advance of his columns. A brisk cannonade ensued, which continued with great spirit for nearly two hours. The manœuvres of the British, meanwhile, manifested a desire to turn the American left, and thus get into its rear. This, as Greene well knew, was practicable. Both the streams from which the Rahway took its rise, were passable, as well by fords as by the bridge on the Vauxhall road. The possession of the hills in his rear would be decisive against him. It was necessary, therefore, that a new position should be taken; and Lee, with the pickets under Walker, and assisted by Ogden, was assigned to the defence of the bridge over the southern branch of the Rahway; to the regiment of Shreve was given in charge the upper bridge, over the chief branch, while Colonel Angel, with a like force, and one field-piece, was left to defend the passage of the principal stream. With the residue of his force, consisting of Stark's and Maxwell's brigades, Greene retired to a strong position among the hills in the rear, his flanks being guarded by militia.

With the first movement of the main body, the British advanced upon the bridge which was held by Angel. Their assault, aiming to force the passage, was fell and furious. They were resisted, however, with a rare spirit, and recoiled from their first onset with loss and confusion. But this success was, necessarily, temporary only. How could such a handful of men resist, for any length of time, a formidable column of the foe, flushed with confidence in experience and numbers, and bringing with them ten pieces of artillery. The assault was renewed, but the struggle was maintained, stubbornly, for fifty minutes, until one fourth of the force of the American colonel were killed or wounded. It was not then, nor until he knew that Greene had reached his destined position, that Angel drew off his division, bringing away with him his artillery and wounded, and coolly, and in good order, retiring to the other bridge, where Shreve was in position.

Equally obstinate was the defence made by Lee at the pass confided to his keeping. Assailed by the right column of the enemy, he met the attack with a firmness and gallantry, which only forebore the struggle in the moment of its utter hopelessness. The stream was already crossed, by a considerable body of the enemy, at an upper ford; and these, having gained a hill by which his position was commanded, compelled Lee, very reluctantly, to abandon the post which he had so nobly held. Pushing on at the heels of these two divisions, the British encountered the detachment under Shreve, now strengthened by the united battalions of Lee and Angel. Animated by the gallant example of the troops under these officers, those of Shreve prepared to give a no less determined reception to the enemy. The onset of the British was met with a welcome of shot and steel which made them shy and reluctant; and, though advancing still, they did so in a manner sufficiently modest, to enable Shreve to retire, coolly and without confusion, upon the main body. Here, with his regular force drawn up in a single line, in a commanding position, flanked by the dragoons and militia, Greene calmly stood in waiting for the general battle. But the enterprise of the assailants had been wonderfully cooled by the obstinate conflicts through which they had already gone. They had been handled too roughly, by the small divisions with which they had been engaged, to venture upon the entire force of the Americans, while they presented a front so determined, and occupied a position so strong. Taught to fear by the loss which they had already sustained, and stung to fury for the same reason, they sought for their victims among those from whose weapons they had nothing to apprehend. Avoiding the conflict which Greene stood prepared to give them, they concentrated their wrath upon the defenceless village; and the flames of its houses soon apprized the American general of the sort of vengeance which the British were disposed to seek. Then it was, that the sharpshooters of the Americans, and the militia, panting to avenge the sufferings of their houseless innocents, were let slip upon the scattered marauders. They stole down to the scene of conflagration; and many a Briton, that day, perished by the light of the very flame which his incendiary torch had kindled. With the general conflagration of the village—for only four, out of fifty, dwellings escaped—the British begun their retreat, hastened, no doubt, by apprehensions of the approach of Washington. Small parties of the Americans were instantly pushed forward, to hang upon their wings and harass their flight; while the brigade of Starke was also put in motion for direct pursuit. Washington had already despatched three hundred men to Greene's assistance, and was, himself, rapidly hurrying to the scene of action. But the celerity with which the British fled, unencumbered by any baggage, and protected by a powerful rear-guard, saved them from any farther injury than that which they had sustained in the encounters of the day, and in the after-gleanings which were made, of deliberately-chosen victims, by the rifles of the enraged militia. The British reached Elizabethtown in safety, and that night recrossed to the city. Their only real achievement, that of the destruction of a harmless village, reflected no credit upon their chivalry; while their failure to effect anything against the vastly inferior force of Greene, was as little creditable to their skill and valor. Greene's reputation as a cool and experienced captain—one of great resources, and of wonderful circumspection—was greatly increased by this affair. The Annual Register (British), speaking of the conduct of the Americans on this occasion, remarks: "It was now evident, that the British forces had an enemy little less respectable in the field than themselves to encounter; and that any difference which yet remained in their favor would be daily lessened. In a word, it was now obvious, that all that superiority in arms which produced such effects, in the beginning of the contest, was, in a great measure, at an end; and that the events of the war must, in future, depend upon fortune, and upon the abilities of the respective commanders."

CHAPTER VII.

Demonstrations on New York.—Treason of Arnold.—Greene appointed to the Post at West Point.—Gates's Defeat.—Greene succeeds him in Command of the Southern Army.—Proceeds to the South.—Joins the Army at Charlotte, N. C.—Treatment of Gates.

WITH the affair at Springfield, ended, for a season, all the active operations of the campaign. The commander of the British seemed disposed to give his troops a respite, and was, perhaps, somewhat restrained from attempting anything at the north, in consequence of the threatened appearance of a fleet and army from France, in co-operation with the Americans. Besides, as already suggested, he was preparing to shift the scene of action, wholly, to the south. By cutting off state by state, in a region whose population was so small, compared with that of the northern portions of the confederacy, the conquest, it was calculated, might be effected in detail, beginning at the extremities, rather than striking at the centre, to which all the defensive energies of the continent were necessarily directed. The south never, at any time, possessed such an army as was maintained, during the whole war, in the neighborhood of the chief cities of the north.

The Americans were inactive from other causes. The succors of France, a fleet and army under De Tierny, arrived early in July. This fleet was superior to that of the British, and, with the troops which it brought, ought to have secured to the allies equal ascendency by land and sea. But this superiority was soon more than counterbalanced by the arrival of reinforcements to the British, under Admiral Graves; and, though the American militia, encouraged by the strong force brought by their allies, had taken the field with new activity and in considerable numbers, yet, this show of spirit was rendered abortive by the position of the French, who were blockaded, by a superior fleet, in the harbor of Newport. Clinton prepared to make a demonstration on Newport; while Washington, equally on the alert, stood ready to make a corresponding attempt upon New York. By the greatest efforts, the means of transportation were procured, and preparations made for a joint attack by land and water on that city. But Clinton was too vigilant to lose sight of this important position. Discovering his enemy's game, he regained his fortresses by a prompt retrograde movement, which put his stronghold once more in a state of security.

With the abandonment of the enterprise against New York, Washington proceeded to Hartford, there to meet and consult with the French commander in regard to future operations. He left the army in charge of Greene. This vigilant general was soon led to suspect that the British commander was meditating a secret movement of great importance. He had established a regular communication with New York, and obtained considerable intelligence through the medium of his spies; but these, though satisfied that an important expedition was designed by the enemy, were entirely at fault when it became necessary to define its objects. Conjecture was nearly equally divided between Rhode Island and Virginia. The casual language of the enemy, and his open demonstrations, looked equally to these points. Greene was not to be deceived. He writes to Washington that he suspects "some secret expedition in contemplation; the *success of which depends altogether upon its being kept secret.*" This letter was written on the 21st of September: the whole mystery was developed on the 23d, when André was taken prisoner, and the treachery of Benedict Arnold discovered. The well-known object of Arnold's negotiation, was the delivery of West Point to the British. The importance of this place to the interests, if not the cause, of American independence, needs no recital. The moment chosen was particularly auspicious for the British, inasmuch as the arrival of Rodney, with his fleet, not only gave them an abundance of water transportation, but enabled Clinton to engage in a distant enterprise, and yet leave New York in a state of security against the enterprise of the Americans.

Greene's first knowledge of the defection of Arnold was derived from a letter of Hamilton, received on the 25th. It explained all that was mysterious in the proceedings of the British. Without delay, he prepared to march the army to the defence of West Point. On the morning of the 26th, his whole force had been put under marching orders, and, with the second division, in obedience to instructions from Washington, he pushed forward with this command, as far as King's ferry, the remainder of the army being held in readiness to move at any moment.

It does not belong to us to narrate the details of Arnold's treachery; and the fate of André is too well known to require more than a passing notice. Sent under close guard to the American camp, Washington, in a private letter, gave Greene his instructions. A court of inquiry was convened, to determine upon the case of the prisoner, which was of many novel features. Greene presided at the deliberations of this court, which was composed of men of the highest worth and greatest dignity in the army. The opinion of the court was unanimous. André was convicted on his own confession.

Painful as was the duty, it was inevitable, and he was sentenced to suffer as a spy. When the report of the sitting, drawn up by Laurens, was handed to Greene for his signature, his head was seen to bend low upon the paper, to hide the tear which he could not suppress. The death-warrant bore traces, also, of the regrets of those who, while forced to condemn, were not insensible to pity. The graces and accomplishments of the criminal, his manly bearing, his youth, his talents and imputed virtues, were considerations which, could they have been allowed before the court of justice, would have been sure to have made themselves felt, for his safety, through the awakened sympathies of his judges. But, the necessity of the example, the peril upon whose verge the country still stood, were conclusive arguments, which no erring weakness of the indulgent nature could, possibly, oppose. André pleaded that the manner of his death might be changed; but this, too, a rigid justice did not dare to concede. To die as a soldier, was not the award of punishment. The true penalty lay in the infamy of the death.

The proceedings of the court were duly communicated to the British commander. Clinton made every effort to save the victim from his doom. Commissioners were sent to the American posts, to argue the propriety of the judgment, and to arrest it if they could. But one of the commissioners, General Robertson, was permitted to land. He was met by Greene, on behalf of the commander-in-chief. The conference took place at King's ferry. We need not, here, renew the arguments urged on either side. Enough that no legal ingenuity could change the firm convictions of Greene; and André suffered, according to his sentence, at the village of Tappan, where, at that time, the principal part of the American army lay encamped.

Greene succeeded to the command of the post at West Point, made vacant by the treason of Arnold. He found it in the most shocking confusion; neglected in most essential respects, and so prepared as to render it an easy prey to the operations of the enemy. To place it in instant readiness against any enterprise, was the pressing necessity, and the proofs remain of his equal wisdom, skill, and diligence. Nor was he suffered to concentrate his whole thoughts and energies upon this one subject. He was the *premier* of Washington, held to a constant correspondence with the commander-in-chief, day by day, on subjects, always of importance, and frequently of the gravest and most complex character. This correspondence still exists in equal proof of his own various abilities and of the unlimited confidence which Washington reposed in his judgment and integrity "Thus," says Johnson, "at one time he is called upon to make a full estimate of all the expenses for a year, attendant upon an establishment of thirty-two thousand men. At another, to sum up the whole annual expense incident to the war, to give a view of the sums paid by each state toward it, and their capacity to continue or increase their present contributions. At another, to consider the expediency of prosecuting the plans of the campaign hitherto pursued, or what changes shall be adopted upon the various exigencies which might occur," &c. These are all hard cipherings, and that Greene should still be required to go through with them, various and difficult as they were, and so little informed by rule as he had been, would go to prove the wonderful facility and resources of his mind, its ready adaptation to novel circumstances, the comprehensiveness of his vision, and the correctness of his judgment—at least in the opinion of the commander-in-chief.

But he was soon to change the scene of his operations, while emerging into a larger scene of action. We have already indicated that change in the plan of invasion by which the British calculated to effect the division or partial defeat, if not the entire coercion of the colonies. The front of war was now fully turning upon the south. Not that the enemy had hitherto withheld himself from this region. Thrice had South Carolina been invaded, twice to the disaster and defeat of the assailants. A third time, overwhelmed with a vastly superior force, at the moment of her greatest weakness and exhaustion, from previous struggles, her capital city had been overcome, and almost the entire regular army assigned to her assistance, with a large portion of her militia, had become prisoners-of-war. Georgia was completely prostrate, bound hand and foot, and the invader had advanced, with rapid strides, into the very heart of both these states. A small and inadequate force of continentals had been pressed forward with too much rapidity, and led headlong to complete overthrow, by the presumptuous rashness of the conquerer of Burgoyne. The news of Gate's defeat at Camden, following close upon the failure of the French allies to effect anything in cooperation with Washington, and the hasty disbandment of the militia, necessarily produced, in the nation, after the first feeling of despondency and dismay, a conviction of the necessity of making new and superior exertions to arrest the progress which the enemy was making in the south. Troops must be raised to reinforce the remains of the southern army, and to restore the strength of its skeleton regiments. These troops were to be drawn wholly from the militia of the southern states, since the eastern soldiers were quite unwilling to be marched away from their own abodes. Contingents were called for from Maryland, Virginia, Delaware, and the Carolinas—from regions which had already felt the drain of such requisitions, and were weary of toils that seemed to promise no results. These were not promptly forthcoming, and a no less serious difficulty lay in the choice of a general who should command them. The fields of the south had been particularly unfriendly to the fortunes of foreign generals. Lincoln was a prisoner-of-war, and Gates, late a favorite, was now a fugitive, under cloud and the censure of his country. The defeat of Gates, in itself a great calamity, since it sacrificed an army, and encouraged wondrously the hopes of the loyalists, was yet not without its advantages, since it took from him that *prestige* which had been wretchedly employed by the enemies of Washington as a mean for his discredit and overthrow. Had the commander-in-chief been consulted, when Gates received the appointment of Congress, Greene would have been indicated to the command which wrecked the fortunes of the hero (so called, but erroneously) of Saratoga. His defeat removed from the eyes of Congress those scales of prejudice, which had hitherto made them blind to the deficiencies in his character. Taught a severe lesson by the terrible disaster at Camden, they were now better prepared to defer their own to the judgment of Washington. He was at length authorized to name a successor of Gates to the command of the southern army. There was no doubt, when this resolve was taken, upon whom his choice would fall; and his preference was confirmed by the declared wishes of the delegates in Congress from the states most concerned in the event. Washington, promptly, and in an affectionate letter, communicated his desires to Greene. The latter, in modest reply, declared his compliance, and only entreated a short leave of absence to "set his house in order," before departing on a distant and perilous expedition. His request was reasonable. He had been more than five years in the service, and his private interests had been almost wholly yielded up, without inquiry or examination, to the control and care of others. But the duty was pressing. In his reply, Washington says: "I wish circumstances could be made to correspond to your wishes to spend a little time at home previous to your setting out; *but your presence with your command, as soon as possible, is indispensable.*" So imperative was friendship, when coerced by duty! But Greene's determination had already been made before he received this reply. He was no less quick to feel this indispensable necessity, than his friend to urge it. He writes, in answer: "*I had given up the thought of going home before the receipt of your letter. My affairs required it;* but I was afraid it would take up too much time, *considering the critical state of affairs to the southward.*" A single day's further delay, and he set forward on the rugged path of duty, not waiting even for the embraces of his wife, momently expected, of children scarcely seen, while departing on a journey of nearly seven hundred miles. A low fever, which had hung upon him for some time, the fruit of exposure and anxiety, did not suffice to excuse a delay which his sense of duty could not justify in favor of his affections.

Greene hastened, first, to headquarters, where his reception was such as declared, not only for the high favor in which he stood with Washington, but for his greatly-increased and lofty reputation with the army. The advice of Washington, solicitous at once for the reputation of Greene, and for the success of his enterprise, was freely given, and all the assistance promised which he should be able to bestow. Here, too, ready and eager to serve under him, he found some of the noblest spirits of the army — Lafayette, Colonel Laurens, Major Lee, and others — who esteemed his personal worth, and did justice to his rare merits as a soldier.

Thus encouraged and assured, Greene hastened to Philadelphia, where he received the instructions of Congress in relation to the campaign, and ascertained the full extent of the resources which were forthcoming for his enterprise. These were few, and sufficiently unpromising. The army itself was a merely nominal existence — a shadow, rather than a substance. The fatal defeat of Gates had lost everything in the shape of stores, baggage, and artillery. Every article was to be supplied, and Congress had no money. A small sum, meant only to defray the expenses of his journey, was all that could be procured; while an attempt to obtain a loan, and contributions of clothing, from the merchants of Philadelphia, resulted only in proving, that government was as singularly wanting in credit as in cash. But for the friendship and activity of Governor Read, Greene must have set forth upon his expedition for the south, almost wholly deficient in every requisite, either for himself or his army. Read supplied him with a certain quantity of arms and munitions from the state magazines, and assisted him in procuring the use of baggage-wagons for their transportation. The annexation of Delaware and Maryland to his military department, from which states, hereafter, he might draw contingents, and very liberal promises of future supplies, constituted the full measure of all the support which Congress, at this moment, could contribute to the maintenance of the conflict in the south. Leaving Colonel Febiger behind him in Philadelphia, for no other purpose than to jog the memories of great men in regard to these promises, and forward the supplies as they might accumulate, Greene set out, on the 23d of November, on his journey to the Carolinas. He was accompanied by Baron Steuben, and his two aids, Major Burnet and Colonel Morris. The journey was a tedious one, which could only have been relieved by the mode pursued by our travellers, of encountering its monotony by an unwearied regard to all subjects, which might be considered, in reference to the great objects which they had in view. As the route lay through the capitals of several states, a brief halt at the seat of each government, enabled the general of the southern army to investigate their resources, and to adopt measures with the leading persons of each for supplying and sustaining his army. To awaken them all to a sense of the approaching danger—to show that the cause was a common one, and was only to be rendered successful and secure by a common action—was a chief employment during this progress. To those more remote from the seat of danger, he showed how certainly the fate of the immediate sufferer must be theirs, unless the assailed parties, struggling for life and death, should be seasonably succored; and insisted upon the policy, in its most selfish aspect, of saving, harmless, the sister state, if only that the wolf might be kept from other thresholds. To those on the verge of the danger, with their apprehensions already awakened for their own safety, he showed the necessity of firmness, promptitude, and a manly readiness to meet and brave the worst, as the true secret at once of security and patriotism. In order the more perfectly to keep the remoter states from indifference and forgetfulness to the claims of those over which the invader was already sweeping with resistless strides, he left General Gist in Maryland, to act as the agent for the southern army in that state and Delaware. The Baron Steuben was left in military charge of Virginia. To these men, urging their duties upon them, his language is full of impressive earnestness. "Let your applications," he says, "be as pressing as our necessities are urgent."—"The greatest consequences depend upon your activity and zeal." To Steuben was assigned the establishment of magazines and laboratories. The south, hitherto, had been almost wholly without them. The sites for these were chosen by Greene, whose eyes, as he approached the field of operations, were addressed to all that was important to his success. This choice of location was one of no small difficulty. In Maryland, they would have been too remote from the scene of action; in North Carolina, much too near. Virginia was the state in which it was necessary to establish them. The point of Fort, at the confluence of Revanna and Fluvanna, was decided upon for the principal laboratory; while the chief depôt of stores and arms was allotted to Prince Edward courthouse. To keep these regularly supplied with powder from the manufactories, and lead from the mines of Fincastle, was one of the special duties confided to Steuben. Greene vested him, besides, with the military command in Virginia, and with the farther task of organizing, disciplining, and expediting, the march of the recruits, from time to time, intended for the southern army. Jefferson was, at this time, the governor of Virginia. He was appealed to, and freely promised, to use all his energies in promoting the preparations of the state in regard to the common danger. Virginia had, at this period, but few regular troops in the field. A considerable body of her militia, with all the draughts and recruits collected to reinforce the southern army, were employed, at this very juncture, under the command of Generals Muhlenberg and Weedon, in watching the movements of General Leslie, which threatened her own safety. Her want of means and credit was quite as great as that of Congress; and her movements were embarrassed at once by the presence of danger, and the absence of adequate resources for defence. The southern army had but little to hope from this quarter. The resources of North Carolina, never ample, were perhaps still less available, at this moment, than those of Virginia. Men there were, perhaps, in sufficient numbers; but they lacked concentration, habits of drill and discipline, equipments of all kinds, munitions of war, and military stores. There was no money in the state, and the granaries of the country were empty. The fall of Charleston, and the defeat of Gates at Camden, had led to an unwise enrolment of vast bodies of militia, by which the country had been ravaged, and in the support of which, such vast quantities of paper money had been issued, as totally to destroy its own currency.

But, with an eye to all things, and every thought addressed to the emergency, devising ways and means, and undespairing in the worst discouragements, Greene continued his way through these states, toward the field of more active operations. With all his delays, his progress was a rapid one, and soon brought him to the encampment of the army at Charlotte, North Carolina, which he reached on the 2d of December. Here, with a noble delicacy, which keenly appreciated the exquisite suffering of a proud and ambitious mind, sinking beneath unexpected, though perhaps not undeserved disaster, he relieved Gates of the command. He confirmed, for the day, the standing orders of his predecessor, whose behavior was marked by a dignified resignation, and a carriage which was, at once, equally removed from the baseness of despondency, and the insolence of a spirit ready to brave public opinion, as it had, unhappily, essayed to brave its fortune. It was also among the delicate duties of Greene, while relieving Gates from the command, to institute a court of inquiry into the conduct by which the battle of Camden had been lost. It was grateful to Greene that he could escape from the prosecution of this painful investigation. The service was not in a condition to allow, nor the army to make it. The order of Washington, requiring that the "officers of the court should consist of such general and field officers, of the continental troops, as were *not* present at the battle of Camden; or, being present, are not wanted as witnesses; or are persons to whom General Gates has no objection," involved conditions which could not be complied with. There were not, in fact, three general officers left in the army who could sit upon the court, unless withdrawn from other places where their presence was indispensable. Under these circumstances, Greene gladly made such representations to Congress as obtained a revision of their orders, by which he was wholly relieved from a duty from which all his sensibilities shrunk. He regarded Gates's case with tenderness; too indulgently, perhaps—but as one of misfortune, rather than misconduct; and his behavior to the unfortunate man—for ever fallen, by this his own catastrophe, from the very heights of power—while it was "edifying to the army," touched the soul of the sufferer himself, and converted him, from a former enemy, into an attached and grateful friend.

CHAPTER VIII.

Glimpses of the past Progress of the War in the South.—Condition of the Country and of the Army when Greene takes Command.—His Difficulties—Resources—Policy.—Moves from Charlotte to Pee Dee.—Marion's Movements.—Cornwallis.—Morgan.—Tarleton pursues Morgan.—Is defeated at the Cowpens.

It was on the fourth of December, 1780, that Greene entered upon the duties of his new and arduous command. It was one of singular difficulty and responsibility, and the means provided for his use and disposal were strangely inadequate to the necessities before him. The condition of South Carolina was one of great destitution, and of a prostration apparently complete. Her resources seemed to be entirely exhausted, and her strong places were wholly within the grasp of the invader. A backward glance at her fortunes, during the war, up to the moment when Greene was appointed to the command of the southern army, would seem, in some degree, to be necessary to a proper comprehension of the duties which were required at his hands, and of the difficulties which lay in the way of their successful execution. South Carolina was one of those states which are at once opulent and feeble. She enjoyed a large commerce, but it was almost entirely in the hands of Europeans who were secretly hostile to her aims at independence. Those aims were boldly urged by her native population, consisting of the high spirited gentry of the lower country. Her causes of quarrel with the mother-country were of a very different nature with those that operated upon the people of New England. They did not arise from feelings of jealousy between the parties in consequence of threatened rivalry of interests. In the south the people engaged in no manufactures, and held no shipping. They were planters, who found a ready market in Old England for all their produce. But they felt keenly the denial to themselves of those privileges of self-government which the possession of many superior intellects, and of a highly-educated state of society among the natives, naturally told them should be their own. They resented the usurpation, not only as a denial of right, but as an indignity, which continually imposed upon them, in places of authority, the foreigner in whom they did not find a superior, and who felt no sympathy with the soil. This prompted them readily to seize upon the common pretexts of the sister-colonies, and to sympathize with the movement in New England, not because of any affinities between the separate people, but as it afforded an occasion for the assertion of their rights. But their motives were not of sufficient influence with the great body of the people of Carolina, to make the cause a common one throughout the state. The people were not sufficiently homogeneous for the attainment of this important object. Large portions of the interior country had been only newly settled, and from European nations. The Germans, having large settlements to themselves, scarcely speaking the language of the natives, were not easily persuaded to forego for the sway of a people whom they did not know, the paternal government of a prince, himself of German family. The Scotch, forming colonies throughout the interior, preserved all their clannish propensities, and their loyalty has always been the distinguishing feature of the national character. The quaker and Moravian settlements, which were also numerous, were opposed to war, on any pretences; and thus it was that in the very heart of the country there dwelt a powerful community ready, at any opportunity, to thwart, by indifference or active hostility, the efforts of the native population, at the great object of national deliverance. Not a few of the natives, also, were unprepared to strike for independence; either doubtful of a policy which would, perhaps, elevate the power of the northern colonies (of which they were jealous) at their expense, or, doubtful if the country was yet ripe for the great experiment of making its further progress alone. For a time, however, these conflicting and opposing interests were kept in abeyance, silenced if not subdued, by the bold and energetic measures which the patriotic party pursued, and the good fortune which attended their initial efforts in arms. Successful, in singular degree, in beating off a British fleet and army at the opening of the war, and scourging into quiet and obedience the insurgents who first made a demonstration in the interior, in correspondence with the movements of the enemy upon the seaboard, it was erroneously supposed that there would be little difficulty a second time from this doubtful quarter. The numbers of the faithful were greatly overrated, in the spirit and vigor which they had shown; the numbers of the disaffected as greatly underrated, in the silence which they kept, and the stealthy policy which held their true feelings secret. A second attempt at the invasion of South Carolina, after the partial fall of Charleston, led the patriots to suspect, in some degree, their own weakness; but as this invasion was again baffled and defeated it was reserved for a subsequent day of danger, to reveal the full extent of the evil from the sources indicated.

The fall of Georgia afforded the British general a *point d'appui* whence he could more easily operate upon the sister-colony. Florida, always in his possession, was another mean of annoyance to South Carolina. Here harbored all the fugitives who had been driven forth in consequence of their uncompromising hostility to the popular movement. A fruitless but expensive attempt to invade Florida—an attempt not more profitable in its results, to recover Georgia—contributed greatly to diminish the resources of Carolina in the *personnel* and *materiel* of war. The bloody conflict in the attempted storm of Savannah, had fallen heavily on the Carolina troops, had diminished her regiments, had burdened her with an excessive debt, and had destroyed the value of her currency. The regular regiment of Georgia had been destroyed, or was in captivity, and her own militia had suffered severely, and been scattered or taken, in the latter state; surprised in the charge of incompetent officers, under the more skilful operations of the invader. Thus circumstanced, she was but feebly prepared to resist the third and successful attempt of the British general-in-chief to obtain firm foothold in her soil.

Charleston, besieged by a vastly superior force of the enemy, under Sir Henry Clinton himself, succumbed, after a siege of nearly two months. The defence had been as well conducted and maintained as was possible by an inadequate body of troops, threatened at once by pestilence and famine, and worn out by unremitting duties in the field. By this surrender, five thousand soldiers of the southern army were lost, temporarily, to the pressing wants of the country. Nor was this the only loss. It involved others quite as heavy and important. While the leaguer of the city had been continued, detached bod ies of the southern militia had still kept the field. This measure had for its object the maintenance of free communication between the seaboard and the interior. It was unfortunate that this division of the strength of the state left neither that portion assigned to the garrison, nor that which kept the field, in sufficient strength for safety. With the fall of the city, and even before that event, the British began to cut off, in detail, the scattered bodies of militia—effecting a series of surprises, which, where the disparity of military discipline and experience was so great as between these parties, was not, perhaps, of difficult achievement. The massacre usually followed the surprise; and, with their capital city overthrown, their regular army made captive, their allies dispersed, their own militia cut up in scattered squadrons, without being permitted to unite—with the loyalists rising everywhere around them, encouraged by the presence of a powerful ally, and eager now, and active in due degree with the apathy and caution which they had hitherto been compelled to show—it was, perhaps, not surprising that the whigs of Carolina yielded for a time to fortune, and lay, *perdu*, in waiting for a better moment. But they did not wait long, or without a hope. The approach of the continental army under Gates, however feeble, once more provoked their activity and stimulated their enterprise. Already, however, had their own partisan leaders—since grown famous—taken the field. Sumter, Marion, Pickens, and others, had already commenced that brilliant career which showed the soldiers of the south to be particularly fitted for guerilla warfare; and these, with the arrival of Gates, were prepared to co-operate with him, by demonstrations happily directed to divert the attention of the enemy, and to distract his purposes. The very hour of Gates's defeat was distinguished by a brilliant affair of Sumter, in which, but for the absence of that caution which is taught alone by a veteran experience in war, his success would have been complete, and would have made partial amends for the catastrophe at Camden. Even after that catastrophe had taken place, it was for Marion to dart out suddenly from his swamps, in the very moment of the British triumph, and to rescue from their clutches a large body of their prisoners. These were proofs that the spirit and enterprise of Carolina were unsubdued by her misfortunes, whatever might be her deficiencies of physical strength. But her contest lay not entirely with the invader. Had this been the case, she had probably been quite equal to her own defence, without needing succor from her sisters. Unhappily, the causes already mentioned, raised an army within her own limits, which was hostile to her independence. Rising in their several districts, the loyalists took ample vengeance for their previous quiet and forbearance. A civil war raged in the country, of so desperate a nature, as to lead Greene, when describing it, to say that the people pursued each other like wild beasts rather than like men. Such is usually the character of civil war. The whole state was thus rendered the arena for unrelenting conflict; and, preying upon each other with a sleepless ferocity, there were but few hands to oppose to those of the national invader. The British looked on grimly, glad of a struggle which relieved them from many of the toils of war; and were content to leave to their auxiliaries, the loyalists, the work of massacre, while they quietly possessed themselves of its fruits. It was not the least of the merits of the Carolina partisan generals, that they could detach from petty broils, and neighborhood conflict, any body of citizens, and rally them, with single aim, for the great busines of national deliverance. That they should still keep alive the spirit of patriotism, in the midst of civil war, with a powerful enemy standing by to sustain the domestic factions by which the movement was opposed, was in itself conclusive that the state might be rescued from foreign clutches, with only a respectable force of regulars, upon which to fall back and rally, and to which to look for support and succor against any overwhelming efforts of the foe. To have continued the conflict, by the native militia alone, so long under the walled places of the British, and with their troops everywhere in the field, was to afford the most encouraging hopes that, in the end, the latter must be driven from their conquests. For such a warfare, perhaps, no general was better endowed by nature, or prepared by training, than Greene. Patient, vigilant, collected—never so eager for success, as to overlook the necessary means for obtaining it—never so sanguine of victory as to forget the caprices of fortune, and the uncertain moods which usually mark an untrained soldier—circumspect and cautious, in the last degree—he was, perhaps, the best captain in the world to restrain and regulate the raw troops whom he had to manage—to curb their impetuosity, methodize their valor, and make them habitually provide against surprise.

Greene did not close his eyes against the difficulties which now rose up in his path at every moment. He found himself, on taking command of the army, sustained by few encouragements. The army itself was a skeleton—the mere wreck of an army—few in numbers, without clothing, arms, or ammunition. It counted but nine hundred and seventy continentals, and one thousand and thirteen militia. This was the force which he found awaiting him at Charlotte. There was a smaller force, but better provided, serving as an independent command under Morgan, which had been detached by Gates, and was now actually operating in South Carolina, and in the neighborhood of the British garrison at Camden. This force consisted of four companies, which had been drafted from the regiments to serve as light infantry; a body of seventy cavalry, under Colonel Washington; and a small corps of sixty rifles, under

Major Rose. We shall have occasion to speak of this command hereafter. With his army weak and ill provided, Greene found himself among friends who were too much abashed by ill fortune and inferior means, to be confident themselves in hope, or to encourage him to boldness. His enemies, on the other hand, warmed with continued victories, were flushed with exultation, and swarming, in the confidence of numbers, on every side. When he looked toward South Carolina, the region which he was to penetrate, he found it everywhere overawed by British garrisons. Its strong points were everywhere seized upon and fortified. Lord Cornwallis had planted himself, with the main body of his army, at Winnsborough. This post enabled him to complete his chain of fortified places, "from Georgetown to Augusta, in a circle, the centre of which would have been about Beaufort, in South Carolina, equidistant from Charleston and Savannah. These posts consisted of Georgetown, Camden, Winnsborough, Ninety-Six, and Augusta. Within this circle was an interior chain, at the distance of about half the radius, consisting of Fort Watson on the road to Camden, Motte's house and Granby on the Congaree. Dorchester and Orangeburg, on the road both to Ninety-Six and Granby, were fortified as posts of rest and deposite on the line of communication; as was Monk's Corner, or Biggin church, and some other small posts on that to Camden." These posts were all judiciously chosen, at once for procuring supplies, maintaining communications, and overawing the country. The British army was divided among these several places, on the assumption by Greene of the charge of the *debris* of the southern army. They consisted of something more than five thousand men, and employed themselves, at all these posts, in recruiting from the tory settlements—a business in which they were uncommonly successful.

Their strength underwent a large increase on the arrival of Greene, being reinforced by a force of nearly three thousand men, under General Leslie, who was, in consequence, diverted from Virginia to Charleston; thus presenting an overwhelming preponderance of force against the American general, which it was difficult to meet.

But Greene's mind — calm, equable, well-trained, and executive — quickly rose to the exigency before it. To ascertain the wants of his men, and to cast about for the sources of supply, were joint operations of the same thought. Clothing, in particular, was the great necessity. The nakedness of the soldiers was the first impressive fact that met his eyes. Many of them could not be seen on parade, and were actually ordered back to their homes on this account. Of those who did appear, the ludicrous exhibition of shreds and patches, odds and ends, of uniforms and old clothes, made a variety, to which no display of a mock military could, possibly, do justice. The munitions of war were equally wanting, and the magazines were as bare as the soldiers. Nor were there means in the military chest to procure supplies, even if they had been within reach of purchase; and it was with great difficulty, and only by the most excellent management, that provisions, from day to day, were procured for the support of the army. The quartermaster's department was in quite as bad condition. Greene's experience in this department enabled him, readily, to appreciate his deficiencies, though it afforded him some advantages, perhaps, in suggesting the means for meeting them. But here, again, the same painful conflict was to be carried on for months, and possibly for years, to encounter necessities without resources, and furnish material without the means; to live by shifts and expedients, striving day by day, with an eternal anxiety, doubtful what the day will bring forth, and ignorant of the sources which shall provide for the exigencies of the morrow. Without a market, or money with which to enter it — without the present means for transporting supplies — and with an army constantly craving, and as constantly required to serve in spite of craving, the genius of the best general in the world might have succumbed beneath his anxieties, unless supported by a generous faith, that hopes everything in a right cause, and from a steady compliance with the requisitions of country and duty.

It was fortunate for Greene that he was consoled and strengthened against these trials and anxieties, by the support and society of some of the most select and noble spirits in the army. His officers were the picked men of the country — brave, enterprising, full of expedients, resolute, generous, and ardent in their sympathies. Morgan, famous as a partisan, distinguished at Quebec and Saratoga; Otho Williams, who had been chiefly instrumental in saving the wreck of Gates's army; Lee and Washington, renowned for the spirit and enterprise which marked their respective characters and commands; Kosciusko, a chief of European fame, and one of the best engineers in the service. These, in their several departments, were scarcely to be equalled; and, with Carrington in the quartermaster's, and Davies in the commissariat department, it may be reasonably supposed that everything which might be done by mortal ability, under like circumstances, must be within the province of his performance. When, to these aids and allies, we add the names of such partisan officers, among the militia, as have never been surpassed — Marion, Sumter, Pickens, Henderson, and others — we may naturally look for achievements, of as much enterprise and daring as belong to the fortunes of any fighting army among any people.

The region of country in which he was to act, required the very best, and the most various, military capacity. Unlike the north, it was a region in which the vicissitudes were equally sudden and extreme. In the north, the fields of controversy were few; the chief points of progress obvious; the means of communication ready; the game always tolerably apparent to the least skilful strategist. There, the population was dense, and intelligence was transmitted with great rapidity. For the same reason, the means of sustenance were more readily furnished, and particularly where the military chest was more amply supplied with the means of payment, than was the case when the war was transferred to the south. In most respects, the theatre of action in the latter region was totally unlike that of the north. Here, the population was sparsely settled; the country, in large tracts, desolate and unproductive; the roads few; the forests unbroken; the swamps impassable; the rivers liable to frequent overflow; foraging remote and difficult; intelligence slow to arrive; the people nearly equally divided in opinion—implacable and fierce in their resentments—always restless, and always suspicious accordingly; and the circumstances, taken together, of such a sort, as to leave an army at no moment perfectly secure from a capital disaster.

It was the peculiar faculty of Greene, to study carefully the scene of action, and to adopt his policy to its conditions. His explorations of the country were singularly searching and thorough. Under his requisitions, the Dan was surveyed by Carrington, the Yadkin by General Stevens, and the Catawba by Kosciusko; and these surveys, which he thus commanded, are supposed to be the first which ever revealed, to any extent, the characteristics of the several rivers. They proved, in the sequel, of immense importance to the progress of his arms. Magazines were established at the head of the Catawba, by which he brought the means of subsistence more immediately within the line which he had fixed upon as the base of his operations. He renewed his entreaties to the authorities of the several states within his province, urging the necessity of immediate supplies, and the most energetic exertions, for the future. He counselled, in the embodiment of the militia, that resort should be had to the draught, in preference to any other form of proceeding; and, in his letters on this subject and others, employs a tone, and throws out suggestions, which have for their object something beyond the matters which they immediately discuss. In plain terms, he seeks to prepare the several governments, which he addresses, for that more decisive exercise of authority which he, himself, was resolved to adopt in the conduct of the war. It belonged to the same policy that he should seasonably begin to enforce that discipline among his troops, which, though essential to their efficiency, had yet been, hitherto, disregarded. It had been the custom of the troops to come and go, almost at pleasure; to retire to their homes without leave, and to stay without limit. For this offence he assigned the penalty of death, and rigidly enforced it. The first offender, after the practice had been forbidden, was made a summary example, being shot at the head of the army, which was drawn out to witness the painful spectacle. It was a terrible lesson, but one rendered necessary by a due regard to discipline.

From his camp at Charlotte, Greene prepared to draw nigher to the scene of more active operations. The duty of selecting a camp of watch and repose; where, without slumbering, the army could yet be tolerably secure; and where, without engaging in conflict, they could yet be kept constantly reminded of the necessity of preparing for it;—was confided to Kosciusko. The spot was chosen at the junction of Hick's creek with the Great Pee Dee, and here the army arrived on the 26th of December. On the same day that the army was put under marching orders for this point, the detachment under Morgan was ordered to cross the Catawba, and approach the position of Lord Cornwallis at Winnsborough. Speaking of his new camp, the object of his movement, and the advantages derived from it, we gather the following summary from Greene himself: "I am here in my camp of repose, improving the discipline and spirits of my men and the opportunity for looking about me. I am well satisfied with this movement, for it has answered thus far all the purposes for which I intended it. It makes the most of my inferior force, for it compels my adversary to divide his, and holds him in doubt as to his own line of conduct. He can not leave Morgan behind him to come at me, or his posts of Ninety-Six and Augusta would be exposed. And he can not chase Morgan far, or prosecute his views upon Virginia while I am here with the whole country open before me. I am as near to Charleston as he is, and as near to Hillsborough as I was at Charlotte; so that I am in no danger of being cut off from my reinforcements, while an uncertainty as to my future designs has made it necessary to leave a large detachment of the enemy's late reinforcements in Charleston, and move the rest up on this side the Wateree. But, although there is nothing to obstruct my march to Charleston, I am far from having such a design in contemplation, in the present relative positions and strength of the two armies. It would be putting it in the power of my enemy to compel me to fight him. At present my operations must be in the country where the rivers are fordable, and to guard against the chance of not being able to choose my ground. . . . Below the falls [of Pee Dee], all through this country, from the Allegany to the seacoast, and from the Chesapeake to Georgia, the country is champaign, and presenting no passes that can be held by an inferior force. The rivers are deep, and their banks covered with impassable swamps, across which, at long intervals, roads have been constructed, which afford the only avenues of retreat. I can not venture to get entangled among the difficulties they present, until I can turn upon my enemy and fight him when I please."

Thus, of the objects and advantages of his position. Hear him now, in the same breath, on the subject of his condition and resources: "I find the difficulties of subsisting an army far beyond all anticipation. Even here, where the inhabitants are generally well disposed, they will not gather in their crops from the field, because depositing their grain in their barns exposes it to be seized by their friends or burnt by their enemies. It is hard to stand so much in need of friends, and be compelled to subsist ourselves by means so well calculated to convert friends into enemies. But we have not a shilling of money, and must collect subsistence by force, or disband. I have had an opportunity of learning the force of the loyalists in these states, and the parts of the country in which they reside, and their numbers and zeal present a formidable obstacle to our future measures. On the other hand, the whig population has been greatly reduced by the numbers that have fled from the distress that friends and foes have heaped on them. The enemy are now recruiting in all parts of this state, and the command of gold, aided by the public distress and loyal feeling, has been too successful in promoting the project of making one conquest the stepping-stone to another. At present they are in possession of all the fertile and populous parts of South Carolina, and until circumstances will admit of my penetrating into the heart of the country, to meet and fight him, we shall have to operate in a country that has been exhausted and depopulated by the swarms of mounted militia that have been impoverishing rather than defending it. Yet I should feel no apprehensions for the event, had I a prospect of being supported by a permanent force. But North Carolina has not a man on foot, and Virginia only a few raw and naked troops, and those enlisted for a short time. The fine troops of Maryland and Delaware, enlisted for the war, are now reduced, comparatively, to a handful, and General Gist gives me no hope of an early reinforcement from that quarter. North Carolina seems disposed to assist us, but her councils are so distracted that I can not hope much from her efforts. The whigs will not serve unless the tories are compelled, and the tories are too strong to be driven, or, if forced to take the field, will run away, desert, or betray us. Virginia, without money and without credit, I fear can do little more; and in both states, militia substitutes are too much in demand to leave materials for enlisting an army, except for very limited periods."

These extracts will afford a sufficient idea of the kind and extent of the embarrassments which beset the commander of the southern army at his camp of repose. Here, however, he was now joined by the long-expected legion of Colonel Lee, from Virginia, a fine body, equally made up of horse and foot, admirably equipped, of three hundred men. At the same time, and from the same quarter, came Colonel Greene, with a body of four hundred recruits. A thousand more recruits had been raised in Virginia, but they could not be sent into the field, from very nakedness. Those who were sent, though marching in the depth of winter, were clad only in summer garments of the meanest description, and chiefly made of linen.

The arrival of Lee at the camp on the Pee Dee, enabled Greene to attempt an expedition which he had contemplated before. This was an enterprise against Georgetown, one of a series in which the enemy should be struck at in detail, in which Lee should operate in conjunction with Marion. The famous partisan had been busy all the while, in his particular way and province. Morgan and Marion were in motion about the same time. The former, not strong enough to attempt the post at Winnsborough, contented himself with keeping Lord Cornwallis anxious about its safety, while achieving some small surprises against the tories in the neighborhood of Ninety-Six. Marion, having Lee with him, succeeded measurably in the attempt on Georgetown. The place was surprised, but, from a failure of proper concert between the assailing parties, and the want of artillery, it was not in their power to retain it, or to gather the best results from the advantages which had been won.

The attempt upon this post, to be followed up by others, had for its object to divert the attention of the enemy from Morgan to the danger of his garrisons in the low country. The surprise of Georgetown was not, accordingly, a simple *coup de main*, but a first step in the prosecution of a great plan which should fetter the enterprise of the British general, distract his regards, and prevent him from that contemplated march upon Virginia, from Carolina, which now constituted the leading policy with Cornwallis. To detain him in North Carolina, until an army of sufficient strength and discipline could be raised to encounter him, was the design and desire of Greene. The measures pursued for this purpose, soon began to disturb the repose of Cornwallis, and to compel his attention to the course of Morgan.

The latter, meanwhile, had taken post on the banks of the Pacolet, where he was joined by a considerable body of the militia of the Carolinas. He had scarcely made his appearance in the neighborhood before he had an opportunity of striking at a strong body of loyalists who had advanced from the Savannah to the Fair Forest. He sent Colonel Washington, with his cavalry, and a couple of hundred mounted militia under Colonel M'Call, who, by rapid riding, came upon them in the neighborhood of Ninety-Six, and struck at them with such emphasis as to kill two thirds of their number. The surprise was complete, and the punishment sufficiently sanguinary. Availing himself of the fact that his appearance was totally unexpected in a neighborhood which swarmed with enemies, and was covered by a strong British post, he succeeded in the attempt to surprise the stockade fort of General Cunningham, and to scatter the garrison. These enterprises, almost at his threshold, disquieted Cornwallis, whose light troops and cavalry, under Tarleton, were then unprofitably urging the pursuit of Sumter, after the battle-field of Blackstocks. Cornwallis felt the evil moral influences of such audacity on the part of the Americans, to say nothing of the direct injury to the service, in the slaughter of auxiliaries and the cutting off of his supplies. Tarleton, accordingly, received his orders to "push Morgan to the utmost." To enable him to do so, to effectual purpose, Cornwallis divided his forces with him, intending, while Tarleton either destroyed Morgan, or drove him out of the state, which he thought most likely, to move forward rapidly himself, and, throwing himself across the path of the American general, cut him off from his place of retreat, and compel him to surrender. Leslie, meanwhile, with another body of troops, was to march up the east side of the Catawba, and interpose to prevent Greene from doing anything for the support of his brigades.

But, events are not within human calculation. They

were destined to disappoint the plans of the English general. Tarleton obeyed the commands of his superior with due diligence; and, with his usual celerity, set forth in pursuit of Morgan. He had with him, in this pursuit, about eleven hundred men, five hundred of whom constituted that formidable legion which had hitherto traversed the country with almost unvarying success. His field-pieces were served by a detachment of the royal artillery. Morgan's force did not quite equal this in numbers, consisting, in all, of nine hundred and seventy men, of whom six hundred were militia. But these militia were now somewhat experienced, and they were under leaders, such as Pickens and M'Call, in whom they had the utmost confidence, and who knew exactly how to manage them. Still, the superiority in artillery and cavalry, was too greatly with Tarleton to render it prudent to await his encounter; and, very loath to do so, Morgan retired at his approach. The pursuit was commenced on the 12th of January, 1781. Morgan might have escaped his pursuer; but he really had no desire to do so—was chock full of fight, and only desired to find for his mood a proper field and fitting opportunity. In this temper of mind, as may be supposed, it was not difficult for Tarleton—with whom, hitherto, in the plenitude of good fortune, it had been only to see to conquer—"to bring him to the scratch." The American brigadier awaited his enemy on the banks of the Thicketty.

Believing that Morgan was only solicitous to escape, and resolved upon the honors of a *coup de main*, Tarleton pushed forward precipitately on the 17th of January, and came upon the Americans—not in the hurry and confusion of a flight, but coolly posted, with the breakfast things just removed, and every man ready, refreshed by a hearty morning meal, and not averse to a very different encounter. The British were fatigued by a five hours' march, the troops of Morgan refreshed by a rest of quite the same duration, to say nothing of the breakfast. But Tarleton, flattered by frequent successes, and, in some degree, the spoilea child of fortune, was not the man to wait. Morgan gave him advantages which, had he been another sort of enemy, his prudence would have scarcely yielded. His ground was upon an eminence, gently ascending for three or four hundred yards, and covered with an open wood. On the crown of this eminence he posted the Maryland regulars, nearly three hundred in number; in line, on their right, two companies of Virginia militia, and a corps of Georgians: making, in all, some four hundred and thirty men. This line, which was the rear, was commanded by Lieutenant-Colonel Howard. A body of picked Carolina militia, nearly three hundred in number, commanded by Pickens, was posted, in open order, some one hundred and fifty yards in advance of the line of Howard; and, in front of these, was another body of militiamen, one hundred and fifty more, scattered, as riflemen, loosely along the whole front. These had their particular duties assigned them, sufciently understood in the words that passed among themselves — "Mark the epaulettes!" and admirably did they mark them. It was by this process, only, that Morgan could equalize the superiority of the enemy, derived from his greater strength in cavalry, and the presence of his artillery, of which the Americans had none. The American reserve, one hundred and fifty in number, consisted of Washington's and M'Call's cavalry, and was posted behind an eminence in the rear of the second line.

Tarleton's attempt to reconnoitre was foiled by the fatal discharges of the scattered riflemen. His cavalry advanced, accordingly, and drove them into the first line.

but not until they had taught their enemy to tremble under the keen close aim and destructive fire of their rifles. Steadily advancing under the fire of his artillery, Tarleton pressed forward. The militia under Pickens, commanded to deliver their fire at fifty yards, coolly awaited the British approach, and obeyed their instructions to the letter. "Here," according to the admission of an officer in the Maryland line, "the battle was gained." So terrible a fire as met the advancing enemy, has seldom been delivered on the field of battle. The officers, in particular, paid dearly for the epaulettes they wore; while a liberal proportion of the troops by whom they were followed, bit the dust in company with their gallant leaders. The service done which was required at their hands—for it was not expected that they should stand the charge of the bayonet—the militia yielded to the pressure of the enemy's battle, and left the way open to the second line. The shouts of the British declared their confidence in the affair as in a battle already won, and hurried forward in a degree of disorder, which soon betrayed the evil consequence, to their ranks, of the loss which they had sustained in officers. The fire of the second line opened upon them, and staggered them while they were thus disordered, and, for nearly thirty minutes, it was maintained with constancy and serious effect. Still, the assailing column advanced, striving to dress and move steadily forward to the charge; but with so much hesitation, that the British commander was compelled to bring the 71st regiment into line upon his left, while his cavalry swept forward against the American right. Morgan perceived the necessity of guarding his flank. But his reserve, under Washington, was already busy in covering the retreating militia, who, pursued by the enemy's horse, and having to traverse the whole front of the second line, upon which they were ordered to rally, were, necessarily, greatly exposed to this danger. To repulse the assailants, and to cover the militia while they rallied, was the work of a few moments with Washington: but, these moments were big with the issue of the day. A retrograde movement of the continental line, occasioned by a mistake in orders, had nearly lost the victory so nearly won. The British line, beholding this retrograde, confounded it with a flight, and rushed forward with shouts of triumph, as to a victory. And such it might have been, but for the fact that, in pursuing the enemy's cavalry some distance beyond the British line, Washington had found their right flank entirely exposed to him, and had a fair view of the confusion prevailing in their ranks. It was at the lucky moment, when the retrograde movement of the American line was becoming too much accelerated for precision, that a messenger from Washington delivered these few words: "They are coming on like a mob; give them a fire, and I will charge them." "Face about!" was the instant order along the line. "Give them a single fire, and the victory is ours." Pickens, with his militia, appeared on the hill at this moment, to unite in effectual obedience to this command. It was obeyed from left to right. With terrible effect did the lightning stream forth from the levelled muzzles, at the moment when their enemies, rapidly rushing forward and tumultuously shouting, were within thirty paces only. The presented bayonet followed up the fire; and, as the glittering blades of the opposing ranks were interlocked, the British dropped their weapons and fell upon their faces. The victory was won. The rifles of Pickens's militia, and the sabres of Washington's cavalry, finished the business of the day; and thus ended the famous battle of the Cowpens.

The enemy lost one hundred and fifty in killed and

wounded, and four hundred prisoners. Of the Americans, but eleven were killed and sixty-one wounded. Morgan retired with two field-pieces, eight hundred muskets, two stands of colors, thirty-five baggage-wagons, tents, and ammunition, and one hundred dragoon horses—the trophies of his victory.

CHAPTER IX.

Morgan's Retreat before Cornwallis.—Greene joins him on the Catawba.—Condition of the American Army.—Militia collects under Davidson.—British pass the Catawba.—Death of Davidson.—Morgan retreats—Passes the Yadkin.—Skirmish with the Rearguard.—Anecdote of Greene.

THE victory of Morgan was complete, but it was one upon which he did not venture to repose. Cornwallis, he well knew, was in force, at a distance of but twenty-five miles, and this space would easily be overcome by the fugitive cavalry of the British conveying the tidings of their own disaster. Reasoning from what should be done in such case, he had every reason to suppose that Cornwallis would put his whole army in pursuit. He halted upon the battle-field, accordingly, only long enough to refresh his men and secure his prisoners; and hurried across Broad river that very evening leaving Pickens, with a sufficient detachment of his mounted militia, to bury the dead and provide for the wounded. With the dawn of morning he was again upon the march, pressing, with all haste, to throw the rising waters of the Catawba between his pursuers and himself. Fortune, and some unnecessary delays on the part of Cornwallis, facilitated his objects. Had the latter set off in immediate pursuit, discarding all cumbrous baggage, all unnecessary *materiel*, the victory of Morgan, burdened as he was, with his spoils and pursuers, might have availed him little. But one or more precious days were lost by the British commander; and, when he approached the Catawba, he found Morgan already on the opposite side, at a distance of twenty miles, with the river roused by freshets, roaring and swelling, as an obstacle between them. Greene, meanwhile, apprized of the victory of his brigadier, and apprehensive for his safety—pushed as he had reason to fear he would be, by the utmost exertions of Cornwallis—set out, with all speed, to join him. His efforts were more successful than those of his enemy. His celerity of movement alone saved him from the dangers of a progress through a country, almost equally occupied with friends and foes, which he traversed for a space of nearly a hundred and fifty miles, and almost without an escort. He had put his army under marching orders, but felt too greatly the importance of being personally at the point of action, at the moment of greatest exigency, to await their movements. His hope was, not yet to cross weapons with Cornwallis, but simply to oppose and foil his generalship; save Morgan, if possible, and so hang upon the skirts of the enemy, like a threatening thunder-cloud, as to paralyze his enterprises until the moment which should make him ready for the fight. To cross weapons with Cornwallis now, was quite beyond his strength. This was the conviction that qualified the delight which he felt at the recent victory. It was one of which he could take no advantage; and he stood, tantalized with the opening, which, with an adequate army, would have been offered him by the field of Cowpens, and the purposeless and unprofitable pursuit of the British. His nominal force, including that of Morgan and the militia, did not exceed seventeen hundred men; while the strength of Cornwallis, joined by Leslie, must have considerably exceeded that number. In equipments, dress, discipline, and munitions of war, the superiority of the latter was very much greater still. In money, Greene was still poorer than in men; not a hard dollar being in the money-chest, even for the most important necessity of an army—secret intelligence.

But, with little to encourage, he was still hopeful. With the waters of the Catawba roaring between the two armies, and forbidding the farther pursuit of the British, he busied himself in recruiting the militia. With a considerable number of recruits, he might even venture, when the river subsided, to dispute the passage with the enemy, and to this labor he addressed himself with his habitual energy. "It is my only wish to be upon an equal footing with Lord Cornwallis, and if I do not give you a good account of him, I will agree to be subject to your censure." Such was his language to Washington. Again, he says: "I am not without hopes of ruining Lord Cornwallis, if he persists in his mad scheme of pushing through the country." To effect this object, Greene required a well-appointed army of five thousand infantry and eight hundred or a thousand horse, equipped for active operations. "Such a force, assisted by the auxiliary aid of the militia, would prove superior to any force the enemy could maintain in the field in this quarter." The militia was forthcoming, but there was no maintenance for them. "There is," says he, "a great spirit of enterprise prevailing among the militia of these southern states;" but they fluctuated in their periods of service, going and coming at pleasure, as well they might do, when they not only got no pay, but were without clothing or provisions. "Early in January, several hundreds of the troops actually could not appear at drill, or perform guard duty, for want of clothing."—"More than half our numbers are, in a manner, naked; so much so that we can not put them on the least kind of duty. *Indeed, there is a great number that have not a rag of clothes on them, except a little piece of blanket, in the Indian form, around their waists.*" That men, under such conditions, should be found in camp at all, is passing wonderful.

Greene made the most of his resources, and bore up against his difficulties with exemplary fortitude and skill. To secure the prisoners taken by Morgan, was a first object, and, to do this without lessening the numerical strength of his army, was not less important. They had been properly sent forward in advance, by Morgan, as soon as he had effected the passage of the Catawba; but there was still a long journey to perform before a place could be reached where they would be secure from rescue. It happened that the term of service of the Virginia militia was nearly out. Greene employed them during the remaining interval of duty, to take charge of the prisoners, and conduct them to Virginia. He was thus enabled to secure his prize without losing the service of a single man. Orders had previously been given for effecting a junction, at Salisbury, of his force with that of Morgan. He had prepared for this junction, collected and camped his provisions, where they lay away from the contemplated route; called in his detachments; given orders to convey stores and valuable property to the interior from the seaboard; and, in order the more securely to provide for the chances of retreat, instructed his quartermaster-general to form a magazine on the Roanoke, and hold his boats in readiness for transportation on the Dan. Despatches to the several governors of the southern states, to supply their several quotas—to Steuben, to hasten his recruits—and to the mountaineers along the frontier ranges of the Carolinas and Virginia, to come forward and renew the glorious examples of courage and patriotism which they had shown at King's mountain—were among the thousand details which furnished employment, at this period of exigency, to his comprehensive and indefatigable mind.

To resume. Greene's exertions to collect a sufficient body of militia for the defence of the passage of the Ca tawba, was not successful, and the stream now began to fall. It was evident that the moment would soon approach when the British army would begin to move; and all that could be done was to retard his passage, and cripple him as much as possible, while the force of Morgan disappeared. For this object, General Davidson, with three hundred mounted riflemen, forming a corps of observation, were to watch and dispute the passage of the river, while a similar force, also militia riflemen, were scattered along the bank, so as to keep eye and aim upon all of the several fords by which the enemy might attempt to cross Greene remained with these, in order to bring them off as soon as the passage was effected; while Morgan, at Beaty's ford, and six miles nearer the place of rendezvous (which was designated, and on the road to Salisbury, some sixteen miles from the Catawba), was prepared to march at the first signal. He did so, hastily and in silence, on the evening of the 31st of January. The river was now falling quite as rapidly as it had risen; no more militia were to be expected, and the British were preparing to force the passage. After several feints, and false demonstrations, the better to deceive the American riflemen as to the true course which he meant to take in crossing the Catawba, Cornwallis, at length, at midnight, on the first of February, approached the ford called M'Cowan's with the main body of his army. This as a private passage, but little frequented, afforded the best prospect of effecting a surprise of the Americans. While he attempted the ford in person, he despatched his favorite colonels, Webster and Tarleton, with a strong detachment, to cross at Beaty's, the ford which Morgan had so recently abandoned. Of course, there was no obstacle to the passage of this detachment, which reached the opposite banks in safety. Davidson, meanwhile, having command of the American riflemen, main tained his station along the banks which commanded the ford at M'Cowan's. He had not been deceived by the *ruse* of the British general, and maintained for him a vigilant watch, which, but for the choice of the time for crossing, and an accident which, seeming to threaten, had really helped the enemy, would have enabled him to exact a heavy toll of blood for the passage. Cornwallis judiciously chose the night-time to effect his object. There was no proper employment of the rifle in the dark; and, in its shadows, the troops were but partially conscious of the appalling aspect of a stream five hundred yards in width, foaming tumultuous over its unequal bed of rocks, overturning men and horses, sweeping the strongest from their feet, and leaving them incapable of defence from their assailants, secure and steady on the river. Their fate must have been inevitable had the passage been attempted in broad daylight. But Cornwallis determined wisely. The heads of his columns entered the river about the dawn of day, but the day opened in storm and rain, and objects were scarcely visible except when near at hand. Davidson, knowing the ford, had posted his men to receive them where they should approach the eastern bank. Crouching among the trees and bushes that lined the river, they waited anxiously for the moment when they should each be able to select the object for his aim. But, in the darkness and confusion of the scene, the strife and roar of raging waters, and the dense mists of the falling rain, the guide of the British lost his way, became alarmed, and finally fled, leaving the column to make its forward progress as they could. This saved them. They wandered out of the track, and, though getting into much deeper water, yet succeeded in reaching the shore at a point where they had not been expected, and where no preparations had been made for them Davidson was soon apprized of this misfortune, and proceeded, with all haste, to repair it, by shifting his position, and bringing his rifles to bear upon them in front. His movement was made with equal judgment and despatch, but, incautiously exposing himself, in the glare of his own fires, he sunk, mortally wounded, under a volley from the British platoons. His rifles, however, were not idle. Wherever they could bring an enemy within range, they covered him with a fatal finger. Lieutenant-Colonel Hall, leading the light-infantry of the British, was among their slain, and Cornwallis himself had a narrow escape, his horse having been killed under him. A sharp conflict, which preceded the fall of Davidson, was terminated in his death, and leaving the passage free, which they could no longer successfully defend, the militia dispersed in search of safety. A small body of these, not more than a hundred in number, stopped at a tavern some ten miles from the scene of conflict, and, supposing themselves safe, prepared to take refreshment. They had nearly paid dearly for their indiscretion. The approach of Tarleton compelled them to take to their horses. Fortunately, their videttes gave the alarm in season, and, accustomed to deliver their fire on horseback, almost as well as on foot, the Americans gave him a Parthian reception, shooting as they fled, and dashed away into forests which he did not think it advisable to penetrate. Seven men and twenty horses fell at this single fire; which the British colonel avenged in the wanton massacre of a few old men and boys upon whom he fell in this expedition, and who neither offered, nor meditated resistance.

The militia of Davidson dispersed for a time, after the fall of their general. But seven miles from the tavern where Tarleton had his encounter with a part of them, he little knew that Greene with his suite, but without any other escort, remained in waiting for them. At a single dash, and with but twenty men, he might have pounced upon this more important prey. Greene waited for Davidson and his militia in vain. He lingered till midnight, before he learned the fate of that brave officer and the dispersion of his troops. Then, with a heavy heart, he proceeded to Salisbury, where he arrived, exhausted in body, and humbled and distressed in spirits. Here it was, that one of those incidents occurred, of which the revolutionary history in the southern states can boast so many, in which woman shows herself not less the angel of patriotism than of charity and love. As Greene made his appearance at Steele's tavern, the disordered state of his garments, the stiffness of his limbs, the languor of his movements, the dejection of his mood and manner, became painfully apparent to every eye. Approaching him, as he alighted from his horse, his friend, Dr. Read, addressed him with inquiries of most anxious solicitude; to which he replied, not able to repress his anguish, that he came alone, exhausted, penniless, and hungry. The reply did not escape the ears of the excellent landlady. His breakfast was soon prepared and smoking; and he had scarcely finished it, when she presented herself, closed the door of the apartment, and, producing a small bag of specie in each hand, she forced them upon him. "Take them," said the noble creature; "you will need, and I can do without the money." Never did help come at a better season. An acquisition so important to the public service, was not to be rejected through scruples of mere delicacy; and Greene rose from the breakfast-table, no longer penniless—no longer succumbing to the condition which had made him feel himself so utterly alone. The obligation was afterward repaid. A few words expressed the gratitude of the American general. He had not time for more. His friends warned him against the numbers and the hostility of the loyalists of this region, rendered doubly eager and active in consequence of the approach of their enemies; and he hurried with all expedition to rejoin the army, then about to effect the passage of the Yadkin.

It was now the aim of Lord Cornwallis to repair the consequences of previous delays, by pushing his adversary with all possible rapidity. Once upon the same side of the river with the Americans, he proceeded to make a second sacrifice of all unnecessary baggage. Destroying his wagons, he was enabled to double the teams for his artillery, and to mount a considerable body of infantry. These he joined to his cavalry, which he pushed forward under General O'Hara. His hope was now to overtake Morgan, before he could pass the Yadkin. But Morgan's command, relieved by the militia under Davidson, had been greatly refreshed by the halt made upon the Catawba; and, having the start of his eager adversary, and urged forward by Greene, he pressed on with a celerity, which was rather increased than lessened, by a heavy rain-storm, which prevailed through the whole of a day and night. Greene knew that a sudden and great rise in the river would be the consequence of this rain, and was anxious to secure the passage before the occurrence of an event which, if he could succeed in doing so, would insure his safety, and enable him to avoid that resort to a last stake, which it was the policy of the British general to compel. The latter concentrated all his resources upon the pursuit, and his troops obeyed his wishes with an alacrity, that showed how well they knew the importance of the prize. But their labors were again taken in vain. Morgan reached the Yadkin without having felt his enemy at his heels; and, here it was that the provident forethought of Greene enabled him to reap all the benefits of his rapid march. Boats had been collected, by his orders, long in advance of the necessity which he yet foresaw; and these, ranged along the river at the several crossing-places, afforded him a quick passage of the Yadkin, whether his purpose be attack or defence. The infantry and baggage of the Americans were transported to the opposite shore without difficulty, and the stream was not yet sufficiently swollen to keep the cavalry from fording. Yet, so rapid had been the pursuit of O'Hara, with his powerful detachment of cavalry and mounted infantry, that he succeeded in crossing weapons with the American rear-guard, which was composed entirely of militia of the country, before it could throw the river between itself and the enemy. This guard had been delayed, in consequence of its being joined by considerable numbers of the whigs of Salisbury, who, with their families, were compelled to fly, as a penalty of their patriotism, at the approach of the British. The baggage of these fugitives proved an incumbrance; but, though retarding their progress, it was not the proper policy of the American general, looking to the future no less than the present, to discard it from his protection. The baggage of the army had been passed; the army itself was in safety on the opposite side; but, before the wagons of the fugitives could be got across, the enemy broke upon them. But the militia stood their ground manfully. It was midnight, and they were favored by the darkness. A sharp skirmish ensued, in which both sides claimed the advantage. That it belonged to the Americans, is beyond a doubt, since they gained their object, saved most of the wagons, and effected their own passage in safety and without loss;—a boast which it was not in the power of the British to assert.

O Hara chafed vainly, upon one side of the river, at the security which his enemy enjoyed upon the other

A fruitless attempt to seize upon some of the boats of the Americans, increased his distemper. He was compelled to draw bridle and wait for the approach of his superior. It was not long before Cornwallis, with the whole British army, appeared on the banks of the Yadkin. The prospect before him was sufficiently mortifying. Thus far, his exertions had been taken in vain. Greene was in possession of all the boats, and the stream was now beyond its bounds, swollen by the rains, and no longer fordable. The artillery was brought up, and long shot were employed to effect a passage which was not within the power of the soldiery. A furious cannonade was opened upon the American encampment on the opposite banks; but it proved an idle waste of ammunition. The camp was sheltered behind a rising ground, while the rocks on the margin of the stream afforded crouching-places of sufficient security for the sentinels. The British general had all this cannonading to himself. In Morgan's command there was no artillery. The two pieces which had been taken at the Cowpens, placed in wagons, had been hurried on, with the prisoners, to Virginia. He could, accordingly, return none of the distant civilities of the British. These do not seem to have occasioned much disquiet among the Americans. It is related of Greene, for example, that he had taken up his quarters in a little cabin, which was partially sheltered by a pile of rocks, a small distance from the river. Here, while his military family were amusing themselves in drawing straws, or doing what else they thought proper to beguile the time, the general was more busily employed in preparing his despatches. At length, however, as if the British had guessed his hiding-place, and were anxious to disturb his occupation, their cannon were pointed to the cabin, the roof of which, alone, was apparent to their aim. Very soon the bullets were seen to strike the rocks in the rear, and to skip about the neighborhood. Soon they travelled nearer and nearer, until the clapboards of the roof began to fly in all directions. What emotions these unruly visiters provoked in the minds of those who were at their innocent games of Push-pin and Jack Straw—the aids of the general—have not been reported; but Greene, himself, is described as showing no sort of concern. He still wrote, heeding nothing but his despatches, and only turning from them to answer the numerous applications that were constantly addressed to him. His pen never rested but at the appearance of some new applicant, who received his answer, distinguished by equal calmness and precision; the pen of the general being again set in motion the moment of his departure.

CHAPTER X.

Continued Pursuit of the Americans by Cornwallis.—Greene meditates a Stand at Guilford.—Condition of his Army.—Continues the Retreat through North Carolina.—Deludes Cornwallis, who pursues a Detachment under Williams, while the main Army of the Americans crosses the River Dan in Security.

THE British general, for a time, was nonplused. With a superior army, in better training and condition, within striking distance of his enemy, he was yet compelled to look on, without being able to strike a blow. It was not merely the interests of his sovereign that suffered by this involuntary inactivity. His own reputation was seriously endangered by the position of his affairs. How had his enemy eluded him? How, encumbered with prisoners and baggage, with a vastly inferior force, had he contrived to escape the pursuit, which he had every reason to apprehend would be hotly urged, and which, thus urged, would, in all probability, have ruined him? True, that, on two occasions, the unexpected rising of the waters had interposed for his safety. But might not Cornwallis have overtaken him before he reached the Catawba? and did not his mounted men and cavalry, a force in itself almost equal to that commanded by Morgan, actually engage the rear-guard of the latter, on the banks of the very stream which now opposed itself to his forward progress? History points to the want of forethought, on the part of Cornwallis, which, unlike the case with Greene, had failed to provide against the rising of the waters; and to the waste of more than forty-eight hours in the destruction of his baggage, which a small detachment might have been left to break up and consign to the flames. It is recorded of Greene, that, when he heard of the pause of the British army to destroy its baggage—an act which indicated the determination to traverse the whole country, if need be, in pursuit—he rose exultingly, with the prophetic exclamation, "Then he is ours!" The prediction was verified; not literally, perhaps, for Greene was not permitted to be "in at the death" of the game—but verified in the capture of Yorktown, as a strict result of this insane expedition.

Standing on the banks of the Yadkin, and surveying the tents of his enemy, secure beyond, there is no doubt that Cornwallis began to entertain some misgivings of his policy and fortune. Perhaps his misgivings with regard to his policy were only due to the unpromising aspect of his fortunes. His efforts, whether urged with sufficient energy and audacity or not, had been fruitless; and it was now due to his safety that he should strike a blow, sufficiently heavy and successful, to do away with the impression of the brilliant victory at Cowpens. But his mind evidently vacillated between its objects; the worst event, perhaps, in the career of a military man. He consumed four precious days in deliberation, which should have been employed in action; and then resolved unwisely. There were still two ways of striking at his enemy. As yet, the junction had not been effected between the two divisions of Greene's army. That under Morgan has employed our attention, and is now before us; but the main body of the army, under General Huger, was in full progress for Guilford. To dart between these two bodies, and strike them in detail, was the desire and final resolution of the British commander. This resolution, of itself, was not amiss, had it not been too tardy of adoption; but it was not till two days after his arrival at the banks of the Yadkin, that he detached parties to reconnoitre the country, and to seek other crossing-places, nor until the eighth of February, that he at length passed the river. Yet the river had been falling on the *fourth*, was fordable the next day, and Greene's army was in motion, after the halt of a day, the moment he discovered the subsiding of the stream. The hesitation of the British general, betraying doubt and incertitude, may have arisen out of his difficulty to decide upon the division which was most proper to assail. It may have been the fruit, also, of some vague general apprehension as to the dangers and exigencies of a long pursuit, through a waste country, filled with bitter foes and doubtful friends, when the important object to be gained, the junction of his force with that of Philips in Virginia, might be baffled; in which event, not only must South Carolina be lost, but he, himself, be destroyed or captured. Whatever may have been his doubts or apprehensions, they certainly produced such a pause in his action, as set at peril all that he had hoped from his previous enterprise. Crossing the Yadkin on the 8th, and resuming the pursuit of Greene, in the hope of cutting him off from the upper fords of the Dan, he gave him opportunities and a start which it was not easy to recover. Not that Greene's object was simply to elude and escape his formidable adversary. His purpose was a more profound one. We find him, for example, halting Morgan at the Catawba, and resting his jaded troops; availing himself of all the respite afforded by the rising of the river, yet without preparing, in this delay to offer battle when the enemy should cross. Starting off, when the passage is about to be effected, we find him keeping just far enough ahead to beguile the British in pursuit.

Crossing the Yadkin as he had done the Catawba, he again halts, and coolly surveys his pursuer. Thus he rests quietly, until again warned by the falling of the waters; and pushing forward for the Dan, again to practise the same game; beguile his enemy yet deeper into the heart of the country, where, in the event of a battle, his resources must be cut off, and where a defeat, or disaster of any kind, would leave him hopeless of help, and at the mercy of the Americans. Cornwallis might well have hesitated to follow this lure. But he probably did not suspect Greene of a scheme so profound. It was one cause of the failure of the British, that they never learned the lesson, till too late, which teaches them to respect an enemy. The pursuit of Cornwallis, and the retreat of Greene before him, has been entitled "a military race," and the credit awarded to the two parties has been limited to the speed with which one of them fled, and with which the other pursued. The subtle policy which governed Greene's movements has but too frequently escaped the notice of historians. It is true, that, assuming it as the cue of the American general to run only, it somewhat worried them to account for his frequent halts. But it was easier to suppose that, in doing so, he only blundered in carrying out his own policy, than to admit that there was a something occult in his progress which they could not altogether fathom. The game of Greene, a sufficiently delicate one, was to amuse his enemy — delay his progress — beguile him with hope, onward and onward, still farther from the base of his operations, from all resources, while the country closed in upon him on all hands, and the militia, springing up from the soil, hung upon his footsteps, cutting off his supplies, and embodying for the final struggle which should give the *coup de grace* to *his* career, as in the case of Burgoyne. We must give Cornwallis some credit for a supposed anticipation of such a fortune. To this, and other causes not apparent to us, we may probably assign that incertitude of conduct which seems to have paralyzed his energies, and was certainly unfavorable to his objects.

Greene, meanwhile, after remaining a day upon the banks of the Yadkin — evidently, with the policy which we have indicated, that of beguiling the enemy still farther in pursuit — continued his march, and, at length, planted himself in a secure position, a short distance from Salem, in the forks of Abbott's creek. Here he again halted, and watched the movements of his adversary. The position was one which not only enabled him to do this effectually, but served, in some measure, to distract the judgment of Cornwallis in regard to the future route which the Americans might take. On that subject Greene had already decided. He had, from Salisbury, sent instructions to Huger, with the main army, to push for Guilford, where he designed to effect a junction of the two divisions; his farther purpose being to make a stand, if advisable under the circumstances, at that place, and if a proper position could be found for fighting his adversary to advantage. He had grown somewhat weary of seeming only to be desirous of eluding his enemy; and there were several causes, besides, which rendered it advisable that he should give him battle. The moral effect of a prolonged retreat was highly injurious, in a region where the population was not only greatly divided in sentiment, but where they had been greatly dispirited by the previous events of the conflict. Even the brilliant victory at the Cowpens, though of the most encouraging character, had failed to make an impression sufficiently deep to exclude from remembrance the repeated disasters of the struggle; and it was highly important that this impression should be renewed, if possible, at this very juncture, when the effect of this victory was still, though beginning to subside, tolerably fresh and vivid in the recollections of the people. Besides, Cornwallis had now been lured sufficiently far from his resources for the purpose of the Americans. He had now reached the centre of North Carolina — was at a great distance from his magazines in South Carolina, and quite as remote from the British army then operating in Virginia. Could he be brought now to fight, on a field selected by his adversary, he must, necessarily, fight under every disadvantage. Even a victory would not materially help his career, could the Americans cripple him in the contest; while any success to the latter, even a drawn battle, would probably result in placing the British army *hors du combat.* Short of provisions, with their munitions of war partially or quite exhausted, and encumbered with wounded, they must fall an easy prey to the militia, rising on every hand, under the encouragement afforded by the prospect of overwhelming the invader. With these calculations, Greene was already contemplating the struggle for victory, while Cornwallis imagined him only anxious to elude the strife. We have seen, already, how industriously he had striven, though with small success, to rouse up and organize the militia. Contemplating the approaching trial of strength with his pursuer, he wrote to the officers of militia in the vicinity of Guilford, to call out their followers, and appear in all their strength at that place. Couriers were also despatched to Hillsborough for the same object, and every preparation was made for the anticipated encounter. A single day's march would bring the division of Morgan to Guilford, and, with advices that Cornwallis was in motion and had crossed the Yadkin, this body of troops began their movement. The junction of the two divisions was effected on the 9th of February, the army being strengthened by the arrival of Lee with his legion, who joined them on the following day. But the militia did not appear in numbers at all equal to the public expectation; and a review of the American forces, showed them to be quite inadequate to the struggle with an army so superior in numbers and equipment as that of Cornwallis. The whole of the force under Greene, of all arms, fit for duty, was but two thousand and thirty-six; of these, but fourteen hundred and twenty-six were regulars. The army of the British, on the other hand, was known to consist of nearly, or quite, three thousand men, all soldiers in the highest state of discipline, and amply provided with the proper clothing and munitions. A council of war unanimously resolved, that to offer battle to the enemy, under such a disparity of strength and resources, would be sheer desperation; and Greene reluctantly submitted to the necessity, sufficiently obvious to himself, of continuing his retreat. Could he have drawn together an additional force of twelve or fifteen hundred militia, his resolution would have been to offer battle; but the wasting policy which governed the movements of the militia—by which, recruited for a short period, half of their time was consumed in marching to and from the service—was fatal to their efficiency and the permanence of an army. The Virginia militia, for example, had been sent into the field for a tour of duty of *three months;* and, in this brief period, how much of it remained unconsumed, when, going and returning, they were required to traverse, without any employment against the enemy, a space of *six hundred miles?* As fast, therefore, as new supplies of the militia made their appearance, corresponding numbers were ready to depart; and the consequence was, such a fluctuation in the strength of the army, as continually to baffle its efficiency, and to leave it in doubt as to its own numbers. Greene's disappointment was great as he contemplated the necessity of farther retreat. He had been hoping against hope. He had baffled pursuit thus far, but it was still humiliating to be compelled to submit to it; and, even though he should not be overtaken by his pursuer, it was to the latter an advantage, next to a victory, if the Americans should still be forced to fly. It was not the least mortifying consciousness of the American general, that his opponent, penetrating a whig country, was already lighting his cruel torch in the blaze of burning cottages. Greene could only sorrow for the sufferers: he could neither save nor avenge them.

The resolution being taken to continue the retreat, the American general lost no time in putting it in execution. Cornwallis was still pressing forward, and, on the 10th of February, a space of twenty-five miles, only, separated the rival armies. The present aim of Greene was to reach the river Dan, and to place its waters between him and his pursuers. This stream, which rises among the mountains of Virginia, soon penetrates the territory of North Carolina, and, pursuing a sinuous progress for a while, in the latter state, finally takes its way back into Virginia. We shall not follow its course. Enough to say, that, in seasons of freshet, the upper fords alone are passable without boats. Cornwallis naturally supposed that Greene would make for this quarter; and the latter so manœuvred, in his progress, as to confirm him in this impression. But the American general had already determined upon the route to the lower and deeper crossing-place. Without artillery, and with an inferior army, the passage, at a point which offered no interruptions to the pursuit of his enemy, would profit him little in any endeavor to elude his adversary. Nor was the route offering by the upper Dan, at all favorable to the hope which he entertained of reinforcements and supplies from Virginia. These supplies were of the last importance to his future strength and safety, and he nuturally sought to increase, by all means, the facilities for their arrival. While Cornwallis was manœuvring busily, to intercept and arrest him in his flight to the upper Dan, Greene encountered his schemes, with others admirably calculated to continue him in his error. He detached from his army a force of seven hundred light troops, the command of which was assigned to Colonel Williams. These troops were composed of the veterans of the army—those who had fought at Cowpens, and who were to be relied upon. Unencumbered with baggage, they could move with the greatest rapidity, and their commander had his instructions to throw himself boldly in the path of the enemy. His detachment, ostensibly a covering force for the retreat of the army, was, nevertheless, pushed forward in a direction which confirmed Cornwallis in the conviction, that Greene was aiming at the upper, or shallow, crossing-places of the Dan. He little knew that his wary adversary had, with excellent forethought, provided boats along the river, at its deepest parts, affording him, at any moment, the means of passage. One of the first measures of his career in the south, when he first assumed the command of the army, was, as we have seen, the exploration of these rivers, and a meet provision of the necessary materiel by which to navigate them. It was fortunate, at the same time, that the agents to whom these duties had been assigned, had performed them with that secresy which is one of the essential elements of success in war. The passage of the lower Dan thus provided for, it brought Greene to the strongest point in his own base of operations, nearer than ever to his sources of supply, his reinforcements, and the magazines which he had also established, long before, upon the Roanoke.

The Dan was now the only river which lay between

Cornwallis and Virginia. To suffer the enemy to pass this line, and to form a junction with other bodies of his army, already within and threatening the latter state, would probably complete the attempted segregation of the south from the confederacy. The eyes of the nation, drawn to the conflict in the south by the brilliant and encouraging affair at the Cowpens, were necessarily fixed upon the progress of the two armies in the inveterate chase which had been kept up by the British. Never had the anxiety of the country been more intense on any occasion. For nearly a month, the whole continent seemed to hang in breathless anticipation, looking momently in dread of some catastrophe which should end the fate of the southern army. Fear had finally given place in some degree to admiration, as the manœuvres of the American general had so completely succeeded in baffling the wolfish rage of the pursuer. But the drama increased in its interest with the continuance of the action, and every moment seemed burdened, in the public feeling, with the weight of an empire. The two rival commanders were fully conscious of this interest, and of the vital importance of the struggle. The junction of the two divisions of the American army having been effected at Guilford, Cornwallis made a brief halt at Salem, even as the tiger draws himself up and seems to contract his dimensions, as in preparation for the final spring upon that enemy, who has also nerved himself with his fullest strength. Everything in their respective fortunes depended upon the gain of a march, and each guarded every movement of his own, and scrutinized all those of his opponent, by all the eyes which armies are permitted to employ — scouts, patrols, and spies — which followed every footstep and reported every conjecture.

A first *ruse de guerre* of Cornwallis had for its object to alarm Greene for the safety of his stores at Hillsborough. These had been delayed at this place, lacking proper means of transportation, and were only now under way to a place of safety. Hillsborough itself, as the seat of government, was a place, it was thought, of sufficient importance to demand the protection of the American army. Its position, on the right of the road to Guilford, was directly accessible from Salem. Should Greene lose ground in this direction, he would be cut off from the Dan. The first demonstration of Cornwallis was made on this route. But the American general was not to be overreached. He adroitly turned the practice of his adversary against himself. The instant progress of Williams, with his select detachment, in the direction of the upper Dan, induced the British general to make a movement to the left, in the hope of cutting off this party. The army under Greene, he fondly assumed to be secure — never dreaming of the ferry-boats — and believing that he had them safely in a *cul de sac*. Williams, lightly enough equipped for a race, coolly kept in front of the enemy, always sufficiently near to be confounded with its own advance. For four days he marched thus, steadily forward, beguiling the enemy still farther from his prey. He had with him a force which could be relied upon in such a progress. His command of the seven hundred veterans who had fought at Cowpens, had been strengthened by the legion of Lee, the cavalry of Washington, and a small select body of militia riflemen. These were all steady soldiers, ready for the most desperate service, and Williams, himself a leader of the most experienced courage, was supported by such gallant captains as Howard and Carrington, from whose fearlessness and talent everything might be expected.

The scheme of Greene was successful. Mistaking this detachment for the rear-guard of the Americans, Cornwallis at once contracted his extended line of operations, and concentrated all his efforts upon the single object of overtaking and bringing his enemy to battle. Greene, meanwhile, was pressing forward in a direct course for the ferry of the lower Dan. His march was a painful one, though utterly unmolested. The cold was intense, and the troops were nearly without shoes or clothing. Hundreds of the soldiers tracked the ground with bloody feet, and in a complaint which one of the American officers utters about this time, we find it stated, that, "as his men were generally barefoot, long marches had, at length, incapacitated them from marching at all." In the corps best equipped, a blanket sufficed for four men, and cloaks and overcoats were luxuries such as the best provided were not even so presumptuous as to dream of. Greene could only sorrow over the sufferings which he had not the power to alleviate. His troops were, happily, constant in all their sufferings, and, with a perfect confidence in their leader, and with the object of their aim in view, they steadily pressed forward, unsinking and unrepining, for four weary days, until, within a few miles of the river, they yielded to toil and night, and snatched a brief respite of refreshing sleep. With the dawn, they resumed their march, and, reaching the banks of the Dan, deeply rolling between, they found the boats in readiness. A few hours sufficed to transport them to the opposite shore. Greene, however, remained on the southern bank of the river, awaiting the light troops, while he sent a despatch to inform Williams that the object for which he had been mystifying Cornwallis had been gained.

This was on the fifteenth of the month. Williams, meanwhile, had pursued his game with great dexterity and spirit. His first movement had brought him directly in front of his enemy, and drew upon him, as his movement was meant to do, all the attention of Cornwallis

So close and unremitting was now the pursuit of the British general, that our little band was permitted leisure for but a single meal per day, and even this was subject to interruptions which sometimes spoiled the feast, if not the appetite. So severe was the duty of the night, in the employment of pickets and patrols, that, but six hours for sleep in forty-eight, were all that the American colonel could possibly allow them. Still they plodded forward with vast perseverance, through wretched roads, in wretched weather, cheerfully, under the necessity, and gratified, as they were conscious that every moment of their pursuit served to insure the safety of the main army. It was not simply a race in which they indulged. They were compelled to maintain a degree of vigilance which allowed them no moment for supposing themselves in security. The enemy's patrols were continually upon their heels, and frequent skirmishes enlivened the otherwise tedious progress. On one of these, the enemy suffered a loss of eighteen of Tarleton's troopers, the Americans losing only a poor boy, a bugler, who was totally unarmed, and was butchered while he begged for mercy. Lee, who commanded the rear-guard in this conflict, would have taken bloody vengeance upon his murderers, several of whom were taken prisoners in the subsequent affair, but for the occurrence of an alarm which compelled his attention to the enemy, while the prisoners who were thus endangered, were sent forward to the main body, under Williams, and thus saved from the sudden wrath of the indignant cavalier. But the escape of the British dragoons from sharp judgment, was an extremely narrow one.

Thus, pressing forward, with little leisure allowed for sleep or supper, watching against surprise, and, with an occasional skirmish with their pursuers, the detachment of Williams pursued a devious progress toward the Dan.

Four days had now elapsed, while he was engaged in the business of deluding his pursuer. Assuming that that there was no longer a sufficient motive for keeping in front of the enemy, he proceeded to direct his course at once for the river. Accordingly, he drew off his detachment cautiously, seeking the nearest road to the crossing place at Boyd's ferry. His *ruse* had been entirely successful. So well had he played his game, that he had completely deceived the British general, who, until this moment, never doubted that he had the whole American army in front. With the discovery of his error, he at once redoubled his efforts to overtake his foe, and, striking a by-path for this object, found himself once more in the rear of Williams's detachment. This sharpened the appetite of the pursuers, and forced the wary American to the continued employment of all his vigilance and activity. Cornwallis sought to bring on a skirmish, in order to retard the flight which he did not seem likely to overtake; but Williams was not to be lured from the proper path of safety by any venture, however specious and alluring. Though frequently within striking distance, the rear-guard of the one army within gun-shot of the advance of the other, the American marksmen were studiously kept from the dangerous impulse which prompted them to use their rifles, though at the risk of bringing on an unequal general action. The stern voice of discipline prevailed to subdue the temper of the Americans for fight, and they sped forward, threatened, wherever their progress was temporarily checked by obstacles of road or river, by the fierce demonstrations of the enemy. But the collision was eluded; the retreating force maintained its advance; and thus, step by step, the British still pressing on their heels, the chase was continued, through storm and snow —through roads, saturated with water, chill with damp, or frozen by cold. Many weary miles yet lay between them and their point of destination, when the night settled down upon their progress. But, suddenly, they beheld the blaze of numerous fires, which they at once felt sure were those of Greene's army. The first impulse was to wheel about upon their pursuers, and, at every hazard, engage them in desperate conflict, in order to save the division of the army which they fancied to be thus reposing in delusive security. But a second thought relieved them of their fear, and saved them from this desperate necessity. Williams knew his commander too well to leave him in any doubt as to that prudence which, had he continued to occupy this position, would have been put to shame for ever. He felt sure, as, in the sequel, it proved, that the fires which he saw blazing were those which Greene had left to burn when he resumed his march. He had put his troops in motion several hours before, and Williams snatched a brief interval of rest, which a halt of the British now afforded him, for sleeping upon the ground which his general had previously occupied.

Here the Americans slept till midnight. The British, having built their fires also, offered no farther present molestation. With the midnight, the former were again in motion. They were still forty miles from the place of safety, and every moment became precious for security. The necessity was equally great with Cornwallis. To suffer his prey to escape him, was to endanger his own security, and materially to discredit his generalship. The detachment of Williams was almost within his grasp, and, not dreaming of the boats which Greene had provided in advance of the necessity, he fondly hoped to gather both divisions, on this side the Dan, at one fell swoop of his superior forces. The chase became more desperate than ever. The energies of both parties were strung to the utmost, a nervous will stimulating exertion almost beyond the endurance of the physical capacity. Over ground now hard and frozen, through the imperfect shadows of the night, pursuer and pursued went forward on their doubtful way. Day dawned, and the British van was once more within speaking distance of the American rear. And thus continued the relationship of the two bodies throughout the morning. Exhaustion craved a respite. One hour, before noon, was stolen for refreshment, and the progress was resumed. Soon, however, the Americans were cheered with the tidings of Greene's safety, with the army, on the opposite side of the river. His express encountered Williams, at noon, with this grateful intelligence. The boats were in waiting for his detachment; and the prospect of a long rest and certain security, was at length before them. It needed but one more effort, and this, with men thus encouraged, was easily made. They would soon link arms with their comrades, and this reflection put new life into their veins. The toils already overcome were all forgotten, in the repose which was promised them at last. When within fifteen miles of the Dan, a movement was made by which the greater part of the detachment was drawn off, and led, by the shortest pathway, to the ferry. The legion of Lee, meanwhile, keeping in front of the enemy, and occupying his attention. The infantry of the legion next followed the march of Williams, leaving the cavalry between them and the foe; and the cavalry, in due season, made their appearance at the river, which had now been passed by all the foot. Night was already over the Dan, when the troopers, leading their horses by the rein, and forcing them into the river, entered the returning boats. They, too, were crossed over in safety, their last files ascending the northern bank of the Dan as the advance of the

British rushed into sight upon the southern. The prey had entirely escaped them. The river was unfordable; the boats were in the hands of the Americans; and, for the present, pursuit was entirely cut off.

CHAPTER XI.

The Armies watch each other.—The Militia collect under Pickens and Caswell.—Cornwallis retires upon Hillsborough.—Greene recrosses the Dan.—Pickens and Lee operate successfully upon the British Detachments.—Sanguinary Defeat of Loyalists under Pyles, and Pursuit of Tarleton.

THE feelings with which Cornwallis contemplated the American army, in safety, upon the opposite banks of the Dan, and, for the present, totally unapproachable, may be better imagined than described. Without a blow being struck, Greene had gained a most important victory; and the reputation of the British general, and the cause in which he was engaged, was destined to suffer proportionally. The remarkable chase and escape which we have just recorded, was one of the most impressive of the incidents of the war. It had riveted the attention of both friends and foes, from the moment of its beginning, on the southern side of tbe Catawba, to the time when it ended by throwing the swollen waters of the Dan between the opposing armies. The public mind of America, sensible of the condition of Greene's army, its poverty in clothing and munitions, its inferior numbers, and the vast stake which the country had in its safety, was naturally wrought up to a pitch of the most intense and eager anxiety. It was not expected that Greene should cope with his enemy at the point of the bayonet. For that, the wide disparity of strength and equipment, between the British and Americans, had rendered impossible.

That he should escape defeat and captivity was their only object; and, his doing this, under the circumstances, was to obtain the victory. He had led his little forces through a perilous extent of country, more than two hundred miles, in the breaking-up of winter, amid cold, hunger, and nakedness, over roads saturated with incessant rains, and with an eager, enterprising, well-clad enemy, in superior numbers, closely pressing at his heels. He had successfully deluded that enemy, and had baffled the pursuit. There was but one opinion as to his superior generalship. Washington writes: "Your retreat before Cornwallis is highly applauded by all ranks, and reflects much honor on your military abilities." Tarleton adds to this the testimony of an enemy, when he says that "every measure of the Americans, during their march from the Catawba to Virginia, was judiciously designed and vigorously executed."

The army, itself, was by no means unconscious of the importance of their escape, and of the superior generalship by which it had been effected. Great was the exultation, and general the felicitation, in the American camp, on the night of the 15th of February. The soldier had a respite from pursuit. He was permitted, once more, to sleep in security. The separate divisions, once more united, could while away the weariness of the night, by comparing their several experiences during the march; and, in full feeling of the success which had crowned their efforts, indulge in delightful anticipations of still more fortunate results, from future enterprises, waged under circumstances more auspicious. But, the care which they could mock, clung still to the side of their commander, and drove sleep from his pillow. We have numerous proofs, in the letters which he wrote this night, while others slept, of a spirit ill at ease—a mind unsatisfied, amid all its successes, that so much remained undone, which should be done, but, for the performance of which, no adequate means had been allowed him. The army was saved, it was true; but, another southern state had been yielded to the ravages of the enemy. The Fabian system, which Greene pursued no less than Washington, might save the troops, but at the expense of the country. The reproach, however, could not be urged against the general, while the troops did not appear; and, borrowing the words of the great Frederick, Greene cried aloud, in the bitterness of his soul: "Oh! that, of the thousand who remain in idleness at home, I had only a few hundred with me in the field." The flames of foreign war were spreading, and he was permitted only to survey them. To arrest them was the pregnant necessity before him, and the safety of the army was but temporary only. Well might care and anxiety drive slumber from his eyelids. His toils had not been less than those of the meanest soldier, and his respite had been even less. From the day when he had ridden, almost alone, through a hostile country, from his own to the camp of Morgan on the Catawba, he had never once undressed himself for sleep. His slumbers had been snatched by the wayside—imperfect moments, in which nature rather yielded to exhaustion, than to a desire for and satisfaction from repose. The days of halt, which were accorded to his troops for rest and recreation, were employed by their commander only in newer toils and fresher exertions. His correspondence, written at periods thus stolen equally from the saddle and from sleep, is singularly various, and in proof of a mind that ranged through all the departments under his care, and suffered the interests of none to escape his scrutiny. The present and future condition of the army—the state of the country, its resources and dangers—the character of the militia, and its improvement—the commissariat and other departments,—these employed him in unremitted labors—in continued appeals; now writing to leading men throughout the nation, now to the governors of the several states, and now to those who were specially connected with the progress of his immediate command. It is surprising, with what equal comprehensiveness and circumspection these letters were written. Nothing, necessary to the detail, is deficient; while the governing intelligence which presides over the whole, exhibits a capacity for generalization, which leaves nothing wanting to thought. Yet, these letters may be said to have been written in the saddle, amid the continual confusion and interruptions of the camp, or in those hours of repose and silence, when sleep would seem to be quite as necessary to the general as to his troops. His correspondence with Patrick Henry, Jefferson, Washington, Steuben, and others, betrays the most indefatigable patience and industry, mingled with an anxiety which the stern sense of patriotic duty, alone, enables him to subdue. He felt that his present respite was temporary; that the game must be quickly renewed; that, with the falling of the waters of the Dan, the British would again resume the pursuit; and that he must, once more, adopt the humiliating necessity of farther flight, unless he could secure seasonable reinforcements. To this object, then, he addressed himself; and, consulting all the difficulties of his situation, calculated, with intense application, the problem of chances, in regard to his own and the movements of his enemy. With reinforcements, the British general was almost in his grasp. But, could he rely on the delusive promises which had been so often, and so fruitlessly, made him? He had been fed on promises, decrees, and resolutions; and his faith was grievously shaken in those assurances of Congresses and governors, which had so frequently held

"The word of promise to his ear,
To break it to his hope."

He was told that the Virginians and North-Carolinians were about to pour in and fill his ranks, and that Steuben was hurrying on a body of recruits for the Virginia regiments; but days and weeks might elapse before these could reach headquarters, and the time for action and successful operations was momentarily escaping him. The river, on the 16th, it was announced, was rapidly falling. This added to Greene's perplexities; it compelled him to determine quickly. The fords were numerous at low stages of the water, and a farther retreat appeared inevitable. In anticipation of this necessity, the baggage of the American army was sent forward to Halifax, and orders were given to prepare means for making good the passage of the river Staunton. The troops were ordered to hold themselves in readiness for marching, as soon as the necessity became imperative for a farther retreat. These arrangements made, the two armies remained in tranquillity, watching the river and each other.

It was, to Greene, the most tantalizing thing in the world, that, with the British fairly in his clutches, he had not the power to contract his folds upon them. The situation of Cornwallis, had the American force been in the situation to take advantage of it, was perilous in the extreme. The British general, in his avidity after his prey, had pursued so far, as to make his advance and retreat equally hazardous. He had withdrawn himself to a distance from his garrisons, and was without stores or magazines. His hope lay in his own audacity, energy, and the errors of his wily opponent. Greene felt this, and his watchfulness was redoubled. Still, he had hopes of something better than being merely able to elude his pursuer. Could he receive his recruits and supplies in season, it might be possible to end the war by the capture of a second British army. But this prospect could depend only on the reinforcements promised him. Small as was the force which he had, the severe marches which he had been compelled to take, had still farther lessened its numbers, and impaired its efficiency. It was still winter, and the clothing of his *best*-clad men was suitable only for the summer. Many were still naked. The effect of this condition may be seen from the returns of the Maryland line, one of the noblest bodies of troops which the war had seen. With eight hundred and sixty-one fit for duty, two hundred and seventy-four were in the hospitals. The whole force in camp, fit for duty, on the 17th, was but one thousand and seventy-eight infantry, sixty-four artillery, one hundred and seventy-six cavalry, legionary infantry one hundred and twelve, and the militia of Pickens one hundred and fifty in number. "How is it possible," Greene asks, "for an army circumstanced like ours, to make head against one organized and equipped like that of Cornwallis?"

But the hopes brightened with delay. At the very moment when Greene was apprehensive that he should be forced to resume the retreat, he had intelligence of a considerable increase to the militia force under Pickens. The latter had succeeded in raising a body of seven hundred men, and was now approaching the enemy's left. General Caswell, at the same time, with another body of militia, was making a similar demonstration on the opposite flank of the British. These movements disquieted Cornwallis. They no longer left him the option of pursuit. The atmosphere was not sufficiently friendly for the health of his troops, and he prepared to change the air. Greene waited for this movement only to recross the river. The waving of a handkerchief from a friendly female, under cover of the bank, apprized the Americans that the British were under march. As soon as this signal was made, the army of Greene was put in motion. A small detachment of picked men, under Major Burnet, led the way across the river, and prepared to hang upon the enemy's skirts and report their movements. They were followed by Lee, with his legion, whose instructions were to harass their progress, and snatch every opportunity for cutting off their pickets and smaller parties. As yet, the main body of the army did not follow. There were reasons why it should remain in reserve, particularly as the destination of Cornwallis was still unknown. Apprehensions were felt for the safety of Halifax, on the Roanoke, a place combining numerous advantages, of such a character as to determine the American general to risk a battle in its defence. To strengthen this position, Kosciuzko had been already despatched, as an engineer, to superintend the construction of fortifications; and the eye of Greene was fixed upon this point, as one which, in the possession of the enemy, would give him a position which might equally control the Carolinas and Virginia. To prevent this, at all hazards, it became important that he should be in a situation to fly to the defence of the place at the first appearance of danger.

But, Cornwallis was not slow in the development of his game. His encampment on the Dan was broken up on the 18th of February. At first, his course left it doubtful whether he meant to cross the river at one of the upper ferries, in order to continue his attempt upon the main army of Greene, or to strike a blow at the militia force of Pickens. As he continued to advance, the magazines on the Roanoke were supposed to be threatened. But, soon, all doubts were ended, as he suddenly wheeled about, turning his back upon the Dan, and marching, direct, to Hillsborough. Here he planted the royal standard, and issued a proclamation to all good and faithful subjects to repair to it. The region was, professedly, a loyal one; and large calculations might, reasonably, be made upon the alacrity with which this summons would be obeyed. At first, the prospect was very encouraging of a large accession to his numbers. His pursuit of Greene, his presence on the spot in force, both conspired to stimulate the tories, and depress and discourage the whigs. Seven companies of the former were reported, in one day, as in course of organization. For three days, the promise continued of this character; but, suddenly, these hopeful auxiliaries disappeared, and their absence was sufficiently accounted for by the tidings that Greene was again on the southern bank of the Dan, while Pickens and Lee were, already, engaged in reconnoitring the camp of the British. It was with increased bitterness that Cornwallis felt his disappointment and perceived his danger. It was on this occasion that he wrote to the ministry, that he was "surrounded by timid friends and inveterate enemies." It was now his necessity to fight with Green, if possible. In no other way could he hope to dissipate his dangers, and break through the meshes by which he was environed.

The Americans had received accessions of force from several quarters. He had suffered none of the movements of Cornwallis to escape him. At first, supposing that the British general aimed to escape to the coast by Wilmington, he determined to throw himself across his path, and delay his progress, until the final issue could be brought about under favorable auspices. "If we can delay Cornwallis for a day or two," is his language, "he must be ruined." Pickens and Lee were pushed forward with the utmost rapidity—the legion of the latter being strengthened by a couple of companies of Marylanders. They were to hang upon his rear, and harass him with all their energies; and better chieftains for such a purpose could not have been chosen

But Cornwallis was not the soldier to retreat while the sword could possibly cut asunder the web which surrounded him. It was soon ascertained that he was in no hurry to depart; and Greene's apprehensions were greatly excited by the reported progress which the British general was making in the enrolment of the tories about his standard. These tidings contributed to determine him upon recrossing the Dan. To close around Cornwallis, to cut off his supplies, prevent a general rising of the loyalists, and cut them up in detail, before they could reach the royal army, was the policy of the American commander. His light troops were everywhere set in motion for these objects. The disposition of Pickens and Lee had already brought them within striking distance of the British camp;—Otho Williams was again in the field, with the excellent legion which he had so lately led in successful retreat;—Stevens, with a thousand volunteers, had returned from Virginia;—Butler was in motion, with a considerable body of North-Carolinians;—and a brisk business was soon begun by these separate detachments, having for their object the clipping of the British claws, and such a contraction of their powers, as to compel their final surrender or annihilation.

It was on the 20th of February that Cornwallis erected his standard at Hillsborough. On the 23d, Greene recrossed the Dan with his whole army. The day before this, a detachment from Pickens's command, led by Colonel M'Call, had surprised and carried off a British picket, only two miles from the royal camp. This was an audacity too great to be endured, and Tarleton was despatched, with a strong force of horse and foot, to keep the Americans within bounds, and afford all encouragement to the rising loyalists. Meantime, Pickens had formed a junction with Lee, and had been advised of Tarleton's expedition. This was so much grist to their mill. They determined to have it so. With dawn they set forth in search of the British legion. Tarleton, with his usual devastating ferocity, had sufficiently traced out his route for the pursuers. They had but to follow his trail of fire — the smoking habitations of the whigs marking, for many miles, his progress. So rapid was the pursuit of the Americans, that, by noon, they were within three miles of the place where Tarleton had stopped to dine. Unconscious of their proximity, he had moved away in season, and had passed the Haw at the first convenient ford. It was while rapidly pressing forward in the pursuit, hoping that he might be overtaken before night, that the path of the Americans was suddenly crossed by a strong party of tories, under Colonel Pyles. These were dispersed, but not without great slaughter, in consequence of a mistake of the unfortunate tories, who confounded Lee's with Tarleton's legion, and only commenced firing at a moment when the effort was fruitless for defence, and served only to provoke the fury of the militia. The delay was a serious hinderance to the pursuit of Tarleton. It brought on darkness. Nevertheless, Pickens resolved not to rest until he had thrown himself between the British dragoons and certain detachments of whig militia under Colonel Preston and others, which Tarleton was aiming to cut off. It was fortunate that he adopted this resolution, as he succeeded that night in uniting Preston's and the other bodies of militia with his own force, adding to its strength, and saving them from the edge of Tarleton's sabre. The force of Pickens, increased by these auxiliaries, was now very decidedly superior to that of Tarleton. It consisted of two hundred and fifty excellent bayonets, three hundred militia marksmen, and the command of Preston, three hundred more. The cavalry of M'Call and Lee, though less in numbers than that of Tarleton, was better mounted, and of far better material. The command of Tarleton composed all the cavalry of the British army, two hundred and fifty infantry, and two pieces of artillery. Could the Americans but overtake and overcome this detachment, the army of Cornwallis was at their mercy. Deprived of his cavalry, and of so large a portion of his infantry, he must have sought safety in flight; and the result of such an attempt, in a country swarming with mounted militia, need not be matter of doubt or speculation.

The fate of Cornwallis lay in other hands, however those of Greene may have paved the way for it. Tarleton, himself, never dreamed of the enemy that was at his heels. He had actually drawn up his men at midnight, arranging for the capture of Preston and his volunteers. But Cornwallis was more apprehensive, and, consequently more vigilant. He had received advices of the advance of the American army, and trembled for the fate of the detachment in the hands of his dragoon. He dreaded lest another affair like that at the Cowpens should utterly ruin him, and courier after courier, to the number of three, was despatched by the British commander in pursuit of Tarleton, apprizing him of his danger, and recalling him instantly to camp. The British colonel obeyed, and with such equal caution and precipitation, that he had gained nearly two hours of his march before his movement was discovered by the scouts of the Americans. With the first intimation of his departure, Pickens was on the alert. His detachment was set in motion, though at midnight, and the pursuit was instantly begun. So dark was the night, when this movement was made, that the troops were obliged to employ torches of *light-*

wood (resinous pine) to light them on their progress. Yet so earnest was the pursuit, that, when the first files of the Americans reached the banks of the Haw, the rear-guard of the enemy was just ascending the heights of the opposite shore. Here the pursuit was arrested. The British colonel, planting his artillery in a position to command the ford, and occupying such a position with his infantry as to give his cannon the best support, rendered the passage quite too hazardous to be attempted. The Americans were without artillery. To attempt the passage at another ford would be only to afford the enemy such an advantage in the race as no subsequent efforts could overcome; at all events, not before he had been reinforced by support from the British camp. And thus it was, that the prey was snatched from the grasp of the American general almost at the very moment when his fingers were about to close upon it. But the expedition had proved of the greatest uses. The recruits of the whig militia had been saved from disaster, their friends had been encouraged, while the tory force under Pyles, four hundred in number, had been cut to pieces, and the loyalists disheartened by a disaster so unexpected, and a punishment so sanguinary.

CHAPTER XII.

Strategies of the two Armies.—Cornwallis surrounded by the Partisans. —Their Activity and Audacity.—He attempts to elude them, and cut Greene off from his Detachments.—He pursues Williams, who escapes him.—Cornwallis retires, and Greene prepares for Action.

THE operations of Pickens and Lee, though only in part successful, were yet productive of the happiest results, particularly in discouraging the loyalists from taking the field. They afforded, thus, an auspicious beginning of that new enterprise, on the part of the commander of the American forces, which had prompted him to recross the Dan. Greene, meanwhile, lost no time in making himself ready for the field. Inferior still, in strength, to his adversary, and sadly wanting in equipments, he felt the necessity of incurring a risk in the endeavor to prevent Cornwallis from utterly overrunning the "old north state," as he had overrun South Carolina. Though not in sufficient strength to measure weapons with the British general, it was still in his power to defeat his leading objects, by cutting off his detachments, arresting the proceedings of the disaffected, and giving encouragement, by his activity and presence, to those who were friendly to the whig cause. For these purposes, he was particularly well provided in the proper officers. With Pickens to conduct the militia riflemen; with Lee to guide the impetuous movements of the legion; with Williams to show himself, ubiquitously with his active and veteran light infantry,—he was possessed of so many wings, rapidly wheeling at every movement of the enemy, harassing him in his enterprises, and keeping him, for ever, in a feverish state of doubt and insecurity. These able leaders were all kept well-informed of the desires of their commander. Attended only by a small escort of Washington's dragoons, Greene made his way across the country, to the separate camps of these several detachments, earnestly, but affectionately, counselling with them on his and their future progress. From the wigwam of green bushes that formed the shelter of Pickens and Lee, he sped to the camp of Williams, suffering nothing to escape his observation in regard to their common enterprise. Hard was the hourly toil which this sort of progress imposed upon him and them. Sorry were the fare and shelter in the forest tent of Pickens; and the two generals, after long consultation, wrapped in their cloaks, were compelled to seek for the necessary warmth, and snatch a brief term of repose, in the folds of a single blanket. The object of Greene in this hazardous visit, in which he narrowly escaped contact with the legion of Tarleton, was to obtain information, to prepare his partisans for the anticipated escape of Cornwallis, and to urge them to the suppression of the loyalists who had appointed the forks of the Haw and Deep rivers as their place of rendezvous. But, soon satisfied that Cornwallis no longer contemplated flight—that he had deluded himself with the idea that the state was fairly in his power—and that his army would be sufficiently strengthened against the Americans, by his tory recruits, to enable him to make a stand, and seek once more the final issue,—Greene saw that nothing, now, remained to be done, but to prepare for the decisive struggle. He proceeded, therefore, to hasten on his reinforcements, occupying, meanwhile, with the main army, such a position as would best enable him to cover their concentration, and cut off the communication of the enemy with the upper country. With these views, the army, having crossed the Dan, was marched toward the head-waters of the Haw, on the route to Guilford. To keep the field between the Haw and the Dan, was a matter of some difficulty; but the very hazard of the service had its recommendation, as it afforded to the volunteers that active employment and constant exercise, which can alone satisfy the eager and impetuous nature, which the unperforming life of the camp would only discourage and disgust. The demonstration had its uses for other reasons. It encouraged, with a show of confidence and strength, the more timorous friends of the cause throughout the country, and impressed upon its enemies a sense of respect, which, necessarily, exaggerated the strength of the Americans, and made them doubtful of their own. The audacity and activity of the light troops of Greene's army, under their accomplished leaders, constituted another guaranty for his security. We have had a sample of their uses, in beating up the quarters of the enemy, cutting off their pickets and detachments, preventing their supplies, and quelling the spirit of their allies. With such partisan officers, the wings and the eyes of the army, Greene's own sagacity, and his knowledge of the character of Cornwallis, enabled him to do the rest. The coolness, forethought, and circumspection of the one, even with inferior forces, were well opposed to, and a sufficient match for, the imperious will, impetuous haste, and sanguine impulse of the other.

As soon as Tarleton had rejoined the royal army, Cornwallis prepared for active operations. He penetrated the objects of Greene, and felt the necessity of counteracting them, if possible. With this view, he abandoned Hillsborough on the 26th of February, and threw himself across the Haw, taking post near Alemance creek, one of the principal tributaries of that river. This movement had for its object to cut Greene off from the upper country, to enable the British troops to cover the uprising of the loyalists, and to forage in a region, the resources of which were, comparatively, abundant. The design was skilfully conceived, and reduced the American general to three alternatives: he might either offer battle to an antagonist who wished nothing better; once more retreat across the Dan, and leave the state to the invader; or advance still farther on the route, by Guilford, toward Salisbury. In other words, the aim of Cornwallis was to compel his adversary to fly or fight; and the policy of Greene was to avoid either necessity. It was a peculiar game to play, and required all the skill of the strategist. It was in this department of war that Greene's particular merit lay. He was thoroughly sensible of the truth, that he can be no general whom the enemy can force to fight at pleasure; and, concentrating all his resources upon the object before him, a series of manœuvres followed, which declared, more impressively than ever, the extent of his abilities, and the strength and confidence with which he managed them. To keep steadily in mind the necessity of covering his own reinforcements, preventing those of the enemy, and saving himself from disaster, was the great purpose which governed every movement in his progress, and counselled every enterprise.

Cornwallis was not insensible to the merits of his enemy, and his own necessities. His mind seemed to rise to the level of his exigencies. His chief object seems to have been to persuade the attention of the American commander in one direction, while he decoyed his reinforcements within striking distance in another. In doing this, he had to keep in mind the necessity of never being too remote from his own stores at Wilmington, which the growing distress of his own army had now begun to render doubly important to his interests. Greene, meanwhile, kept even pace with the march of the British general. Vigilance and activity were his prevailing dictates. Carefully did he avoid every risk which might bring on a general action; and his arrangements never failed to contemplate an open avenue, either for advance or retreat. He thus armed himself against every manœuvre of his enemy; but no labor could have been more exhausting, as no game could be more full of perplexity and doubt. Thus counselled, he pressed forward, and crossed the Haw, near its source, and chose for the scene of operations, the ground which lies between Troublesome creek and Reedy fork.

Here were Greene's headquarters, but he was in no circumstances to be fettered by an arbitrary choice of position. His place was changed nightly, and the capricious front which he displayed, served the double purpose of not only leaving the enemy uncertain of his position, but of his numbers. His detachments, strengthened at his own expense, were active in correspondence with their strength. His light troops were continually hovering about the enemy, darting upon his foraging-parties, cutting off his supplies and intelligence, beating up his quarters, vexing his march, and exhausting him, by incessant provocations to fruitless service. In this occupation, it is difficult to say which of the partisans was most conspicuous. Williams, Pickens, Lee, and Washington, equally distinguished themselves upon the flanks, and in the front, of the enemy. The former, maintaining always a proper position for supporting the detachments, was equally careful to be sufficiently near to co-operate, when necessary, with the main army. Joined by Pickens, while manœuvring in the vicinity of the Haw, the two bodies now threw themselves in front of the enemy, one on each side of the Alemance creek. Their force, strengthened by large accessions of militia, had become so considerable, that, on one occasion, they seriously meditated a combined attack upon the British general. Such had been the secresy and celerity of their movements, that he had been utterly bewildered by them. He could form no idea of their numbers, and was only conscious of their presence, by feeling them—in military language—throughout the night. That these two leaders did not make their attack, arose from counsels to a delay for a more auspicious moment, which, unhappily, did not again occur.

Thus operating, at once in front, flank, and rear, doubling upon their grounds daily, like a fox, now approaching and now retiring, but never so far as to relieve their adversary's detachments from a wholesome fear of danger, the several divisions of Greene's army contrived still to keep the region into which he had been bold enough to penetrate. No will-of-the-wisp ever sported more capriciously with the benighted traveller, than these partisans with the British general. He knew not in what quarter to look for the foe, whom, but the last night, he had felt in this—knew not where to apprehend the danger to-night, which had threatened him, equally, on all quarters, the night before. Every source of intelligence seemed to be cut off. His horizon was bounded to a span. His cavalry seemed adventurous no longer. The wondrous energy and success of Tarleton were suddenly at an end; and, as for the anxious tories, lately as fussy and full of exercise as an overflowing hive about to send out its swarms, they dreaded to make the slightest humming, which should declare their vitality, lest it should waken sharp echoes from the sabres of Washington, or the fatal rifles of Pickens

Cornwallis was naturally anxious to relieve himself of such troublesome attendants. His position was becoming exceedingly delicate and doubtful. His skill, though considerable, had hitherto been unavailing. It was in vain that he urged the genius of Tarleton into enterprise. A single brush of that desperate dragoon with the legion infantry, gave him no encouragement to press his fortunes, and suggested additional reasons to Cornwallis, for an effort of deeper policy, and more decisive endeavor, than had yet been made. Circumstances seemed to favor his desires. He had succeeded in procuring some certain intelligence of these detachments of the Americans, whose ubiquitous career had been so distressing to his forces. Like some great animal, assailed by inferior forces, which only escape his rage in consequence of their superior agility, he affected to sleep in his position. For six days he remained almost quiet on the Alemance, with an occasional demonstration on the road to Cross creek. His quiet was meant to lull the Americans into momentary security; his demonstrations in the direction of Cross creek, to divert their attention from his true object. He almost succeeded in this *ruse*. Greene, meanwhile, with the main army, lay at Boyd's ferry, fifteen miles from the camp of Cornwallis. Williams was more within his reach, and, on the night of the 6th of March, lay but a few miles off, on the left of the enemy. Could the British general succeed in surprising Williams, or in darting by him, so as to reach the High Rock ford, in advance of Greene, then would the latter be most effectually separated from his detachments, and be compelled to leave them to their fate, or hazard his whole army in a battle, to secure the junction with them. Suddenly, then, in the hope of achieving this object, Cornwallis set his army in motion early on the morning of the 6th. His movements, though unanticipated, were not wholly unprepared for. He did not succeed in his surprise of Williams; who, keeping good watch, discovered his march when he was yet two miles off, and instantly set his detachment in motion. His course, like that of Cornwallis, was for Wetzel's mills, across the Reedy Fork. Throwing himself in front of his enemy, he despatched advices to Greene of the threatened danger, and then proceeded to strain every nerve to attain the pass by which alone could he unite his force with that of his superior. Throwing out light flanking parties, under Colonels Preston and Campbell, to annoy the advance of the enemy, he succeeded in keeping the start which he had had at the beginning, and the race continued, with great spirit, until the passage of the ford, at Wetzel's mills, was effected. Drawn up on the opposite bank of the stream, they were prepared to dispute the farther progress of the British, whose advance, under Tarleton, soon made its appearance, but, awed by the presence of the American cavalry under Washington and Lee, they forbore to attempt the passage. The detachment under Preston engaged the enemy in a smart skirmish, the advantages of which enured to the Americans. A few prisoners were taken on both sides. Here, on the east bank of the Haw river, Williams became informed of the true purpose of the British general. Greene was apprized of it in season; and though Cornwallis had stolen a march on Williams, and had very adroitly managed his enterprise, he failed entirely to secure his prey, when almost within his grasp. A series of well-concerted movements on the part of Greene, and the leaders of his detachments, were admirably successful; and, when the British general reached the point at which he expected to intercept his adversary—compelling him either to abandon his advancing reinforcements, or forcing him to an action in their defence--he had the mortification to find that the Americans had gained the opposite bank of the river, where, both divisions of their army being united, they could safely oppose his passage across the stream, and be secure of the junction with their rapidly-approaching reinforcements.

This was the last contest of skill between the rival captains. Cornwallis, at length, despaired of outgeneralling his antagonist. His only hope, now, lay in suffering him to accumulate his forces in sufficient strength to engage boldly in the struggle, where the arbiter should be the sword. Returning sullenly from the pursuit, he took post at Bell's mills, on Deep river, while Greene, in his camp on Troublesome creek, gave his troops a brief respite, while waiting the arrival of his Virginia corps and militia. A few days enabled these to make their appearance, bringing with them stores and supplies, which were, of all things, most needed by the suffering army. The North Carolina militia began to pour in, while detached parties of militia and volunteers, from time to time, added to the bulk of the army, so as to swell its numbers to a complement of more than four thousand men. With these, Greene was superior to his adversary. Fifteen hundred of these troops were regulars. A considerable body had been well-trained, and had enjoyed much valuable experience in the field. They were such as could be relied upon, as well for steadfastness as courage. His volunteers and militia were by no means wanting in resolution and spirit. Their deficiencies lay wholly in their want of training. Unaccustomed to long endurance in the field, to concerted action, to rapid movements, and subjection to discipline, their efficiency lay rather in their quick employment in actual conflict, than in the more slow and tedious, but not less important duties of marching, manœuvring, and rapid evolution. To employ these sufficiently, who constituted so large a part of his army—to confirm the spirit of his troops—to raise that of the people, to respond to the call of public opinion, which now began loudly to demand a battle—Greene prepared to afford his adversary the opportunity which the latter had appeared so long and so earnestly to seek. The forces of Cornwallis did not number more than two thirds of his own; but they were all picked soldiers, men of tried courage, of long experience in the field, and admirable training. In numbers, Greene was the superior to Cornwallis, but far his inferior in discipline and equipment; and the former did not regard the approaching issue with so much confidence as hope. He was in a measure compelled to seek the fight. He could expect no more regulars, and he was to employ and encourage the militia. The hopes of the British rested upon their loyalist auxiliaries, and these were best quieted by a conflict, in which, even if successful, the British army should be greatly crippled and disorganized. A few days devoted to the drilling of his militia, calling in and dissolving his detachments, reviewing and concentrating his strength, and making the other needful preparations, and Greene advanced to Guilford Courthouse, taking post, on the 14th March, 1781, within twelve miles of the enemy. To approach within this distance to an enemy is a military challenge. Its purport was understood; nor was Cornwallis unwilling for the encounter. Both armies accordingly prepared themselves for action

CHAPTER XIII.

The Battle of Guilford.—Its Vicissitudes.—Duel between Colonel Stuart and Captain Smith.—Slaughter among the Guards.—Retreat of the Americans.

The scene of battle on the present occasion, had long before attracted the military eye of Greene for this very purpose. He had noted its susceptibilities, on his first retreat from the Yadkin to the Dan, particularly for the employment of irregular troops, in which an undisciplined militia, with certain advantages derived from the inequalities of the surface of the field, might successfully be brought to oppose the steadier onset of a veteran enemy. The country was, in fact, little better than a wilderness. The settlements were few, and the unbroken forest spread itself on every hand, leaving but a few openings here and there, indicative of the mere dawn of cultivation. The road wound its way between thick masses of forest and undergrowth. The defile was narrow; dense coverts of copse and brush shadowed it on all hands and with few open intervals; while the ground, ascending gradually, with occasional undulations, from hill to hill, conducted finally to the superior eminence, which was occupied by the courthouse. With the ascent of these hills, the road begins to enlarge and expand. The brushwood begins to disappear; open fields, and small clearings, let in the more frequent light; while the fences of the farmer, which the approaching armies had not yet torn away, were standing in proof of the humble first beginnings of art, in its conflict with nature. These fields were mostly abandoned. A stunted growth, such as naturally occurs in like cases, had begun to appear, but not in such degree as to offer obstruction to the progress of troops in battle. The ascent of the ground was gradual, sloping gently from the courthouse, and subsiding at last, into a rivulet, which wound its way along the edges of a piece of swamp or bottom-land. The open tracts were divided by a dense mass of forest, which concealed them from each other. The space immediately about the courthouse was partly sheltered by a growth of saplings, which also formed a partial border for the high-road to Salisbury. Occasional ravines, which traversed the open grounds, afforded additional strength to the position, and contributed to recommend the spot to the eye of the American commander. He had reached the field in sufficient season to examine and to choose his ground, to arrange the order of battle, complete his preparations, and give his troops an encouraging night's rest.

With the dawn of the 15th he was stirring, and full of anxious expectation. He had no reason to doubt that he would be sought by his enemy. The day opened brightly, and with pleasant auspices. The troops were in the best of spirits; and Greene, at length, congratulated himself on the prospect of a victory, or, at all events, a struggle, such as should confirm the hope of his soldiers. and answer the expectations of the country. His force of regulars and militia-infantry consisted of four thousand two hundred and forty-three men. Of these, two thousand seven hundred and fifty-three were militia. Of his whole army, something less than two regiments had ever been in battle. It was in this lack of discipline and experience, among the Americans, that the inferiority of the British in numbers was more than equalized. The force under Cornwallis had been rated, and with every apparent probability, at about three thousand men. It certainly could not have been less than two thousand five hundred, not including cavalry. These were all disciplined troops, accustomed to victory, and doubly urged, at the present time, by their necessities no less than their desires, to seek it with the most desperate earnestness and valor.

Early in the morning a detachment under Lee, consisting of his legion and a body of riflemen, had been sent out to reconnoitre. They encountered the British advance, under Tarleton, and engaged it with spirit and success. But, feeling that they had to do with the van of an army, they withdrew to the main body, giving due notice of the approaching conflict. Greene at once made his preparations. His officers were soon in station, and his troops arrayed for battle. His army was drawn out in three separate lines, presenting so many successive barriers to the assault of the enemy. The first of these, consisting of the North Carolina militia, one thousand in number, under the command of Generals Eaton and Butler, were placed upon the skirts of a wood at right angles with the road upon which the enemy was approaching. In front of them stretched a long and narrow cornfield, whose crumbling fences of rail afforded rather a show of protection and shelter than any positive defence. It was supposed that a few rounds might be delivered under their cover before the defenders were compelled to retire under the push of the bayonet. The weapons of this line were mostly rifles. Practised marksmen, from habitual exercise, it wanted but steadiness of nerve to make their bullets tell. Unfortunately, they had not only never been in battle, but they had never been subject to the severe mechanism of that drill and discipline which, in military training, accomplishes quite as much. In the road, in advance of this line, were placed a couple of six-pounders, under Captain Singleton. On the right of this line, extending behind the west side of the open fields, obliquely toward a swamp, was a covering party under Colonel Washington, consisting of Kirkwood's Delawares, eighty in number, and a battalion of two hundred riflemen under Colonel Lynch. Washington's cavalry was drawn up in the woods at a little distance. The left of the line was covered by a party under Colonel Lee, consisting of the legion-infantry, and a detachment of riflemen under Colonel Campbell, two hundred and fifty in all. Lee's cavalry held a corresponding post on the extreme left, with Washington's on the right.

The second line of the Americans was drawn up about three hundred yards behind the first, and under shelter of the woods. This line was formed of Virginia militia, raw troops also, but they were fortunate in being led by officers who had been in the continental army, and possessed considerable experience in the field. The line was commanded by Generals Stevens and Lawson. The former, whose experience in militia was considerable, and who had suffered extreme mortification by their misconduct on a previous occasion, adopted a stern and sharp remedy against their timidity in future. He stationed, in the rear of his brigade, a line of sentinels, picked men upon whom he could rely, whose instructions were to shoot down any individual who broke the ranks. The remedy has usually been found unfailing against the infirmity it seeks to cure. This line, as well as the first, crossed and completely covered the road.

The third and last line of the Americans consisted of continentals, under the command of Generals Huger and Williams. It was composed of the brigades of Maryland and Virginia, the former under Williams, the latter under Huger. This line was stationed about three hundred yards in the rear of the second; the Maryland brigade, on the right, fronting the southwest; the Virginians, in regard to the peculiar formation of the hill, facing southeastwardly. Between the right of the one line and the left of the other, the angle was occupied by two pieces of artillery. The Virginia line consisted of two regiments, led by Colonels Greene and Rudford; the Maryland of two also, under Colonels Ford and Gunby. That of Gunby was the only veteran regiment. Two roads, directly in the rear of the Americans, left avenues for retreat, a necessity which, considering the peculiar objects of General Greene, was not, certainly, a humiliating one. His game was to cripple the enemy by his light troops, if possible, and insure their safety in retreat, by the intervention of his regulars. His third line was, in fact, his only reserve, and it commanded both the roads by which to secure the escape of the fugitives, in the event of disaster. No doubt the arrangement was one of many advantages; but we are half inclined to doubt the policy which exposes a militia wholly inexperienced and untried, to the first shock of battle, when, the judicious intermixture with them of select bodies of regulars, would fortify their courage by example, and sustain them with firmness under pressure.

The appearance of the van of the British army, at about 1 o'clock in the day, drew upon them the thunders from Singleton's two pieces in advance. The response was quickly made by the British artillery, from an eminence which commanded the road, over the heads of their own columns. Watching his opportunity in the intervals of the fire, Cornwallis rapidly pushed his sections across the defile, displaying them, as they severally passed, according to arrangement, under cover of an intervening wood. The right of the British was com manded by General Leslie, the left by Colonel Webster. The troops forming the line, consisted of the Hessian regiment of Boze, the 71st, the 23d, and the 33d regiments, in succession. The first battalion of the guards was drawn up, as a support to that wing in the rear of the right. The second, with the grenadiers of the same corps, under Brigadier-General O'Hara, acted as the support of the left. The Yagers and light infantry of the guards, when the line was put in motion for the assault, attached themselves to the 33d regiment. Tarleton's cavalry was held in reserve, and kept pace, under cover of the wood, with the progress of the artillery, which could only advance upon the open road.

These arrangements completed, the British pushed on to the attack. The first line of North-Carolinians still wore an aspect of firmness, and their officers began to exult in the hope that, under the partial cover of the fence, they would deliver such a fire as would fatally cripple the enemy in his advance, and possibly effect his utter discomfiture. But, a few moments sufficed to dispel these pleasant anticipations. With the advance of the British, a scattering fire was began by the militia, and a single discharge from the whole line may have been delivered. But the inexperienced woodsmen were not equal to the terrible shock of battle, when opened with the earnest pressure of the bayonet. Coming on with a fierce halloo, an army with banners and a most gorgeous array, the British rushed forward in a wild torrent, pouring in their fire as they came, and hastening, with the most determined resolution, to the close business with cold steel. The militia were not equal to the trial. A panic seized upon the line. Those who were fearless, and would have fought, were isolated in the wild disruption of their ranks, and compelled to obey the necessity which seemed to hurry them in flight. It was in vain that their officers threw themselves across the path of the fugitives, and strove by blows, no less than words, to arrest the torrent. The flood was irresistible. Their fears, superior to self-rebuke or shame, were not to be restrained by arguments or threats. Bewildered by their terrors, they darted through the woods, or sought shelter in the rear of the second line, which opened, with hisses, to receive and shelter them.

The British, exulting at this first advantage, rushed forward in pursuit, with triumphant shouts, as if secure of victory. But they were welcomed by crossfires from the flanking parties of Washington and Lee, which silenced their clamors, and, for a moment, cooled their hopes. These flanking parties had witnessed, without dismay, the sad misconduct of the militia. They kept their ground steadily, and delivered their fire with a rapidity and precision, which taught Cornwallis the necessity of moving with more deliberation to the conflict. A halt was ordered; while the regiment of Boze, half-wheeling to the right, and the 33d, with the light infantry and Yagers, to the left, addressed themselves, on each hand, to the business of dispersing the flanking parties. Washington and Lee, thus entreated by a superior force, gradually yielded before the enemy, delivering steady and sure fires, at every chance, from tree and thicket, and only giving ground under the pressure of the bayonet. In thus retiring without losing their order, these separate bodies were soon brought into a corresponding relation with the second line of the Americans, which they had occupied in regard to the first.

Meanwhile, the British line, which had again closed for the encounter with the Virginia militia, hurried on, with confidence, to the assault. But the Virginia militia, uninfluenced by the shameful example of the North-Carolinians, presented an unbroken front to the assailants.

Their fire was delivered with equal coolness and precision. Armed, numerously, with the rifle, no single shot was expended idly, but each bullet had its mission for a special mark. Wide gaps were soon opened in the British files by a fire so destructive; and the faltering and derangement which followed in the British line, under this handling, proved, conclusively, that their doom must have been inevitable with better behavior on the part of the American first line. But, the steady valor of the British prevailed, under the tenacious and trained spirit of veteran experience. Animated, by their officers, to the most determined efforts, they continued to press forward. Then it was, that, under the superior influence of the British bayonet, Lawson's brigade, on the American right, began to yield. But they gave back slowly, and without losing their coolness or order; the American left, and the British right, becoming, respectively, the pivots upon which the two lines appeared to revolve. It was at this moment that Washington, who commanded the flanking party on the right, following the sweep which had been made by the right of the American line, and faithful to the charge of covering it, came out upon the road. Here, discovering that the retreat of the line was inevitable in the retreat of Lawson's wing, he separated his infantry from it, and made his way to the third or continental line, taking post on the right of the Marylanders. The fight still continued on the left of the second line of the Americans, which, supported by the riflemen of Campbell and the legion of Lee, were enabled to protract the issue, if not to change its character.

The disappearance of Washington, with his detachment, from the right wing of the Virginia militia, had left Colonel Webster free to pursue his progress in this quarter. Webster was in command of the British left. He pushed forward, accordingly, until he came in contact with the first regiment of Marylanders, forming the extreme right of the continental or third line of the Americans. This regiment was, *par excellence*, the tenth legion of the American army. It was the same which, under Colonel Howard, had crossed bayonets with the British at Cowpens, compelling them to succumb. It had a fame to keep and cherish, which was not difficult, with its almost veteran experience. Commanded by Colonel Gunby, it was in fit condition to maintain its laurels. It was an evil hour for Webster that he pushed forward in this quarter. His approach occasioned no emotions. The Marylanders were prepared for him, and coolly awaited his approaches. Their fire was withheld until the British were within proper range, and then delivered with an effect so fearful as to produce almost instant discomfiture. Not waiting to note the effect of their fire, but seemingly assured of what it should be, the Marylanders followed up their fire, by descending into the plain and administering the bayonet. The rout which followed was complete. The British left was sent off reeling in confusion; and, had either of the two squadrons of American cavalry been present, the enemy could never have recovered from the disaster. Webster, himself grievously wounded, was yet enabled to draw off his crippled regiment, and, covering them behind a ravine in the cover of the woods, to wait for succor from his general. Greene did not dare to pursue his advantage, having no such confidence in his remaining regiments as would justify him in a close grapple, on the plain, with the whole British army, discarding all the advantages of his position, and relying on the struggle hand to hand.

It was during the conflict between these two parties, that the artillery of the British, under Lieutenant M'Leod, had made its way along the road, and at length reached the field of action, taking a commanding position on a rising ground at the edge of the wood. This was an event of considerable importance in determining the final event.

The battle, meanwhile, was still raging fiercely between the left of the Virginia militia, and the right wing of the enemy. Stevens, the brave commander of the former, had been disabled by a severe wound in the thigh; but this did not dismay his followers. Still using their rifles, with coolness and precision, they were clinging to the wood, as they retired, and making their way slowly to the cover of the continental line. Their rifles, though no match for the British bayonet, were yet speaking audibly, at every second, to the very hearts of their assailants; but they were not now in sufficient force to render necessary the employment of so large a division of the British army as had engaged them, and leaving them to the care of the first battalion of the guards, and the regiment of Boze, General Leslie drew off the 23d and 71st, and hastened to follow the footsteps of General O'Hara, who, with the 2d battalion, and grenadiers of the guards, had hurried to interpose between Webster and the Marylanders. His march brought him into collision, not with the first regiment of Marylanders, whom, we have seen, under Gunby, encountering the onslaught of Webster with such severe handling, but, with the second regiment from the same state, under Colonel Ford. Here the American general was doomed to a mortifying disappointment. Ford's regiment, uninfluenced by the noble example of Gunby's, recoiled from a conflict with the splendid line of British guards that bore down upon them. Their admirable bearing, and brilliant appearance, imposed too heavily upon the apprehensions of the Marylanders, and instead of a brave, manly struggle, they yielded, with scarcely an effort, before their foes, breaking entirely, after a brief trial, and in spite of all the exertions of their officers. This misfortune threw Singleton's two pieces of artillery into the hands of the enemy; and they rushed forward, secure now of victory, with shouts that shook the field. But their exultation was premature. They had not noticed the approach of other foes of more steadiness and spirit than those whom they pursued. Gunby's approach, with the first Marylanders, had been concealed by the copse-wood by which the field was skirted, and equally silent and unsuspected had been the approach of Washington, with the cavalry of his command. In an instant, the British shouts of victory were changed to shrieks of death. Wheeling upon the left, the regiment of Gunby dashed in among the guards, and a terrible struggle, hand to hand, ensued. The contest was for life, no less than for victory. Gunby was wounded, and put *hors de combat*, his place being supplied by Howard. Disordered by their own wild pressure upon the recoiling ranks of Ford's Marylanders, the British guards no longer maintained any compact order, under the charge of Gunby's. Then it was, that, while they struggled pell-mell, in all the mazes of the conflict, Washington's cavalry burst in upon them from the rear, and threatened their total annihilation. A series of individual conflicts followed in this struggle, some of which find their places in regular history. One of these may well deserve our attention. The combatants were Colonel Stuart, of the guards, and Captain John Smith, of the Marylanders. Both of these champions were distinguished by nerve and muscle. They had met before, and a personal provocation had resulted in the mutual declaration that their next meeting should end in blood. The present was a fitting occasion, and they singled each other out, with a

9

fierce passion for revenge, which made them totally regardless of the wild confusion and red horrors of the *mêlée*. Their weapons were at once crossed, with a desperate fury, which promised but one result. A moment decided the conflict. The adroit pass of Stuart's smallsword was admirably parried by the left hand of the American, while with his right, he drove the edge of his heavy sabre through the head of his enemy, cleaving him to the very spine. The next moment, he himself was brought to the ground, stunned, not slain, by the graze of a pistol-bullet, sent by a devoted follower of the fallen Briton, who was stricken to the heart, almost in the same moment, by the bayonet of an American, who was equally watchful of the safety of his superior.

But the duel between these furious combatants did not arrest the business of the field. That went on, with increasing animation and interest. The British guards were overwhelmed in the struggle. Broken and scattered, reeling in confusion and dismay, pressed with inveterate rage by Howard and Washington, they were allowed not a moment to recover their organization or their breath. The crisis of their fate had arrived, and Cornwallis beheld in it the shadow of his own. He hastened to the point of danger, the whole field beneath his eye, covered with his flying guards, and their vindictive pursuers. The desperate condition of his fortunes required one of those desperate remedies, at the employment of which quite as much nerve as judgment becomes necessary. The stern Briton adopted his resolution in an instant. He wheeled from the spot for the purpose of putting it in execution, and narrowly escaped captivity or death, at the hands of Washington. A petty accident, the falling of his cap, at the momen when our colonel of cavalry was about to dart upon his prey, as he rode off, enabled the British general to escape this danger, of which he was, possibly, at the time, unconscious.

His care was in another quarter. The necessity be fore him was a fearful one. His fortunes hung upon a thread. The rout of the guards was irretrievable, and must be followed by the worst consequences, if, in the scattered state of his troops, the fierce onset of the cavalry under Washington should remain unchecked. He had no forces in reserve. By this time the whole strength of the British army had been more or less engaged in the action. But one dreadful expedient remained to him, and, hurrying to the hill on which M'Leod had posted his artillery, he gave the terrible order to repel the progress of the American cavalry, by pouring out torrents of grape upon the field. Mingled in masses upon the plain, were his own troops with the Americans. Every storm of bullets swept necessarily through the ranks of friends and foes. His own guards must feel the storm as heavily as their adversaries. But they were already compromised. No remedy could avail for their safety, and none but this for his own. He gave the orders. Bleeding with previous wounds, O'Hara expostulated with his chief: "It is destroying ourselves." His remonstrances were made in vain. "True," was the answer of Cornwallis, "but it is now unavoidable. The evil is a necessary one, which we must endure if we would escape destruction." O'Hara turned away from the cruel spectacle, while the floods of grape tore their way in frequent tempest over the plain. The expedient was fatally successful. It repelled the American cavalry. It rescued the victory from their clutches; but one half of the splendid battalion of the guards was swept to ruin in the storm.

The battle was not yet over. The conflict still con tinued between the parties engaged in the woods. For the safety of his detachments in this quarter, Greene felt the greatest anxiety. The British commander, resolute on victory as the only source of safety, was newly forming his line, bent upon the renewal of his endeavors. Forming under cover of the brush along the roadside, his operations were greatly concealed from sight; and, pressing too cautiously forward, for the purpose of discovery, Greene incurred as great a peril of captivity or death as Cornwallis had done but a little while before. His coolness and presence of mind alone saved him from a shower of musketry. Occasional volleys were still heard from the edges of the wood, with now and then a mutual bellowing from the cannon of the rival forces, posted on separate heights. The regiment of Boze was still kept busy in the woods, with the left of the American second line. There the riflemen of Campbell, the infantry of Lee, and the broad-swords of his legion, still maintained the conflict, firing from every cover, and retreating only at the approach of the bayonet. In this kind of warfare the Americans had all the advantage. They could be driven by their enemies, but not far; and the moment the halt was made again, it was only to send forth new volleys of winged bullets, every one of which had its billet. The British, still advancing, were, nevertheless, dropping fast, and Cornwallis ordered Tarleton with his dragoons, to the succor of the regiment of Boze. It happened, unfortunately, that Lee's cavalry had been withdrawn, with some other object, from the wing of Campbell's party, when the descent of Tarleton was made. Had they been present, the fortunes of the day might have been made triumphantly secure. Unsheltered by this arm of the service, Campbell's rifles were compelled to disappear ir double-quick time, having nothing to oppose to the British broad-sword. This, alone, saved the regiment of Boze, and enabled it tc recover the British line. With its reappearance, and the disappearance of Lee's corps, for the fate of which his anxiety was now painfully awakened, Greene felt that the chances of the day were about to go against him. The British troops, though dispirited and greatly thinned, were yet again in line, and presenting a formidable front. To oppose them, the mere numbers of Greene might have been still sufficient; but how could he rely upon the regiment of continentals which had so shamefully emulated the flight of the North Carolina militia, at the very brunt of conflict? He had too much at stake to peril his troops unnecessarily in a struggle for which no training had yet prepared them. A drawn battle, for all moral purposes, would suffice for his objects. The policy of the Americans counselled delay rather than risk. With every moment of pause, the British army was losing in numbers, health, confidence, and resources Fortunately, Greene had kept his regiment of Virginia continentals in reserve. With these he could draw off his troops with safety, the former interposing with unbroken front, to cover the retreat. A reckless courage, an audacity that would stake all on the hazard of a single cast of the die, might, with this regiment, sustained by those who still kept the field, have rendered the affair a glorious victory. But so, also, might such audacity have worked the entire ruin of the cause and the commander. Such boldness could only be justified by the desperation of the case, such as Cornwallis felt, and by a perfect confidence in the coolness and steadfastness of the regiments from which the service was expected. Wanting this confidence, and feeling no such necessity, Greene prudently determined not to renew the engagement. He had gained, perhaps, quite as much, or even more, than he had anticipated from the trial of strength, in crippling the enemy, and encouraging his own troops. Both of these had resulted from the engagement, in spite of all its disappointments and vicissitudes.

The order, accordingly, was given to retreat. The North Carolina and Virginia militia had, by this time, generally gained the rear of the army, and were on their way to the designated place of rendezvous. Colonel Greene, with the Virginia regiment, fresh and entire, was employed to cover the retreat. With the first indications of this movement, the enemy advanced, with two regiments and a strong body of cavalry. The firing opened on both sides with great spirit, and was continued for some time with considerable animation. But the Americans were too firm, and the British too much crippled, to make the pursuers eager for the renewal of the conflict. The pursuit was soon arrested, and, bringing up the rear in person, Greene made his first halt for several hours, within three miles of the field of battle. Here he picked up his stragglers, arranged for the care of the wounded, and snatched a momentary rest from fatigue, before resuming his march, which he did in a cold and pitiless rain, reaching his encampment at the iron-works of Troublesome creek, about the dawning of the next day

CHAPTER XIV.

Cornwallis retreats—Is pursued by Greene—Escapes.—His Condition, and that of the Americans.—Greene's Policy.—Discontinues the Pursuit of Cornwallis—Marches to South Carolina—Appears before Camden—and offers Battle to Lord Rawdon.

Thus terminated this long and bloody conflict, the caprices and vicissitudes of which, for a long while, held the issue in suspense. But for the miserable failure of Greene's first line, the victory must have been with the Americans—as it was, nothing but the superior discipline of the British secured it for them. Cornwallis was at the head of two thousand troops, as fine as any in the world. Of Greene's army, not more than five hundred had ever seen service. Yet no troops could have behaved better than a certain portion of his force. The habitual training of the British, when made to recoil, enabled them quickly to recover, and to form themselves anew for battle. But with Greene's militia the case was otherwise. Defeat was dispersion also. Even the Marylanders of Ford, though saved from the onset of the guards by the timely interposition of Gunby and Washington, could not again be brought to look the enemy in the face. The steadiness of the infantry of the former, and the cavalry of the latter, could not have been surpassed; and the spirit exhibited by both, united the audacity of chivalry with the discipline of the regular soldier. Could Greene have saved his artillery, the loss of which is not adequately accounted for, he would probably have had little reason to complain of the results of the conflict. One fourth of the British army had been put *hors du combat* in the *mêlée.* Most of their officers were hurt. Cornwallis and Leslie narrowly escaped, the former having had two horses shot under him, while, at one moment of the struggle, the sabre of Washington was almost literally brandished over his head. His gallantry deserves every credit, and was such as to prove how vitally important to his safety did he estimate the issues of the day. His loss, in killed, wounded, and missing, was six hundred and thirty-three. Of these, one colonel and four commissioned officers were slain on the field; Colonel Webster and several captains died of their wounds; the recovery of General O'Hara was, for a long time, doubtful; Tarleton was wounded, and a General Howard, who volunteered in the engagement, besides twenty other commissioned officers.

The Americans were far more fortunate. Their loss did not reach half this number—a result attributable, purely, to the superior excellence of the rifle in their hands, over the musket in the hands of the British. General Huger, at the head of the Virginians, was slightly wounded in the hand; Major Anderson, an able officer of the 1st Marylanders, was killed; General Stevens was severely wounded; and about a dozen other officers suffered from wounds also. The greater loss of the Americans consisted in the flight of the militia. One half of the North-Carolinians and a large number of the Virginians, when they left the field, continued on their way, long after the danger was over, and retired to their homes. The whole force of Greene, reviewed on the 19th, four days after the battle, amounted to three thousand one hundred and fifteen, including every description of soldier. The trophies which he left in the hands of his adversary, consisted of his artillery, a couple of baggage-wagons, and a portion of his wounded. It is one of the curious proofs of the doubtful and capricious character of the conquest, that he carried off a greater number of prisoners than he lost.

The victory certainly lay with the British; but it was a victory, as was remarked by Fox, in the house of commons, like that of Pyrrhus, which left the conqueror undone: "another such would ruin the British army." Greene, himself, upon a survey of the result, was enabled to make the same estimate. "He has gained his cause," said he, speaking of Cornwallis, "but is ruined by its cost." The British general, himself, was, probably, not not less satisfied of the justness of this judgment. Returning from the fruitless pursuit of the Americans, he was enabled to review his troops and the field of battle. The scene presented a spectacle, in open land and woods, which must have admonished him of the growing peril which hung about his camp. Nearly seven hundred of his best troops had been cut off. There they lay, on every hand, where the rifles of Campbell had dropped them, step by step, as they came — where the fierce charge of Gunby's regiment had swept them down, and where the flashing sabres of Washington had smitten them as with an edge of fire. There, too, covering the broad space before his eyes, were the numerous victims to his own unsparing artillery, when it became necessary, in arresting the cavalry of Washington, to sweep, with the same besom of death, the scattered and staggering guards whom he could no longer save. The British general, with a drooping spirit, prepared for the burial of the dead and the care of the wounded. History records, to his honor, that he did not discriminate between friend and foe in the performance of these melancholy duties. Night found him at this gloomy work, and the aspect of the heavens had become gloomier with cloud and rain. The chilling gusts of March swept the field, laden with sleety showers, that added to the sufferings of the wounded, and increased the cares and anxieties of those who were burdened with the charge of them. The baggage had not arrived. The soldiers were without tents; and, after the dwellings within reach had received all whom they could shelter, there were still hundreds, even of the wounded, who were exposed to all the rigors of the night and season, with no other cover than the clothes they wore. More than fifty of these wretched sufferers had perished ere the dawn.

Encumbered with his wounded, with his best officers slain or incapable from wounds, with the moral of his army greatly impaired, surrounded by doubtful and timid friends, or by vindictive and impatient enemies, far from his resources, and equally uncertain of reinforcements, the barren victory of Cornwallis was really a disaster of the worst description. He put on a face of the utmost confidence, while grief and anxiety were heavy at his heart. His proclamation, issued from his camp at Guilford, set forth, in glowing colors, the brilliancy and importance of his recent victory, even at the moment when he felt that his necessities counselled a retreat. He summoned the loyalists to his standard, and held out terms of pardon to the whigs at the very moment when his retrograde movements had begun. He could no longer venture to hunt his enemy. He felt that the fugitive must soon become the hunter. It was impossible to struggle longer against the difficulties that encompassed him. When he destroyed his baggage, after the affair at Cowpens, it was with the full persuasion that he should be in security in the British camp in Virginia, or in the richest counties in that state. He was now almost as far removed from this prospect as before, and in less condition to attain it. His numbers were reduced one half—his men were barefoot—his stores were exhausted—and the enemy was still at hand, threatening an early renewal of the conflict—that enemy whom he had found it impossible to conquer, and whom he could no longer venture to pursue. In a precipitate flight lay his only means of security.

On the 18th of March, three days after the battle, he commenced his retreat. His design was covered by every possible artifice. His boastful proclamation was intended to disguise his purpose; and the better to attain his object, he conveyed his wounded in his wagons and litters, taking for granted, that, with such incumbrances, nobody would suspect his purpose of retreat.

But Greene had been too well advised of the condition of the British army, to leave him in doubt as to the necessity before his adversary. The excellent spirits of his own army, officers and men—nowise daunted by the issue of the late struggle, but proud of the stand which a portion of them had made, and anxious to efface the discredit and reproach which had fallen upon the whole, by the misconduct of those who had faltered—all encouraged the American general to take the initiate in the future trials of strength with the enemy. With the first intimation, therefore, of the march of the British, Lee was detached to hang upon his rear, and harass his progress. A deficiency of ammunition, under which Greene's army at present labored, alone prevented him from a more decided demonstration with his whole force.

The advance of the Americans hastened the movements of Cornwallis. He could no longer pursue his march at leisure, encumbered with the litters of his wounded. Seventy of these he left behind, under the protection of a flag; pursuing a progress which was designed to keep his opponent in doubt as to his real destination and purpose, pressing forward across Deep river, in the direction of Salisbury. This route, looking quite as much to a return to South Carolina as to any other point, might have persuaded any commander, less wary and sagacious than Greene, to take a direct course for Camden, in order to intercept his progress to that place. But, entering into all the calculations of Cornwallis, Greene was prepared to fathom, or to suspect, the real purpose of his adversary. A few hours sufficed to satisfy him of the propriety of his doubts. Recrossing Deep river, Cornwallis marched down its east bank, leaving it no longer uncertain that Wilmington was the place which he aimed to reach. The light detachments of the Americans hung upon his skirts, while the whole force of the army was pressed forward by a nearer road, which left the British troops but little advantage in point of distance. The contest was now not only one of speed, but one of skill—the former, indeed, depending greatly upon the degree in which the latter should be shown. In this contest, Cornwallis put forth all his strength. Greene pressed forward with all the energy which was possible, in bad roads and inclement weather, and, at one moment, when near Buffalo creek, had hopes of bringing on an engagement, under favorable circumstances. But a re-examination of his resources of ammunition, showed such a scanty supply, as greatly to discountenance the desire; and the British sped forward, without farther interruption than could be suggested by the harassing vigilance of picked squadrons at their heels. This survey of Greene's resources, resulting so unprofitably, occasioned some delay in the pursuit, of which Cornwallis took due advantage. Pressing forward his pioneers, he commenced throwing a bridge, at Ramsey's mill, across Deep river, near its confluence with the Haw. This indicated an intention to cross at that place, and was calculated to direct the march of the American army, crossing above him, down the opposite bank. This left Greene in a dilemma. He saw that if he pursued this route, the British, having an alternative, would cross the Haw, and securely descend on the east side of the Cape Fear. So well planned, in this proceeding, had been the measures of Cornwallis, that there was no method of counteracting them. A movement directly forward, would only force the enemy across his bridge, which, broken down behind him, would leave to the Americans no means of passage, but by fords across the Deep or the Haw, in seeking which, the loss of time must utterly baffle the pursuit.

For a moment, Greene was compelled to hesitate in doubt. But twelve miles separated the two armies—the British at Ramsay's mills, the Americans at Rigdon's ford, both on Deep river. A day elapsed, in which the forces lay in patient watch of one another. But Greene soon reached his conclusion. His only hope lay in a forced march, and *coup de main.* He resolved to push forward his light troops, with orders to engage the enemy, if possible, and keep them employed until the army could overtake, and share in the conflict. The movement was made before day on the morning of the 28th. But the British commander was too wary, and was too fully conscious of his peril, to be caught napping. He kept himself well informed of all the movements of his adversary, and was soon apprized of the approach of the detachments. His flight was resumed, and he passed the bridge in safety; but so hot was the pursuit, that he had not time to destroy it effectually, to bury his dead, or carry off his beef, which was found hanging in the stalls. The light troops of the Americans were enabled to cross, and continue the pursuit; while the army pressed forward to overtake them, with an energy and eagerness, under which their sufferings were immense. Many of them, exerting themselves beyond their strength, fainted upon the wayside. No halt was taken for refreshment, but the calls of nature were suspended, in an earnest desire to bring the enemy to the final issue of the sword. What was their mortification, reaching the mills, to find the prey escaped! It was then that they broke down utterly—the stifled necessities under which they had toiled, speaking out, desperately, in their disappointment. The volunteers and militia refused to follow any farther. Exhausted with toil, wanting provisions, and with their terms of service long since expired, they demanded their discharge. This was a surprise to their commander; but it was one which he had no power to resist. He could only entreat, but unsuccessfully; their engagement was really at an end. The cares of agriculture were at hand, and their farms summoned them to the performance of duties, upon which, indeed, rested the future hope of provisioning the army. He was compelled to yield to their requisitions, and this necessity was fatal to any hope which he might entertain of overtaking his enemy. Cornwallis, meanwhile, had passed into a region abounding with loyalists, where his resources improved at every step, and in which he could obtain easy and early intelligence of every step taken by the Americans. Greene reluctantly gave up the pursuit.

Fixing his quarters, temporarily, at Ramsey's mills, in order to recruit his troops, and make his preparations for future service, Greene found his situation quite as mortifying, at this moment, as at any period during the campaign. He was now, after the discharge of the militia, numerically inferior to his enemy; yet he was now in possession, for the first time, of proofs which showed how easy it might be, with moderate assistance, to ruin the army of Cornwallis. But he applied for this assistance in vain. His own army was in a state of extreme suffering and prostration. They had scant provisions. Lean beef in small quantities, and corn-bread baked in the ashes, were their chief supplies; and, not unfrequently, the vulture was robbed of his garbage, by the fierce hunger of the starving soldier. Equally wretched was the condition of the troops in regard to clothing. Shoes there were none; and their garments were such as remained from long and wearisome marches in wild countries, through pitiless weather. It was covering, perhaps,—but not clothing. That they were cheerful under their privations, was, perhaps, quite as much due to the influence of their commander, who freely shared their sufferings, as of that cause and government by which they seemed to be, almost entirely, disregarded.

Having abandoned the farther pursuit of Cornwallis, as no longer proper or profitable, the natural inquiry of Greene was, in what manner he should now employ his army. Merely to maintain a position of *surveillance* upon the movements of his enemy, was neither agreeable to his own desires, nor of much promise of advantage to the objects which he aimed to effect. To achieve successfully, in conflict with an enemy already in partial possession of the country, it was necessary to dislodge him. This required the exercise of constant energies, and enterprises at once frequent and decisive, by which his attention would be distracted, and his strength worn out, in the harassing toils of a watch and defence, which exhausted his resources without leaving him in security.

We have seen, that, on Greene's first assuming the command of the southern army, he fixed his eye upon the numerous posts with which the British had covered all the vulnerable and commanding portions of that state. These, in fact, constituted their base of operations. To dispossess them of these, became, naturally, a first policy of the American general; and a series of separate enterprises for this object was meditated, beginning, as we remember, with the attempt to surprise Georgetown by Marion—an attempt which was only partially successful. Circumstances now prompted Greene to the determination to renew these attempts and, at once, boldly again to make his way into South Carolina. There was much to encourage him in this purpose. The partisans of that region had not been idle, while he was engaged in his protracted trial of skill with Cornwallis. Sumter had been beating up the British quarters on various occasions, had cut off their detachments, obtained numerous smaller successes, and, by his rapidity of movement and continued activity, had given frequent occasion for disquiet to Lord Rawdon, whom Cornwallis had left in command behind him Marion had been equally busy; and Pickens, who had been detached by Greene, with this object, some time before, was busily engaged in recruiting the whig militia for similar uses. The day after the battle of Guilford Colonel Hampton, another of the famous partisans of Carolina, arrived at the camp of the Americans with such tidings as renewed all Greene's anxiety to direct his steps rapidly upon the enemy's garrisons. His decision was accordingly taken. His calculations were simple and conclusive. If Cornwallis continued his progress to Virginia, his posts in South Carolina would be exposed to ruin, one by one; and if, on the other hand, he wheeled about to follow the American army, he would be diverted, necessarily, from the conquest of North Carolina and Virginia, both of which states, relieved from his presence, would be enabled to concen trate their energies upon the completion of their broken regiments. In any point of view, the resolution to carry back the operations of active warfare into South Carolina, seemed to promise results of far greater benefit than any other proposed plan of future campaign. But, in deciding upon this measure, General Greene incurred the greatest of perils—that of offending public opinion. He was about to depart from the ordinary rules of warfare. Military men are not often permitted to forego the pursuit of an enemy, already weakened in conflict, to direct their efforts against a foe, strongly posted, and, as yet, unimpaired for resistance by previous struggle. This, which, in ordinary cases, would seem equally the impulse of temerity and caprice, was, however, in the present instance, dictated by considerations of the profoundest policy. Greene's reasons were given at length, at the time when his resolves were taken, in ample letters to Washington, Lafayette, and others. He argued, in addition to what has been already stated, that, by moving south with his troops, he should be enabled to provide them with the supplies which must else find their way to the enemy; that, whether Cornwallis pursued him or not, North Carolina, at least,—which was paralyzed by his presence,—would be rescued from his pressure; that the very boldness of his scheme, which seemed startlingly full of dangers, would have a large effect upon the public mind, as it would seem to indicate the possession of resources which were unsuspected by his adversaries; and that the necessities of the country, and the moods of the people, were such as to justify and render it necessary that some considerable perils should be incurred—something, in short, left to fortune, in the expectation of results which could not accrue from any mere exercise of patience and circumspection. "The manœuvre will be critical and dangerous," was his lan guage to Washington; . . . "but necessity obliges me to commit myself to chance." "The troops will be exposed to every hardship; but I shall share it with them."

The moment that his determination had been taken, he sent an express to Jefferson, governor of Virginia, to forward fifteen hundred militia. Captain Singleton was despatched to Virginia to procure artillery; magazines were ordered to be formed on the banks of the Catawba; the partisan generals of South Carolina were apprized of his designs, and instructed to get the militia under arms for a series of separate enterprises; and every means was put in exercise to secure, in advance, abundant supplies of provisions. The route of the army lay through a country, at once sparsely settled and in the hands of enemies; and every precaution was necessary against failure and disappointment. All things being ready, the camp at Ramsay's mills was broken up on the 7th of April. The heavy baggage, and all the stores that could be spared from present use, were sent another route, by Salisbury, to the head of the Catawba; while the army, still seeming to press the pursuit of Cornwallis, crossed Deep river, and, for a day, continued the direct route to Wilmington; then, suddenly taking the first convenient road to the right, he turned the heads of his columns in the direction of Camden, South Carolina. His hope was to surprise this place. He flattered himself, that, preceding all relief from the army of Cornwallis, his march would be unknown to, and unsuspected by, Rawdon. But he was disappointed. The distance which he had to traverse was one hundred and thirty miles. His progress was unavoidably slow. The country was sterile and exhausted, and in the hands of enemies. His every movement was watched and reported. The runners of the tories preceded him in his march; and a delay of several days at the Pee Dee, in consequence of the want of boats for crossing, enabled Rawdon to receive full advices of the danger, and to provide against it. Greene reached the neighborhood of Camden on the 19th, and found its garrison fully equal to all the strength he could bring to bear against it. Reconnoitring it with the view to assault, he was compelled to forego the hopeless enterprise. Camden is situated on a gentle elevation, extending from the swamps along the Wateree river, to Pine-tree creek. Covered, to the south and west, by these streams, it was still farther closed against assault by a chain of redoubts, which guarded it on every open point, while the defences were made complete, by strong lines of stockade in the rear of the redoubts. Without battering cannon, any attempt to subdue it must have been hopeless; and nothing remained to Greene but to choose such a position as might tempt the enemy from his strong-hold. He took post, accordingly, on a small rising ground, on the Waxhaw road, within half a mile of the British lines. But, Rawdon manifesting no disquiet at this challenge, and no disposition to accept it, Greene retired, with his army, a mile and a quarter farther, to a place called Hobkirk's hill, where, with his left covered by a difficult morass clothed with woods, and his right approaching an almost impenetrable thicket, he pitched his tents for the present.

CHAPTER XV.

Cornwallis pursues his Route to Virginia.—The Partisan Warfare in Carolina.—Marion.—Captures Fort Watson.—Greene's Movements.—Rawdon marches out from Camden and gives him Battle.—Battle of Hobkirk's Hill.

Cornwallis was greatly surprised by the unexpected march of Greene into South Carolina. The boldness of the proceeding confounded him, and awakened his serious apprehensions for the safety of British power in that state. His resolves seem to have been troubled by serihus perplexities. At first, he meditated to follow his adversary; and the scheme was full of plausibilities, which proposed to place the army of Greene between his own and that of Rawdon. From this, indeed, lay the greatest danger of the American general. But Cornwallis paused so long before reaching his conclusion, that it became evident that Greene was quite too far on his route to be overtaken. Rawdon must have either triumphed, or succumbed to his opponent, before he could possibly arrive to share in the struggle. To proceed to Hillsborough, with the hope of drawing off the regards of Greene, to that point, from South Carolina, was another suggestion, which seemed to betray the perplexities of the British commander, occasioned by the movements of the Americans. On either side were doubt and difficulty; doubts which no decision seemed likely to overcome, and difficulties which appeared to increase the more he examined them. Greene's wisdom, in the adoption of his course,was never more strikingly shown than in the trouble and anxiety which it occasioned to his enemy. The situation of Cornwallis's army was such as materially to interfere with his enterprises. It had been terribly crippled by the affair at Guilford, the subsequent harassing pursuit, and the exhausting marches. For three weeks after his arrival at Wilmington, he was employed in recruiting the strength of his shattered regiments; and when he did put his army in motion, it was to commence the invasion of Virginia, where, following the finger of his fate, he was destined, at Yorktown, to yield to other hands the laurels, to which, in some degree, the commander of the southern army might have urged his claim. Leaving him to his fate, which no longer concerns our progress, we return now to the field of former and future struggle in South Carolina.

In that state, at no period, had domestic opposition to the invader been entirely at an end. Crushed for the moment, her partisans simply held themselves aloof in shadow, in reserve for the moment when a reasonable prospect of success might attend the effort at open struggle. The numerous small enterprises which were undertaken by Marion and Sumter, with the many brave officers who followed in their commands, during the various progresses, already recorded, of the main army, will not require our enumeration or description here. Enough, that their effect was such as to carry dismay everywhere among the settlements of the loyalists. Marion, in particular, succeeded for a time in breaking up, almost entirely, the communications between Charleston and the army under Rawdon, and by intercepting detachments and supplies for the several posts across the country, reduced them to the most serious straits and exigencies. Greene was by no means insensible to these services, and in approaching South Carolina, a second time, he despatched Colonel Lee, with three hundred men, to co-operate with Marion, who was at this time lying, *perdu*, in consequence of an active pursuit, which Colonel Watson, with a select and superior force had been required by Rawdon to institute after the wary partisan. Lee narrowly escaped Watson, who might easily have prevented his junction with Marion. This, however, was effected successfully, and the partisan general lost no time in proceeding to action. His first demonstration was against Fort Watson, a strong stockade fort, raised on an ancient mound near the Santee. This post was captured, after a short defence. From this service, Marion turned to that of intercepting the march of his former pursuer, Colonel Watson, who was supposed to be making his way with all speed to the assistance of Rawdon at Camden. It was in aiming at this object, throwing himself across the path of Watson, and pressing on, himself, to the neighborhood of Camden, that Marion contributed to give a new impulse and new activity to the proceedings of Lord Rawdon. The British general was growing uneasy at the augmentation of the American forces; and determined to take the risks of a battle, before they should have been so far increased as to put the issue beyond all doubt. He was unaware that Greene had been strengthened by a timely arrival of two pieces of artillery, one of which, as soon as received, had been sent to Marion, while two other pieces, sent from Virginia, reached the camp of the Americans, on the very day when the British general marched out to give them battle. Prior to this, some movements which Greene had made, on the 22d of April, which Rawdon very naturally construed into an attempt on the part of the American general to intercept the approach of Watson with his reinforcements, contributed to his uneasiness, and aided in inducing the determination to precipitate the issue. For this, Greene was in perfect readiness. It was an event which he had too eagerly sought, and too earnestly desired, not to have provided against with all necessary precautions. The army was encamped in order of battle. They were held in constant expectation of attack. Patrols ranged all the approaches, penetrating as near to the town as the forest cover would permit, and the front of the camp was guarded by double pickets, against all the points from which danger was likely to approach. A becoming vigilance guarded against all danger of surprise.

On the morning of the 25th of April, the day which Lord Rawdon had selected for the attack, a convoy much needed and long expected, bringing supplies of artillery and provisions, made its appearance in the American camp. The troops were at breakfast, with a keen relish for the creature comforts so seasonably brought, and Greene, with his aids was enjoying the unwonted luxury of a cup of coffee, when the sound of fire-arms, in the distance, announced the approach of the enemy. The men, many of them, were still busy in the more grateful occupation of dressing their food; while some washed their clothes at a neighboring rivulet. With the alarm, and the roll of the drums which followed, they were instantly in arms, and but a few moments sufficed to place them in array for battle. They were in number nearly or quite equal to the force of the enemy, and they exhibited a cheerful steadiness which gave to their commander the most grateful anticipations of the issue. The whole regular infantry of the Americans, fit for duty at this moment, was eight hundred and forty-three. The cavalry under Washington numbered but fifty-six men who were mounted. The artillery, commanded by Colonel Harrison, nominally a regiment, did not comprise men enough to fight three pieces; and the militia force was but two hundred and fifty. Portions of the American force detached, left the strength of Greene very nearly that of his adversary. That of the British has been estimated at nine hundred men. These were chiefly Americans, and mostly first-rate marksmen. Greene's regulars had seen service also. He had with him the favorite Maryland regiment of Gunby, which had behaved so gallantly at Guilford; others of his troops had seen service in the same field; and all of them wore such an aspect of coolness as to leave him in no apprehension of the result. Still, he omitted none of his precautions. His baggage was despatched to the rear, a distance of several miles, and nothing was left to hazard, which the exigencies of battle did not make it necessary to expose.

Hobkirk's hill is a narrow and slight elevation — a sandy ridge — which separates the head springs of two small rivulets. The encampment of Greene occupied this ridge. By his order of battle, the left wing rested upon the swamp of Pine-tree creek; the right extended into the woods, and rested, in military *parlance*, in air, — somewhat protected by the nature of the ground, and the brush and felled timber which was spread in front. The high-road to Camden ran through the centre of the line, dividing the two wings, and was covered by the artillery, which had been received just in season to be wheeled into position at the enemy's approach. Ignorant of this timely arrival, and assuming Greene to be wholly without artillery, Rawdon brought none — his forbearance to do so enabling him to advance by a route on which his cannon could not operate. The better to take advantage of this ignorance, on the part of the enemy, Greene masked his pieces by closing the two centre regiments of his line upon the road. His whole force enabled him to form a single line only. The two Virginia regiments under General Huger, occupied the right of the road; the two Maryland, under Colonel Williams, the left. The first Virginia, commanded by Colonel Campbell, was on the right of the whole; the second Maryland, under Lieutenant-Colonel Ford, on the left. The second Virginia, under Lieutenant-Colonel Hawes, and the first Maryland, under Colonel Gunby, constituted the centre. Colonel Washington and the small militia force, about two hundred and fifty in number, under Colonel Reid, were held in the rear, at the foot of the hill, forming a second line or reserve.

Lord Rawdon's line was composed of the 63d regiment on the right, the New York volunteers in the centre, and the king's American regiment on the left. The right was supported by the volunteers of Ireland, the left by a detachment under Captain Robinson; a South Carolina regiment was posted with the cavalry, forming, with these, nearly one half of his troops, which, accordingly, presented a very narrow front. Rawdon had taken a hint from the Americans, and had employed flanking parties of loyalists, as riflemen, moving abreast of his wing among the trees. This judicious arrangement served greatly toward giving him the advantage of the day. His advance was by a route which rendered it impossible to announce his approach, except by the fire of the videttes. These were nearly a mile distanc from the encampment. The picket guards, under Morgan and Benson, behaved with great courage and coolness, gathering in the videttes, retiring deliberately, and forming in good order under Captain Kirkwood, who was posted, with the remnant of the Delawares, in an advanced position on the right. These and the advanced parties maintained the contest with an obstinacy that afforded ample time to the American army, and a beautiful example, as they retired, of deliberate and unshaken valor. The auspices seemed highly encouraging to Greene, as the British army came in sight; having forced their way, step by step, through the thickets into the open space, where the Americans were calmly awaiting their approach.

Their appearance was the signal for the unmasking and opening of the American artillery. The effect may well be imagined of such a surprise upon them. Showers of grape among their ranks, when they had been taught to believe that Greene was wholly without artillery, produced instantaneous results of confusion and dismay. At this moment, struck with the extreme narrowness of the British front, Greene seized the instant of their greatest confusion, to give orders for a charge. To close upon their flanks with his regiments on the right and left, and cut off the fragments of the broken column, seemed to require but a single order: "Let the cavalry make for their rear—Colonel Campbell wheel upon their left, Ford upon their right—and the whole centre charge with trailed arms." Such was the prompt command delivered to his attendants, in what seemed the very moment for its execution. His aids flew to convey it to the proper captains. The roll of the drum announced their tenor. The infantry stretched forward right and left; and the cavalry of Washington disappeared among the trees, making the necessary circuit which would bring them into the British rear.

For a moment, nothing could have been more auspicious to the hopes of the Americans. Their fire had shown itself superior to that of the enemy. The artillery had done its work; and the ranks which had suffered from its terrific discharges, had failed to recover from their panic. The regiments under Campbell and Ford started forward, under an impetus at once swift and steady; and the manœuvre, right and left, upon the flanks of the enemy, seemed to promise the most conclusive finish to the grateful beginnings of the day. A feeble and ineffective fire from the flanking companies of the British, served rather to stimulate, than to discourage, their assailants; and nothing remained to prevent the entire success of the Americans, but one of those capricious whirls of fortune, which sometimes lay the best plans, and the fairest prospects, prostrate in the dust.

Greene had no ordinary opponent in Rawdon. His steady eye, deliberate and stern resolve, and ready resources, made him a formidable adversary. He, too, beheld the danger which awaited him, and of which the American general had taken such instant advantage. He saw the force by which his flanks were threatened, and, with equal promptness, he ordered the protrusion of the supporting columns of his army. In an instant, the Americans were outflanked, their wings enfiladed, their rear threatened, and they themselves exposed to the very same peril in which they had calculated to take their enemy. A momentary recoil followed in the American regiments. With equal discipline to that of the enemy, the result must have been otherwise. But the firing of the British drew the fire of the American centre when their orders had been to reserve it. This centre was composed of the very flower of the army,—one of its two regiments being that of Gunby, or the 1st Maryland, whose conduct at Guilford had been so conspicuous for its bravery. Firing against orders, was one proof of confusion, which was increased by the fall of Captain Beatty, of the right company of the regiment, who was much beloved, and who was stricken down by a bullet that pierced his heart. His fall checked the progress of his command. The halt influenced the other companies. It became a panic; it spread from right to left, from front to rear; and, finally, produced the recoil of the whole regiment. Unhappily, while Williams,

Gunby, and Howard, were exhausting themselves in the most earnest efforts to restore firmness and consistency, Colonel Ford fell, mortally wounded, while gallantly leading the other Maryland regiment on the American left. The death of their leader, and the halt of Gunby's veteran command, determined their career. They recoiled also. An unhappy error of Gunby, who hoped to recover his first line by halting it, instead of boldly pushing forward the second to its support, was easily mistaken for an order to retreat. A retreat it became, accordingly—and one, which all efforts soon proved fruitless to prevent or to repair.

Greene, at this period of disaster, was on the extreme right, leading on Campbell's regiment in person. Called away by the panic in the centre, he in vain labored to restore order amid the confusion which prevailed, and to bring the panic-stricken soldiers, once more, to face the enemy. His voice and presence were not without effect. A brief halt was obtained; but, by this time, they had reached the opposite foot of the hill, and he was recalled to the field by the exulting shouts of the British. Galloping back to the scene, where the action still continued, Greene was enabled, at a glance, to perceive the whole extent of his misfortune. The regiment of Hawes was that only which remained entire. By the advance of this regiment, and the retreat of the other centre regiment, the artillery was left, uncovered, upon the summit of the hill. The field was lost, and the danger was that the artillery would be lost also. Greene perceived its peril and his own. He was on one of the most conspicuous stations of the hill, with showers of bullets continually flying around him; but he gave his orders with a degree of coolness and promptness, which readily communicated itself to his followers. His only hope was, to draw off the right and left regiments from the now unequal struggle, and form them on the regiment of Gunby, which had now rallied; while Hawes, with the 2d Virginia, should cover the retrograde movement. The order was given and well executed. Hawes's regiment retired firing and fighting, and with so firm a front, as, in the issue, left to the American commander a choice, whether to renew the conflict, or effect a regular and orderly retreat. But it threatened to be at the price of the artillery. For the safety of his cannon, Greene had ordered to the spot a select corps, of forty-five men, under Captain Smith, the same officer whose duel with Colonel Stuart, of the guards, formed so conspicuous an incident in the battle of Guilford. But, before Smith could reach the spot, the enemy, with loud shouts, was making his way up the hill; and Captain Coffin, at the head of the British cavalry, was darting forth from his cover in the woods, to join in the pursuit. The American matrosses were already quitting the drag-ropes, when Greene galloped up alone—his aids being all engaged in conveying his orders—and, throwing himself from his horse, with his own hands seizing upon the ropes, set an example of perseverance and resolution, which the most timid found it impossible to resist. Smith's corps now made its appearance, and his men, their muskets in one hand, applied the other to the ropes, and made their way along the hill with the artillery. But the approach of Coffin's cavalry arrested this progress. Then it was that, forming in the rear of the artillery, Smith's little band encountered the charge of their enemy, pouring into the advancing cavalry a fire so destructive as to compel their flight. Again and again, however, did they return to the charge, and again were they foiled and driven back by the deliberate aim and steady nerve of this little squad, who, in the intervals, still pulled the ropes of the artillery, only throwing them aside when it became necessary to form and receive the charge of cavalry. But this game could not be continued long. The British infantry began to arrive. Their marksmen were scattering themselves among the trees, and their dropping fire began to thin Smith's company. His forty-five were soon reduced to fourteen. He himself was badly wounded; and, though he held his ground with unflagging resolution, it was evident that, but for timely succor, he must be lost. Unhappily, before this succor could arrive, an irregular fire was drawn, by some accident, from his little squadron, and Coffin, with his cavalry, succeeded in forcing his ranks. Every man was slain or taken. The artillery now seemed lost. The batmen had run the limbers into the woods, cut the horses out, and made off upon them. It was at this moment that Colonel Washington charged in upon the road, and put an end to the contest. This officer had, unhappily, burdened himself with prisoners. He had taken more than two hundred; his humanity revolting at those summary processes by which Tarleton would have escaped the encumbrance. Each of his troopers bore his captive behind him, when the disaster of the army rendered necessary the final charge which extricated the artillery. Flinging off his prisoners for the onset, Washington drove the British cavalry up the hill, and checked their farther pursuit of the retiring regiments. The artillery was carried off in safety, and Greene, without farther molestation, continued the retreat.

Two miles from the field of battle, he halted to collect his stragglers, renewing his march in the afternoon, and encamping for the night on Saunder's creek. Here he remained until the 25th, not without the hope that Rawdon, encouraged by his success, would attempt to renew the battle. But the enemy did not venture to repeat the experiment, and it is a curious fact, that by a stratagem of Colonel Washington, the field of battle really remained in his possession. Rawdon, with the retreat of Greene, had taken up the line of march for Camden, leaving Coffin with his cavalry and a detachment of mounted infantry, on the ground. Advised of this arrangement, Washington placed his cavalry in a thicket on the roadside, having pushed forward a small party, with instructions to suffer themselves to be seen by Coffin's troops, and then, by flight and a show of panic, to beguile them into pursuit. The bait was taken, and the entire troop of Coffin darted headlong in the chase. Brought within the snare, Washington's cavalry dashed out upon them, and the whole party were either cut to pieces, or compelled to disperse for safety.

Grateful as he was for this success, the mortification of Greene, at the issue of the combat, was almost wholly without consolation. The cup of victory had been snatched from his lips while the draught was most grateful and ready for the taste. He had made the most skilful disposition of his troops; he had omitted no precautions; he had placed in the post of danger the soldiers whom he had reason to suppose the most assured and steady; and fortune had pronounced against all his plans and all his calculations. The victory was already in his grasp. The effect of his artillery had produced consternation in the ranks of the enemy—they were already faltering, and the cool obedience to his orders, as shown by the flanking regiments, had only to be sustained by the steady advance of the centre with the bayonet, and the British, from wing to wing, must have been swept from the field. The fall of Camden must have followed, and this must have brought with it, as a necessary consequence, the rapid surrender of all the British posts from the mountains to the seaboard. Bit terly did Greene reflect upon the inauspicious fortune which had so frequently interposed to snatch the cup of hope from his lips to replace it by the cup of trembling!

His troops had not behaved badly. They had fought, on the whole, with great spirit. A portion of them had shown the tenacious courage of veterans, holding on to the foe with a bulldog resolution which gave the most flattering assurances of success. It was the unhappy error of Gunby, whose order to his first line to halt, when he saw them faltering, was unwise and unmilitary. "Gunby," says Greene, in a letter, "was the sole cause of the defeat. I found him much more blameable afterward, than I represented him in my public letters." A court of inquiry pronounced upon his conduct. They approved equally his courage and activity. His zeal and spirit were beyond all cavil. They censured the order which he had given to his regiment, but as an error of judgment only, and from which flowed all the evil consequences of the day. The battle had been sufficiently bloody for the number of troops engaged, and the loss of the opposing armies was nearly equal. "The enemy," according to Greene, "had more than one third of their whole force engaged, either killed or wounded; and we had not less than one quarter." If the Americans lost the victory, the barren honors of the field were all that his success secured for Rawdon.

CHAPTER XVI.

Rawdon attempts the Camp of Greene.—Evacuates and destroys Camden.—Capture of Fort Motte and other Posts by the Partisans.—Rawdon at Monk's Corner.—Marion takes Georgetown—Pickens Augusta.—Greene besieges Ninety-Six—Attempts to storm it, and is defeated with Loss.

THE event of the battle of Hobkirk's hill, though unfavorable to the Americans, did not materially change the situation of the parties. Any successes of the British which failed to destroy their adversaries, or drive them out of the state,—any advantage, falling short of a complete victory,—would fail in effecting for them any advantageous change in their situation. The army of Greene was chiefly important to the southern states, at this juncture, as it afforded a countenance to the whig population, and, by keeping the foreign troops of the enemy in constant anxiety and expectation, gave an opportunity to the native partisan leaders, to cope with the British detachments and their tory allies. There was nothing, therefore, beyond the natural mortification of defeat, in the recent battle, to discourage the hopes, or compel a change in the plans, of the American general. On the other hand, there was much to qualify the satisfaction which Rawdon felt in his victory. The spirit of his troops, his own merits and good fortune, had brought him success; but it had been dearly paid for, and it was incomplete. His strength had been lessened in the struggle, while that of his adversary ap peared undiminished. He had been compelled to retire within his works at Camden, and the Americans still gathered in his neighborhood. They had been driven, but not out of sight; and he was in no condition to renew the attempt at their destruction or expulsion—not, certainly, with his present force, encumbered with wounded, nor until the arrival of his reinforcements under Watson. The fate of this command was necessarily, a subject of the greatest anxiety.

To prevent the junction of the force under Watson—estimated at six hundred men, with four field-pieces—with that of Rawdon, was the first subject of consideration with Greene. Marion and Lee were employed to cover the intervening country, and arrest his march, should he make for Camden. The last intelligence reported him to be still in Georgetown, and inactive; and Greene had no difficulty in persuading himself, that, with the vigilant eyes of Sumter, Marion, and Lee, upon his movements, it would be impossible for him to make his way to the stronghold of Rawdon. But the troops under our partisans, however swift and vigilant, were not sufficiently numerous to compass such an extent of country, so as to guard equally all its avenues; and Watson had large merits of his own as a partisan, which his own and the necessities of his superior compelled him to put in active requisition. With the co-operation of Major M'Arthur, an intelligent and adroit captain of cavalry, he succeeded in masking his real movements, and eluding the vigilance of his enemies. They had attempted too much with their small commands, and Watson succeeded in making his way into Camden.

The junction of this force with that already in the garrison at Camden, by increasing the strength of Rawdon very much beyond that of Greene, rendered the situation of the latter somewhat critical. In connexion with rumors of the approach of Cornwallis from Virginia, it compelled him to exercise all his vigilance with regard to his own safety. He foresaw that Rawdon's increase of strength would naturally prompt him to resume active operations in the field, and a proper reflection taught him to look for the first blow from the enemy. His first duty was to evade the conflict, to which he was still unequal; and, accordingly, on receiving the tidings of Watson's good fortune, he set his army in motion to increase the space that separated him from Rawdon. Retiring to a strong position on the farther side of Colonel's creek, he drew up his army in order of battle, and awaited his enemy.

Rawdon was not long in making his appearance. He drove in the American pickets, reconnoitred their position, and, finding it too strong to be forced he drew off his army, and returned once more to Camden. This respectful behavior carried with it few consolations to the mind of Greene. His condition, and that of the country, can be shown in no more forcible language than that of Colonel Davie. "This evening," says he— the 9th of May, the day after Rawdon's demonstration— "the general sent for me earlier than usual. I found the map on the table, and he introduced the business of the night with the following striking observation: 'You see that we must again resume the partisan war. Rawdon has now a decided superiority of force. He has pushed us to a sufficient distance to leave him free to act on any object within his reach. He will strike at Lee and Marion, reinforce himself by all the troops that can be spared from the several garrisons, and push me back to the mountains. . . . You observe our dangerous and critical situation. The regular troops are now reduced to a handful, and I am without militia to perform the convoy or detachment service, or any prospect of receiving any reinforcement. . . . North Carolina, dispirited by the loss of her regular troops in Charleston, stunned into a kind of stupor by the defeat of General Gates, and held in check by Major Craig and the loyalists, makes no effort of any kind. Congress seems to have lost sight of the southern states, and to have abandoned them to their fate; so much so, that I am even as much distressed for ammunition as for men. We must always calculate on the maxim, that your enemy will do what he ought to do. We will dispute every inch of ground in the best manner we can; but Rawdon will push me back to the mountains. Lord Cornwallis will establish a chain of posts along James river; and the southern states, thus cut off, will die like the tail of a snake."

These were melancholy forebodings. The mind of Greene, naturally cheerful and elastic, was overborne, temporarily, by the pressure of defeat and the grief of hopes deferred. But, however gloomy, he did not yield to despondency. The native hue of resolution did not abandon his heart. Nor was the case so bad as his melancholy mood had painted it. He had been driven rather than defeated, and his disappointments had never been coupled with any real occasion for the exultation of the enemy. His great prudence had served, in almost every instance, to save him from material injury. His recuperative faculties were great, and there were circumstances, in the progress of the struggle, that were full of future promise to the cause. The increase of Rawdon's force at Camden did not imply anything but a temporary gain. It gave him a momentary advantage over his enemy, but was not adequate to the necessities which grew around him. His chain of posts, already broken by the loss of Fort Watson, was still farther threatened by the active partisans of Carolina. Marion was even now besieging Fort Motte, while Sumter and

Pickens were preparing for the investment of Granby Augusta, and Orangeburg. These, unless with timely succor from the main army, must soon fall into the hands of the Americans; and, thus threatened with isolation, with the several detached parties of tbe native militia assembled in co-operation with Greene's army around Camden, that garrison must succumb also. The prospect was scarcely more grateful to Rawdon than to Greene; and a progress that we have forborne to touch upon, had contributed to awaken the most lively apprehensions on the part of the British and their tory allies. This had arisen in consequence of the unexpected growth and appearance of new bands of whig partisans in every part of the state. In addition to those which followed Sumter, Marion, and Pickens, they were everywhere rising in proof of a revival of the revolutionary spirit. The career of Major Harden had exercised a highly important influence in the lower country. Detached by Marion with seventy select men, well mounted, he had crossed the enemy's line of communication; and, penetrating the country southwest from Charleston, he had roused a spirit of hope and resistance, which was full of the most beneficial results. Rapid in movement, appearing unexpectedly in the settlements, he had taken the enemy by surprise everywhere, and rendered himself the terror of the loyalists of that region. His force gathered with its progress. His seventy grew to hundreds; and, after scourging summarily the disaffected along the banks of the Savannah, in Georgia as well as South Carolina,—mocking all plans to entrap, and all efforts to subdue or overtake him,—he darted upward in season to unite with Pickens, then operating against Augusta.

This was but one instance of many similar progresses which were calculated to encourage the hopes of the

Americans, and alarm the British general with regard to the growing dangers of his fortune. Rawdon felt too surely that his successes had been illusory. They could not suffice to lessen the perils of his situation. His only hope would be to beguile his enemy into a pitched battle; but his recent attempt to do so, satisfied him that his antagonist was quite too wary to incur any unnecessary perils, in a game which circumspection must secure. In this lay his only hope, and it was one which the character of Greene forbade him to indulge. Denied this hope, he felt, momently increasing, the apprehension of being cut off from the seaboard. It was now known that no help was to be expected from Cornwallis, whose march to Virginia was beyond dispute; and, with this knowledge in the American camp, Greene felt fully assured of the course of his opponent, in consequence of a just appreciation of the critical exigency of his situation. A single day altered the aspect of his fortunes, and his own. We have, again, the testimony of General Davie: "I employed the whole night in writing, until an orderly-sergeant summoned me to headquarters, about daylight. On entering the general's tent, I soon perceived some important change had taken place. 'I have sent for you,' said he, with a countenance expressing the most lively pleasure, 'to inform you that Lord Rawdon is preparing to evacuate Camden. That place was the key of the enemy's line of posts. They will now all fall, or be evacuated. All will now go well."

The orders of Rawdon had already gone forth for the abandonment of Ninety-Six. Cruger, who commanded at that place, was to remove his command to Augusta, which was threatened by Pickens. Rawdon, himself, meditated, by his own march, to save Fort Motte, and, possibly, the farther posts of Orangeburg and Granby. At all events, the British general was preparing to yield before the army which his increase of strength had not enabled him to subdue. The departure, like the approach, of the British, was usually marked by desolation. Camden was given to the flames, and left in ruins. Had the militia promised from Virginia been sent to Greene in season, the British general would, in all probability, have left Camden as a prisoner, rather than a destroyer. He had not moved a moment too soon. The garrison was already straitened for provisions; and the arrival of the Virginia militia, or the co-operation of the several commands of Sumter, Marion, Pickens, and Lee, after the fall of the several posts against which they operated, must have had but one issue in his overthrow.

Rawdon's movement was not in season for the relief of Fort Motte. It had already fallen into the hands of Marion. The posts at Orangeburg and Granby had also been surrendered to Sumter and Lee, before he could approach them, and his own march was watched by Marion's parties. He pursued the route toward Charleston. Greene had also put his army in motion, in order to cover the detachments of Marion and Lee, which he supposed still engaged in the leaguer of Fort Motte. Sumter, whose impetuosity and enterprise were ever the most striking elements in his military character, now strenuously urged upon Greene the plan of uniting with Lee and Marion, and making an attempt upon the army of Rawdon. But the American general preferred the safe game to the perilous one, however brilliant; and the conquest of the posts of the interior, presented themselves to his mind as the most legitimate object.

Rawdon, meanwhile, made his way forward, without interruption, until he reached Monk's corner, where, for the time, he established himself, leaving the country all above him in the hands of the Americans, with the exception of the posts at Ninety-Six, Augusta, and its neighborhoods. The latter, pressed by Pickens and Lee, were soon yielded to the skill and courage of the assailants, though not without a fierce and bloody resistance. The capture of Forts Grierson and Cornwallis was distinguished by one of those instances of sudden and terrible retribution, which conferred a character, so personal and vindictive, on the warfare in South Carolina. Colonel Grierson had become, with other obnoxious enemies, particularly odious to the Americans by his savage barbarities. It was while Pickens was absent from the camp, that a person unknown—disguised, perhaps, sufficiently to escape identification—dashed on horseback into the house where Grierson was kept, and, without dismounting, shot him dead, wheeling about and escaping before he could be arrested. The incident reminds us of one in Scott's poem of Rokeby, where the outlawed Bertram rides into the church, amid the assembled congregation, and shoots down his victim at the foot of the altar. So obnoxious had the prisoners, taken on this occasion, become to the majority of the militia of Pickens's command, in consequence of their monstrous and frequent atrocities, that the lives of others were attempted, and their commander was compelled to send them to Greene at Ninety-Six, in order to protect them from the unsparing revenges of the families they had outraged by their crimes.

Greene, meanwhile, almost for the first time with an open field before him,—his apprehensions of Rawdon at rest for the moment,—pressed forward, with all diligence, for the purpose of investing Ninety-Six. The task of holding Rawdon in check, and confining him to the neighborhood of the sea, was confided to Marion and Sumter. In the execution of this duty, they closed upon the British general, until he found it necessary to fence himself in with a new chain of fortified places, extending from Georgetown, by Monk's corner, Dorchester, and other points, to Coosawhatchie. But the partisans, daily becoming bolder, did not hesitate to dash at intervals within the limits of this *cordon*, and to ruffle the dovecotes even within hail of Charleston. Marion, strengthened sufficiently to leave a strong force of volunteers for the protection of the country along the Santee, directed his attention to Georgetown, which he took, expelling the garrison and demolishing the works. His lieutenant, Horry, had succeeded in silencing and subduing the loyalists along the Pee Dee; and, in the activity of the several parties under these commanders, Rawdon soon found himself greatly straitened in his resources, and threatened in his securities. They were not in sufficient strength for any open demonstration in his neighborhood; but they traversed the country almost beneath his eyes, sweeping off the herds, and cutting off his foragers. Thus watched, pursued, and environed by the most sleepless and restless foes, Rawdon was compelled to gnash his teeth in inactivity, while Greene was making his approaches to the important and strong post of Ninety-Six.

The siege of this place constituted one of the most stubborn and animated contests of the campaign. It was a position of great strength, well fortified, and with a numerous garrison. Greene, soon after reconnoitring it, expressed his apprehensions of failure. "The fortifications are so strong, the garrison so large and so well furnished, that our success is doubtful." It was held by Colonel Cruger, an American loyalist of skill and courage; and no pains, that zeal and industry could suggest or employ, were spared in preparing for the leaguer. Numerous slaves were employed to relieve the garrison from laborious services; while abundant supplies of provisions precluded all hope of starving them into submission. Originally a stockade, raised by the first inhabitants as a barrier to Indian incursion, the post of Ninety-Six, or Cambridge, became the site of a village bearing the latter name. Lying a few miles to the south of the Saluda, and less than forty from the Savannah river, it constituted an important position for the control and keeping of a large and exposed frontier The name of Ninety-Six was derived from the distance at which it stood from Fort Prince George, another post which had been planted among the Cherokee towns along the Keowee. The spot was otherwise distinguished as the scene of the first conflicts in the southern, and perhaps in the revolutionary war. At this place, in 1775, commenced that dreadful civil war between the patriots and loyalists, which, afterward, desolated the country. Many of the present defenders of Ninety-Six, under Cruger, were natives, who had distinguished themselves by their ferocity, and who now fought with halters about their necks. That they should fight desperately and well, it is easy to conjecture.

The simple works of defence which originally covered the spot, were strengthened by others of superior character, as soon as Cornwallis resolved that it should be occupied. Select British engineers were employed for this purpose, and new works were raised, with a due regard to all the requisitions of military science. Among these works was a redoubt, in the form of a star, with sixteen salient and returning angles. It stood within rifle-shot to the southeast of the village. It was manned with three pieces of artillery, worked on wheeled carriages, which enabled its defenders to sweep any point along the horizon; while the rifles of a numerous garrison covered the more limited range with crossing fires, from which it was scarcely possible that any assailants should escape. A dry ditch, frieze, and abatis, by which it was sur rounded, still farther increased the strength of the position, and lessened the chances of successful assault upon the defenders. Opposite, at a distance of nearly two hundred yards, a stockade fort, which enclosed two blockhouses of strength, occupied the crown of a small eminence. A little valley, traversed by a streamlet, which afforded water to the garrison, divided this fortress from the village, and was reached by a covert way. Contiguous to this valley, and as a protection on the right, the county jail had been converted into a castle, and was strongly garrisoned also. The several places of defence lay within easy reach and support of one another, and numerously held, with ample supplies of food and ammunition, might well discourage the inferior and ill-provided army with which Greene prepared to undertake the leaguer. His force, exclusive of militia, did not exceed a thousand men, and left him without the means of assailing the garrison except on a single side. He had sat down before the place on the 22d of May, commencing his examination in person, accompanied by the celebrated Kosciuzko, his chief engineer, and one of his aids, and, under cover of a thick and rainy night, approaching so near the works as to be challenged and fired upon by the sentinels. The star redoubt was selected as the most conspicuous object for attack, as it commanded all the others. Yet Greene was totally without battering cannon, and in such a deficiency, the only modes of procedure were by simple blockade, by mining, or by storm. The former process, the garrison having abundance of provisions, it was useless to attempt: Greene resolved upon trying both the remaining modes. Had it been known that the garrison had failed to procure water by digging within the redoubt, it would have been easy to cut them off from the stream which wound through the valley;—but, as, on a previous occasion, a well had been sunk within the redoubt, affording ample quantities, the besiegers had no reason to doubt that a similar experiment would be followed by the same result.

The besiegers broke ground on the 23d; and, proceeding by regular approaches, on the 3d of June the second parallel was completed. Numbering but twice the force of the garrison, the duty fell severely upon the Americans of fighting and working, with little relief or cessation. On completing the first parallel, a mine, directed against the star redoubt, was commenced, under cover of a battery which had been thrown up on the enemy's right. Day and night, the work was pursued by the besiegers. Now laboring in the ditches,—now watching over those who labored,—and sleeping, where they toiled, on their arms, with the view to repel the sallies of the besieged—their hours of rest and respite were exceedingly limited. The besieged showed neither want of energy nor spirit. Their sallies were frequent, marked by great audacity, and usually resulted in prolonged and bloody conflicts. The steady progress of the American works sufficiently prove, that, however bold, the sallies of the garrison were without any productive results. They proved rather their courage and daring, than their ability and strength. Not a night passed without battle and the loss of life.

With the completion of the second parallel, the garrison was summoned to surrender. A courtly defiance was Cruger's answer. The third and last parallel was immediately begun, and prosecuted with a degree of vigor which the exhausted state of the army would have scarcely promised. It was at this moment, when most he needed his recruits, that Greene was apprized that the Virginia militia, two thousand in number, for whom he had been looking so long, had been diverted in another quarter by the governor of that state. He had commenced his operations against Ninety-Six, in anticipation of this body of men. The militia of South Carolina and Georgia were barely adequate to the duty of keeping Rawdon and the tories in check. Those under Pickens were still engaged in the siege of Augusta. Could the Virginians have arrived in season, the siege could have been pressed at once to conclusion, and the place, in spite of the vigor of its defence, must have soon fallen into his hands. What rendered the proceeding particularly ungracious, which deprived him of the Virginia militia, was the fact, that, for the defence of this very state, he had voluntarily deprived himself of his whole disposable force. It was at his instance, when Cornwallis was found to be pressing upon Virginia, that Lafayette had been ordered back,—that the troops of Pennsylvania, on their way south, had been halted and made to act under Lafayette and Steuben,—and that the North-Carolina levies, actually on their way to join him, had been sent in the same direction to the succor of the sister state. And this magnanimity had been shown by Greene immediately after the battle of Camden, when he was lying in front of a superior enemy, and destitute of almost everything.

He could only complain and remonstrate against this treatment. He had no other remedy. To issue new orders to the North-Carolina levies to join him instead of proceeding to Virginia,—to make a new effort to raise troops in South Carolina and Georgia,—and to concentrate all his present strength upon the present object—that of bringing the garrison of Ninety-Six to their knees with all rapidity,—were the tasks before him, and to which all his energies were now addressed. With the commencement of his third parallel against the star redoubt, the sallies of the garrison were increased in frequency and spirit. The fighting was incessant Their three pieces were used with equal vigor and judgment, and it became necessary to silence them if possible. Rude towers of roughly-hewn logs were raised, of sufficient solidity to withstand the weight of the shot thrown by the garrison. These were manned with marksmen, whose fire, from a commanding position, soon picked the artillerists from their guns. Red-hot shot were employed, by the besieged, for the destruction of these towers; but the green wood of which they were constructed, baffled the fervor of the flames. Silenced during the day, the artillery of the garrison was employed for a while, fruitlessly, at night; but this practice was soon abandoned, as it was found how ineffectual was the aim. The *cordon* was contracting around the brave defenders of the fort; and the arrival of Lee, with his legion, from the siege of Augusta, which had now surrendered, enabled Greene to direct his efforts against the stockade fortress also. He had reason to urge all his efforts to shorten the duration of the siege. Des patches from Marion had brought him intelligence of the arrival, in Charleston, of three British regiments, to the support of Rawdon. The acquisition of this force would give the latter the immediate and complete ascendency in the state, and, as Greene well knew, would set him instantly in motion for the relief of the beleaguered post. To press his leaguer with all his strength and energy, and to keep the garrison from any knowledge of the increased ability, or of the efforts, of Rawdon to relieve them, were the immediate objects of the American general. To secure the latter object, Colonel Wash ington, who had now rejoined the army with his cavalry, and the cavalry of Lee's legion under Major Rudolph, were ordered to reinforce Sumter, who was instructed to form a junction with Marion—the whole force, thus united, to hang upon the enemy's march, retard his movements by every possible means, and completely cover the country over which tidings of his approach could be transmitted. Assuming the reduction of Ninety-Six as a matter certain, could the necessary delay be secured, Greene's determination was, after that event, taking with him the Georgia and South-Carolina militia, to join his forces with those of Sumter and Marion, and give Rawdon battle on the march. But the reduction of Ninety-Six was the first object.

The siege of the star was urged with the desperate energy of those who knew how much depended on the event. Lee, meanwhile, made regular and rapid approaches to the stockade. He, too, had to encounter numerous and spirited sallies of the besieged;—but his advance was equally swift and steady; and very soon, between his fire and that of the third parallel, the enemy could no longer venture to the rivulet for water in the light of day. Naked negroes were now employed, by night, for the purpose of bringing in the necessary supplies to the garrison of both places; and those who know the singular consideration of self which marks this class of people, may easily imagine how limited must have been the supply thus furnished to the garrison. To increase their disquiets and discomforts, an attempt was made, such as had been employed by Marion at Fort Motte, to set fire to the buildings within the fort by means of burning arrows. But Cruger instantly unroofed his houses, and thus escaped all farther peril from this source of annoyance. An attempt of Lee to destroy the abatis of the stockade by fire, in open daylight was similarly unsuccessful, and resulted in the destruction of the whole party engaged in the attempt. But these disappointments did not discourage the besiegers The fate of the brave garrison seemed to be a thing written. It was evident that the defence could not much longer be maintained. Their works were all overawed by the superior fire of the besiegers, whose wooden towers approached within thirty yards of the ditch, from which the riflemen swept everything human that rose within vision above the ramparts. A battery, twenty feet high, for cannon, within a hundred and forty yards, so entirely commanded the star redoubt, that it became necessary to give its parapet, already twelve feet high, three feet more of elevation; which was done by means of sandbags, small intervals between which were left for the use of small arms. The withdrawal of the bags by night, left embrazures for the cannon, which could thus be pointed capriciously, without suffering the assailants to conjecture in what quarter they would next appear.

Thus, with a stubbornness and perseverance, on both sides, which amply testified the common origin of the several combatants, they lay watching each other. The pressing energy of the one, was nobly met by the unflinching constancy of the other. For eighteen days had the conflict continued: and, at this moment, not a man could show his head on either side without drawing the fire of his enemy. It was seldom that the bullet was sped in vain. Much blood had been already shed. Many were the gallant deeds performed on both sides—on that of the garrison, apparently, in vain. Sanguine of the result, now apparently at hand, the soldiers of Greene looked forward to a grateful termination of their toils in the surrender of the fortress. A corresponding gloom, which was only not despair, had fastened upon the hearts of their opponents. Their resources were diminishing, their strength momently lessening, their hope exhausted. They knew nothing of the reinforcements received by Rawdon—knew nothing of his approach for their relief. Their minds were prepared for the catastrophe which seemed inevitable; when, at the moment of their greatest despondency, they received tidings of succor, and were invigorated to new efforts in the contest. The facts were these; —they mingle a little romance with the dull details of ordinary matters.—

There was a young lady, the daughter and sister of tried and honored patriots, who resided at a place not far distant from the American camp. Unsuspected, she visited the camp, with a flag, on some pretence of little moment. She was received with civility, and dined at the table of the general. It was not known that she was the betrothed of a British officer then in the garrison. Subsequently, however, it was discovered that she had remained for a day or two at a neighboring farm-house. In this period, a young loyalist, well mounted, dashed through the American line of pickets, and, by the rapidity of his flight, baffled the sudden fire which he drew from the sentinels. His audacity, and the narrow escape which he ran, were a sufficient passport for his admission to the garrison. He brought the tidings, in a verbal message from Lord Rawdon, which gave new life to the garrison. His news was too grateful to be questioned. Their huzzas, and an animated *feu de joie*, announced his mission to the besiegers, and indicated the newborn resolution which now defied their utmost efforts.

It now became necessary that the place should be carried by storm. With Rawdon approaching, and the garrison in possession of the fact, there was no chance of a more pacific termination of the siege. Accordingly, the resolution having been taken, the several detachments of the besiegers were ready by twelve, on the morning of the 18th of June, to attempt the assault; —hot work for hot weather. Lee was to command in the assault upon the stockade. His forlorn hope was led by Rudolph, supported by the infantry of the legion, and the remains of the gallant Delawares under Kirkwood. The forlorn hope against the star redoubt was led by Lieutenants Duval and Seldon,—the one with a command of Marylanders, and the other of Virginians. They were followed by Colonel Campbell at the head of the first Maryland and first Virginia regiments, by whom the assault was to be made. The American forts, the rifle-towers, and the advanced works, were all manned, with orders to sweep and clear the enemy's parapet during the advance of the storming party. Parties bearing fascines to fill the ditches, others armed with long poles barbed with hooks of iron to pull down the sandbags, followed in the footsteps of the forlorn hopes, the tasks of which, particularly in the attempt on the star redoubt, were sufficiently perilous. They were to advance, under the numerous crossfires of its angles, to clear the abatis, and, driving off the defenders, occupy the curtain opposite them, while the hookmen drew the sandbags from the walls. This service done, Campbell, with his two regiments, was to gain the summit and finish the work.

The American works were manned, accordingly, with riflemen prepared to sweep the enemy's parapets. Precisely at noon, the signal for the assault was given. Then followed a blaze of fire from artillery and small arms, from right to left, all concentrating on the centre of attack. Under this cloud of fire and storm, the assailing parties rushed to the assault. No effort could have been more nobly impulsive, or more resolutely maintained. In an instant, this gallant little band had crossed the ditch and commenced the work of destroying the abatis. They were encountered by a terrible fire from within the works, the severity of which naturally increased with the increased destruction of the abatis.

From every crevice in the sandbags, the rifle poured forth its deadly missile — a constant stream, to which the assailants could oppose nothing but unflinching obstinacy in the prosecution of their tasks. It was in vain that they opposed their constancy to this destructive fire. Pikes and bayonets bristled above them, defying their approach, and mocking their endeavors. Between two angles of the redoubt, the discharges of both swept their columns with unsparing rage. Their bravest were the first to fall. The gallant Captain Armstrong, of the 1st Marylanders, was struck down, among the first, at the head of his company. Duval and Seldon were both severely wounded. But they pressed forward, encouraging their commands, till the curtain was won, and the hookmen, promptly following while the other fought, strove to pull down the sandbags from their elevations. The attainment of this object might have secured the victory; but they had greatly miscalculated the depth of the ditch and the height of the parapet. The sandbags were above their reach, and their toils were taken in vain.

This was a melancholy misfortune. Greene saw with anguish the fruitlessness of the struggle. The prey was about to escape his grasp. The fight had continued for nearly an hour, and but little had been achieved. The stockade had been won, with little risk, by Lee's party, led by Rudolph; the enemy having concentrated themselves, for the final struggle, in the star. But this advantage was of little moment. No impression had been made on the formidable redoubt, which had been the main object of the enterprise. The greater part of the assailing party had fallen, either slain or wounded, in the ditch. It was possible that success might attend a continuance of the conflict. Lee was prepared to sustain the movement on the right. The assailing party had been, comparatively, a small one, and repeated efforts, with larger parties, might result more fortunately. But, with Rawdon approaching with a fresh army, Greene dared not wait the doubtful issues of the conflict. Even if successful in the storm, yet what could be his hope against the now full regiments of the British, with a greatly crippled army. Reluctantly, he gave the order to retire. Lee was recalled; Campbell commanded to desist; and the survivors in the strife, bringing back with them the greater number of their wounded comrades, escaped in the face of a galling fire, which the garrison delivered as thev retired.

CHAPTER XVII.

Greene retreats from Ninety-Six.—Is pursued by Rawdon.—The latter evacuates Ninety-Six, and retires toward the Seaboard.—Greene turns upon and pursues him.—Various Movements of the Armies.—Rawdon at Orangeburg.—Greene offers him Battle.—He declines it.—Is strengthened by Cruger, and Greene retires and encamps among the High Hills of Santee.

THE cup of triumph was once more plucked from the lips of the Americans, at the very moment when the precious draught seemed to be secure. Greene was not much the favorite of fortune. What he achieved seemed to be in her despite. The siege of Ninety-Six had lasted twenty-eight days. In its progress he had lost nearly two hundred men killed and wounded; but, even with this disappointment of his object, and this diminution of his force, he found some reasons for hope and consolation. The constancy and spirit which his troops had shown, were full of the happiest auguries. They were beginning to reap, obviously, all the advantages which qualify the mortification of defeat, and prepare for a grateful change of fortune. There was no longer danger that they would again suffer from such a panic as lost them the field of Hobkirk, and Greene had not so much to regret in his failure before Ninety-Six except the loss of so many admirable soldiers. With adequate numbers, trained like these, he should no longer shrink from a pitched battle with his enemy. In his despatches to Congress, he expresses this confidence and satisfaction. "The behavior of the troops on this occasion deserves the highest commendation... They have undergone incredible hardships during the siege. . . Had the Virginia militia joined us, agreeably to orders, success would have been complete." He did not withdraw from the leaguer too precipitately. Rawdon's army was almost within striking distance. He was but a few miles off when the last struggle was made, and the storming party was rushing to the breach. The force of Rawdon was more than two thousand men; too large a force for the detachments under Sumter and Marion to oppose. He was also strong in cavalry. They could only hang upon his flanks; and even in the performance of this duty, an unfortunate facility of route, which enabled Rawdon to choose at pleasure, and almost at any moment, required that the forces of the partisans should be so scattered as, if possible, to keep a watch on all. The same circumstance prevented Sumter from calling in his detachments, and pressing for Ninety-Six in season to enable Greene, thus strengthened, to advance and choose the proper ground for an advantageous meeting with his lordship. For this Greene was anxious. He writes with great earnestness on this subject to all the partisans. "It is my wish to meet him," is the language of one of these letters, "and I doubt not of victory if the virtuous militia collect and fight with their usual gallantry. Come on, then, my good friend, and bring Lieutenant-Colonel Jackson with you, and all the good troops you have collected. Let us have a field-day, and I doubt not it will be a glorious one. No time is to be lost,—be here to-morrow evening at farthest." This was written on the 17th. It was on the 18th that the attempt was made to storm the post at Ninety-Six. But the virtuous militia did not arrive in season, and the approach of Rawdon rendered the attempt to storm, and the subsequent retreat, indispensable. Greene, therefore, on the 19th, moved off, on the track of his baggage, previously sent, across the Saluda.

This retrograde movement, as usual, affected the enthusiasm of the militia. Of four regiments of volunteers, under Sumter, every man left him in a single day. Marion was only less unfortunate. The fluctuations of the spirits of an army can only be counteracted by the imperative necessity of the service; by the conviction on the part of the soldiers, that, through good or ill fortune, they have no refuge but in camp. The lessons of the revolutionary war were incessant, and of the most impressive character, which taught the absurdity of any other process for raising troops among the militia, than that which binds them to the business for the whole war.

Greene's retreat, once begun, was pressed with little intermission for twenty-two miles. It was well that he could retreat. He had shown his troops that such a necessity implies feebleness but not discredit, and sometimes, indeed, supplies what is equal to a victory. At all events, his soldiers had learned to endure, without too great a degree of humiliation, this usually humiliating necessity. Had Greene been a more rash and impulsive man, he might have recoiled, at the risk of their safety and his own reputation, at the inevitable misfortune; and by giving way to his pride against his judgment, have forfeited the stakes he played for. But, in truth, retreat did not imply, in his case, the disappointment of his objects. He was simply driven, for the moment, from his prey, which, events had shown, was destined to fall into his hands at last. Thus had he been hunted and pursued by Cornwallis, yet the latter had been exhausted by the very advantages he had won, while the American general, soon recovering, was pressing forward to a renewal of his efforts. To Cornwallis, Rawdon had succeeded; and Greene was twice — soon to be thrice — driven before him. Yet, all the while, the strongholds of the British were falling into the hands of his detachments, and he was ready, the moment that his pursuer had given up the chase, to turn upon his footsteps and renew his enterprises. These characteristics of the warfare he pursued, well understood among his followers, had now taken the sting from partial defeat, and the humiliation from flight. Retreat was only a part of the game, and not an unforeseen disaster. It was, in other words, that process of muscular contraction which is necessary to a becoming future exercise of strength; such a contraction as the individual makes, when, seeking to spring far, he crouches low. Cheerfully then, and in good spirits, strengthened by their past experience, the troops of Greene made their way over Bush river, and, with the tidings of Rawdon's advance, sped on yet farther across the rivers Enoree, Tyger, and Broad, halting, on the 25th, at a place called Tim's Ordinary, about half way between the Broad and the Catawba rivers. Rawdon pushed forward to the Enoree, but found the pursuit to be equally impolitic and vain. Greene had swept the country in his progress, and was in due route to his magazines on the Catawba. Rawdon, moving from his own, felt momently the increasing want of supplies, his foragers not daring to venture far in the face of two strong detachments of cavalry and light-infantry, under Washington and Lee, accompanied by Greene himself, that sullenly preceded the pursuit. The army of the Americans, meanwhile, continued its march under Colonel Williams. Greene had gained another of his victories when Rawdon abandoned the pursuit. He had the fate of Cornwallis before him, whose pursuit of Greene, continued into three states, had, by a curious coincidence, begun at the very spot where his successor deemed it wiser to forbear. It might be that Rawdon was less influenced by this ominous coincidence than we have reason to suppose. Other considerations may have governed him in abandoning the chase. His troops were fresh from Europe, had marched nearly two hundred and fifty miles in less than twelve days, and, clad in thick garments, were far less able to withstand the melting heats of the climate in midsummer, than the Americans, who were little burdened with any clothing. His return to Ninety-Six revealed still farther the difficulties of his government. That place was to be abandoned also. Remote from the seaboard, it could no longer be maintained. The toils were closing momently around the invader, and he was compelled, however reluctantly, to draw in all the troops from his outposts,—to contract his antennæ.

This necessity, if humbling to the British, was pregnant with still worse conditions to their tory allies. Ninety-Six had been the very centre of their wantonness and power. Here, encouraged by the foreign emissary, they had run full riot over the whig inhabitants. In the simple consciousness of strength, they had indulged it in excess, and the surrounding country had been ravaged by their gross and terrible barbarities. When, therefore, summoning their chiefs around him, Rawdon declared the necessity of withdrawing the British garrison from the post, a terror which they had never felt before seized upon their apprehensions. This was to abandon them to the just vengeance of their enemies. The day of retribution was come. They felt what was due to their atrocities, and shrunk from the tender mercies of the avenger. There was but one alternative before them, and that they adopted. This was to abandon the country and to follow that foreign power to which, and their own passions, they had sold themselves, and which alone could give them protection. Melancholy was the spectacle that followed. Trooping slowly and gloomily in the van and rear of the British army, went the families of this unhappy faction. For days the roads from Ninety-Six were crowded with a wretched cavalcade, men, women children, and slaves, with cattle and wagons, seeking the protection of the British army on its way to the sea-board. They were leaving their homesteads at the most endearing season. The whole country was looking most beautiful in the vigorous warmth of the maturing summer. Their fields, paved in green and gold, with the growing harvests, and fruits and flowers on every hand, imploring them to stay, compelled tears from eyes that had not often shown pity to their fellow-creatures. Conscious of their own brutal rage and the hardness of heart with which, in the season of their prosperity and power, they had regarded their unhappy brethren among the whigs, they could hope for no mercy from them in the day which found the position of the parties reversed. They did not dare to make the experiment upon sympathies which they had so commonly joyed to outrage; and, followed by keen eyes of vengeance, as they clung to the shelter of the British, on their downward march, they made their way, a melancholy and doomed community, to the neighborhood of Charleston, where a miserable hamlet, called Rawdontown, in the suburbs of the city, gave them temporary shelter; but where pestilence, and the diseases of an unfriendly climate, soon thinned their numbers, leaving but few to burden the retiring vessels of the enemy when they finally left the country. Such as remained in the interior suffered more summarily, but it is doubtful if from a severer fate. The returning whigs, desperate from ruined circumstances, and protracted injuries, pursued their vengeance with a sleepless appetite wherever they could find a victim. The country was depopulated, and in spite of the strenuous efforts of Greene to meliorate the sufferings of the people, or, rather, their rage, he was but too frequently compelled to hear of cruelties which shocked humanity, and of bloody revenges for past crimes, over which humanity could only weep. The time that he could spare from the enemy, was devoted to the most earnest endeavors to soothe the passions and disarm the fury of the people; but his toils were only in part successful. It is estimated that the civil war in Ninety-Six District alone left fifteen hundred widows to deplore its horrors.

In retracing his steps toward the seaboard, and withdrawing the forces from Ninety-Six, Lord Rawdon divided his army into two nearly equal bodies. One of these bodies, under Cruger, was employed to cover the departure of the Loyalists; while the other, consisting of eleven hundred infantry, sixty cavalry, and two companies of artillery, under his own command, took up the line of march, on the 29th of June, for Orangeburg, at which place he had instructed Colonel Stuart, with a strong detachment, to meet him. The signal for his departure was that of the return of Greene upon his track. He had already anticipated the necessity for the retreat of Rawdon, and provided against it. Lee, with his legion, was ordered to hover about the post of Ninety-Six, and to strike whenever an opportunity offered. Washington, with his cavalry and the infantry of Kirkwood, was to keep near the enemy at Orangeburg, with a similar purpose. Sumter was instructed to descend the country, and to co-operate with Marion in pursuit of the common object; while Greene, himself, with the main army, taking the route toward Granby, was to determine his own by the movements of the enemy. The progress of the latter seemed to indicate a design upon the posts which the Americans had recently reconquered; and the apprehensions of Greene were still lively lest Rawdon should organize garrisons along the route from Ninety-Six, out of the bands of loyalists about him, with which his foreign reinforcements enabled him to dispense for the present. Greene's object, in this pursuit, and in the employment of his light troops, was to prevent any such design from being put into execution, and, gradually, to compel his adversary to retire once more within that range of inferior posts with which he had environed himself in the neighborhood of the sea. This was his desire and design — a design to be put in execution only when his recruits should sufficiently increase the strength of his army. This was still greatly inferior to that of Rawdon, but improving daily under the active agency of Marion and Sumter. The militia were once more gathering about their favorite leaders, under the encouraging effect produced by the retrograde movement of Rawdon; and a small detachment of continentals, and some two hundred and fifty North Carolina levies, under Major Armstrong, presented themselves at camp at a moment when it most needed favoring auguries. But the season was unfavorable to enterprise. The heat was excessive; and Greene found it necessary to give his army a couple of days of rest. Meanwhile, the objects of the British commander continued doubtful, and the American general remained in a state of the most anxious suspense. His opinion was, that Rawdon meditated a retreat; but this might only be a feint. He might really desire to fall within his new line of posts; but it might be his purpose to establish himself on the Congaree, and compass, within his power, the country between the Edisto to the west, and that of the Congaree and Santee to the north and east. Such, really, was his intention; but it was not until the first of July that his object became known to the American general. A letter of Stuart, which Washington had intercepted, advised Rawdon of his march, but gave him to understand that he could not reach Granby, whither the latter had summoned him, by the time specified — namely, the 3d of

July. Advised, at the same time, by Lee, that Rawdon, relying on this junction with Stuart, had ventured to divide his forces equally with Cruger, and was marching toward Granby in the fullest confidence that the meeting would be effected at the designated time, suggested to Greene the prospect of an enterprise for which he immediately put his troops in motion. If he could succeed in throwing himself between Rawdon and his detachments, he might destroy him in detail. Disembarrassing itself of everything which might impede the march, the army was put under the command of General Huger, with orders to press on to the Congaree. Greene, himself, with a small escort of cavalry, hurried off in search of Colonel Washington, and in order that he might observe more nearly those indications by which his ulterior measures were to be directed.

The forward movement of the American army, and possibly the nonarrival of any courier with advices from Stuart, appears to have awakened the apprehensions of Rawdon. He now urged his own march with an obvious anxiety to reach Granby in anticipation of the Americans. His progress was attended with some misfortunes, which probably increased his desire to hasten forward. Lee's cavalry, by which his retreating footsteps were harassed and haunted, succeeded in cutting off nearly the whole of the British horse, taking forty-five of them prisoners when within but a mile of their army. This event exaggerated the alarm of Rawdon, and his speed was increased with but small regard to the health and comfort of his troops, more than fifty of whom fell dead from heat and fatigue, in the progress from Ninety-Six to Orangeburg. But he succeeded in his object, and reached Granby two days in advance of that which he had appointed for the rendezvous with Stuart, and, consequently, before Greene was ready to present himself at the same point of junction. This point gained, Raw don lingered only long enough to destroy the boats for some distance along the river, and then, chiefly solicitous for his detachments, pressed forward immediately to Orangeburg, where he took up a strong position, awaiting the arrival of Stuart and Cruger. He had gained a position of safety, with desperate exertions that did not scruple at great sacrifice of life in the prosecution of his purpose.

Foiled of his prey, Greene had other hopes in reserve. Apprized, through a deserter, of a large supply of stores which were on the march to Orangeburg, he laid a plan for securing them. These stores were of vital importance to the British, and their loss might eventually lead to the destruction of the army. They were a tempting bait to the Americans, to whom they were almost as important. But the well-concerted measures failed, and the next object was to attempt the detachment under Stuart. Greene, at the head of the corps of Marion and Washington, resolved to lead this enterprise in person. He succeeded in passing Lord Rawdon on the 6th of July, and Marion placed himself in waiting for his prey. But the good fortune of the British general had not deserted him. Sallying out, at one o'clock, on the morning of the 8th, expecting to take his prey, Marion, to his utter discomfiture, found that Stuart had passed him in the night. Unconscious of his danger, and influenced only by a choice of roads, the British colonel had turned aside into one, while his enemy was seeking for him in another. The miserable deficiency of force, thus frequently prevented the Americans from realizing the best-laid plans of enterprise. On the day of the junction of Stuart with Rawdon, a letter from Marion shows how little the British army was in a condition to fight or fly. He writes: " Their troops are so fatigued that they can not possibly move. Three regiments were going to lay down their arms, and it is believed they will to-day, if they are ordered to march. They have no idea of any force being near them."

Greene was anxious, but in no condition, to take advantage of this disorganization in the ranks of the enemy, Rawdon soon recruited his troops by repose, and his position was too strongly sheltered to be attempted by the troops of the American general. With the defeat of the attempt upon Stuart, he had retraced his steps to the army, and calling in his detachments on the Congaree, and finding himself in unusual strength, with fully two thousand troops, including the men of Marion and Sumter, he prepared to march down and offer battle to his enemy. The advantage of numbers was with Greene. The force of Rawdon, with that of Stuart, did not exceed fifteen hundred; but they were all disciplined troops, and well equipped and supplied with necessaries. Of the American army, but eight hundred were regulars. The cavalry of the latter was, however, much the best, that of the British being exceedingly feeble in numbers, and deficient in that confidence in itself which alone insures the usefulness of this important arm of battle.

It was highly important that Greene, if he hoped to engage the enemy, should do so before the junction with Cruger should be effected. In that case, his strength would so greatly preponderate as to leave the contest hopeless. Cruger was on his march, and rapidly approaching Orangeburg, only watched by the militia under Pickens — a force neither sufficiently strong nor sufficiently practised to retard the advance of the British detachment, consisting of twelve or fourteen hundred men. To anticipate his coming, Greene appeared within four miles of Orangeburg, and offered Rawdon battle. The latter took no notice of the demonstration, and the certainty of Cruger's approach compelled Greene to move up with the hope of forcing his adversary to the deadly issue. But a careful examination of Rawdon's position, determined him against the measure, and, very reluctantly, and against the advice of many whom he was disposed to respect, he withdrew from the field. The temptation was not inconsiderable, but the risk was still less so. He dared not peril unnecessarily a cause which he felt that patience and caution must eventually secure. Accordingly, withdrawing, by slow and easy marches, he retired to a camp of repose among the high hills of Santee, a beautiful and salubrious region, where he gave to his wearied soldiers the rest and respite which they so grievously required. Cruger, meanwhile, reaching Orangeburg, so strengthened the command of Rawdon as to leave him in no present danger of a challenge from his enemy. The former had not descended from Ninety-Six without leaving his mark upon the country. Left at Ninety-Six to cover the flight of the loyalist families, and while awaiting their assembling, he despatched a swarm of tories, accompanied by a small regular force, into what was called the Long-Cane settlement. This expedition afforded to the vindictive loyalists a chance of striking a last blow at their ancient enemies. Their ravages were of a kind to afford a sufficient sanction to the assertion that orders had been given by the British commander to lay the country waste — a measure of wanton barbarity which had no justification in necessity. They swept the country with sword and fire, checked only by the timely arrival of Pickens and Clarke, with their followers, by whom the dastardly marauders were once more driven to seek shelter under the guns of their British allies. Pickens could only watch, and follow, and threaten. His force was too small to retard the progress of an enemy whose aimless barbarities had entirely placed him without the pale of humanity and mercy. The junction of Cruger with Rawdon would have soon brought the latter out from his place of security, in search of Greene, but for the timely retreat which placed the Congaree between the rival armies.

CHAPTER XVIII.

Incursion of the Partisans under Sumter into the Lower Country.—Capture of Dorchester.—Alarm in Charleston.—Attempt on the Post at Biggins.—Abandoned by the British.—Pursuit of Coates.—Affair at Quinby Bridge.—Battle at Shubrick's.

A RETROSPECT of the campaign just closed, affords us a curious illustration of the caprices and fluctuations of the war. We see Cornwallis, superior in strength and eager for combat, pursuing the American general from the Catawba river, in South Carolina, across the Dan, in Virginia. We remark that, at the very moment of the greatest seeming superiority in the former, he wheels about and recedes before his adversary. We see that adversary, conscious of inferiority, yet pressing on his heels; and the combat which follows, while giving the victory to the enemy, secures most of its fruits to the defeated Americans. The game is again reversed, and Cornwallis, the pursuer, is pursued, and finally escapes to Virginia. Greene resumes his plan of invading South Carolina and recovering its territory in detail. He crosses weapons with Rawdon, is compelled to fly before him, yet grows stronger from every defeat, seemingly like the ancient wrestler, to receive new life and vigor at every fall upon his native earth. His adversary pursues, until, in a state of exhaustion, he pauses for breath, only to find his enemy upon his path again. In the meanwhile, his fortresses are taken by assault, or he is forced to abandon them. Steadily and inflexibly the American pursues his object. Retreat forms a part of his system.

as in the case of the Parthian, and his followers are encouraged even by seeming discomfiture, as it usually results, under their present leader, in a large increase of strength. His calculations have all been realized; his schemes have been successful; he has conquered without loss: and, when baffled, it has been chiefly still at the expense of the enemy. His very caution, which has sometimes had the effect of lessening the brilliancy of his exploits, has economized his forces, and left them assured and confident of the wholesome authority which they obey. His camp of rest upon the hills did not imply repose. In this salubrious region, in which his soldiers found refuge from the diseases of summer and the climate, not a moment was consumed in idleness. The combatants had separated for a season, only to recruit the strength necessary to a renewal of the conflict. The task before Greene was one of unremitting watchfulness and study. His troops were suffering from sickness and exhaustion. To refresh the whole, to restore the sick, to accumulate clothes and provisions, and discipline the inexperienced, were employments of the camp which employed every hour of his time. There were other cares of a more general and comprehensive character. To invite the co-operation and assistance of the contiguous states, by earnest and frequent entreaty and expostulation—to suggest and indicate their measures—to establish magazines in secure and convenient places—to connect his several points of communication—to secure the means of transportation—these were tasks which kept him wakeful through the weary watches of the night.

The repose of the regular army among the Santee hills did not imply the inactivity of the partisans. It was one of the chief uses of a regular army in South Carolina, that it enabled the whig militia to rise into activity. As the presence of a British army, in force, had overawed the whigs and encouraged the audacity of the tories, so the army of Greene, in due degree with its ability to restrain and watch the movements of the British, gave opportunity to the friends of the revolution to encounter their ancient enemies. With the increase of popular confidence in the prudence and soldiership of the American general, the partisan militia gathered to their favorite leaders. These, accustomed to the climate, familiar with the country, and mostly mounted, were capable of rendering active service while the two opposing armies were in summer-quarters. Accordingly, the moment that Greene crossed the Congaree, on his march to his camp of repose, he organized an expedition of the partisans, directing their operations in the lower country. The command of this expedition was given to Sumter. Under him were such chieftains as have not often been gathered under a single leader. Marion and Lee, the Hampdens, and Colonels Taylor, Horry, Maham, Lacy, and others, gave ample assurances that the work in hand would most probably be well done. The command consisted of all the troops of the state, of Lee's legion, and a small detachment of artillery with one field-piece —in all about a thousand men. Its object was to strike at outposts, inspirit the whigs, and divert the attention of Rawdon from the country above, by provoking his fears for the security of that below him. In his orders to Sumter, Greene writes: "There is no time to be lost. Push your operations night and day. Keep a party to watch the enemy's motions at Orangeburg, as they move down. Should they move in any other direction, I will advise you. Keep Colonel Lee and General Marion advised of all matters from above, and tell Colonel Lee to thunder even at the gates of Charleston," &c.

Sumter's detachments were soon sweeping down by

every road that led to Charleston. He, himself, with the main body of his force, pursued the Congaree, on the south side of that river, then the east side of the Cooper. The incursion, thus begun, was full of the happiest results. For a while it prostrated every appearance of royal power almost to the gates of the metropolis, and drove the enemy from all quarters to seek shelter within its walls. Lee made his appearance at a fortunate moment before the post at Dorchester. It was a field ripe for the sickle. The garrison had been greatly reduced by the draught made on it by Stuart, and a bloody mutiny among the residue, which was only quelled by the massacre of more than a hundred men, almost entirely deprived the place of all power of resistance. At the approach of Lee it was hastily abandoned, the garrison making their escape to Charleston. The Americans succeeded in seizing a valuable spoil, consisting of a couple of hundred horses, and some wagons of fixed ammunition. This done, Lee, in connexion with Colonel Wade Hampton, passing on to the east of Dorchester by the Wassamasaw, to Goose creek bridge, cut off the communication between Dorchester and Monk's corner, and between the latter place and Charleston, by the route west of Cooper river. A detachment of Marion's men, under Colonel Maham, passing the head of Cooper river and Watboo creek, penetrated below, eastward of Biggin church, in order, by destroying the bridge over the creek, to obstruct the retreat of the garrison at the latter place. Meanwhile, the better to hold these several parties advised of any movement of Rawdon's troops at Orangeburg, Colonel Henry Hampton seized and held, with a strong party, the bridge over Four-Hole creek, he, himself, moving off afterward to co-operate with Lee. It would be difficult to conceive a plan of operations better calculated to effect the objects of the expedition. With the abandonment by the British of the post at Dorchester, Colonel Wade Hampton, anticipating the march of his confederate, Lee, dashed down the road to Charleston, capturing more than fifty dragoons in the march, and, suddenly appearing almost beneath the lines of the city, spread terror and confusion within its walls. With the conviction that Greene's whole army was at his heels, the bells were rung, alarm-guns were fired, and the entire population was mustered out in arms. Content with thus disquieting them, Hampton retired, and proceeded to unite himself with the force of Sumter. Lee moved in the same direction, and with the same object. The particular point at which Sumter aimed to strike, was the post at Biggin church. This church, within a mile of Monk's corner, was a strong brick building which the British had fortified and garrisoned. It covered the bridge which crossed Biggin creek, which is esteemed the head of the West branch of Cooper river. On the east of this creek the road to Charleston passes Watboo and Quinby creeks, between which the road forks and crosses the latter, considered the East fork of the river, at two several points; the left at Quinby bridge, the right at Bonneau's ferry. From Biggin bridge, the only route westwardly to Charleston, crosses at Goose creek bridge. To destroy the bridge at Watboo, was the object of the Americans, as the eastern route then became impracticable. The bridge, accordingly, became the object of interest with both parties. It happened, unfortunately, that Sumter, on his march, received false intelligence of a British detachment appearing at Murray's ferry. This place lay without the line of his march, and he lost time in sending a force of three hundred men to strike at the hostile party. The delay and the movement suggested the danger to the garrison at Biggin's, and gave time for it to obtain reinforcements. When Mayham, who had been sent by Marion to destroy the bridge, drew nigh for this purpose, he found the enemy in too much strength to permit him to make the effort. He was obliged to wait patiently for the approach of Sumter. The garrison at Biggin consisted of five hundred disciplined infantry, being the 19th regiment, under Col. Coates, with a piece of artillery and a full complement of one hundred and fifty horse. On the 16th July, Sumter marched up to support Mayham's attempt upon the bridge. Reinforcing his party with a detachment under Col. Horry, the command devolved upon the latter, who instantly proceeded to the destruction of the bridge. To prevent this, the enemy's cavalry advanced, and were encountered with such rough handling that they were driven back in confusion. The Americans then proceeded to their work, but were soon driven off by the appearance of the British in such force as to compel the retreat of the detachment to the shelter of the main body. Under the impression that the enemy had marched out to give him battle, Sumter retired to a defile a little distance in his rear, which he had selected as a favorable spot for receiving the attack. But the purpose of the British colonel was more profound. His object was to amuse his antagonist and wear out the day. Retiring, accordingly, as the evening approached, after such a demonstration as served to keep up the impression that he was in search of a fight, he obtained the time that he desired. Night came on, and it was only at three in the morning that the flames bursting from the roof of the church, declared the enemy to be in motion. He had collected all his stores within the church, set them on fire, and moved off by Watboo and Quinby, on the road to the eastward

The pursuit was instantly begun, led by Lee and Hampton. When the Watboo was passed, it was discovered that the cavalry of the British, separated from the infantry, was pursuing the road to the right. Hampton struck off in pursuit of this body, and reached the river only to find the enemy on the opposite side, with all the boats in his possession. Darting back upon his route, he arrived in season only to witness the escape of their infantry; an event accruing, perhaps, in consequence of the diversion in pursuit of their cavalry. This body of troops had been pursued by the legion cavalry, seconded by that of Marion under Mayham. About a mile to the north of Quinby bridge, they succeeded in overtaking the rear of the retreating army, with nearly the whole of the baggage. This division of Coates's force, consisting of one hundred men, was commanded by Captain Campbell. At first, they made a show of resistance, but such was the furious charge of the cavalry, that it overwhelmed them, and they threw down their arms without firing a gun. This imbecility had nearly involved the fate of the whole regiment. Unapprized of their disaster, since not a shot was fired, Coates, having passed the bridge, had made his dispositions for destroying it as soon as his rear had passed in safety. The planks which covered it had already been loosened from the sleepers, and men stood ready to throw them off at the proper moment. A howitzer at the opposite extremity was planted for the protection of the party assigned for its destruction, and the commander of the British force stood waiting impatiently at the bridge for the coming of the rear. It was fortunate that he was thus prepared, and thus present, at the place of danger. The American cavalry dashing into view, instead of the British rear, warned him of his danger, and found him ready to employ the proper means for meeting it. His measures were promptly taken. His main body was, at this time, partly on the causeway on the south side of the bridge, and partly crowded into a narrow lane beyond it, in a position which not only disabled them from present service, but left them particularly exposed to destruction, should the impetus of the American cavalry carry them across the bridge. To despatch orders to his troops to halt, form, and march up, and to make his artillerists ready to employ the howitzer, while his fatigue-party were opening a chasm between his assailants and himself, by thrusting the planks into the water, were necessities instantly conceived and as instantly set in motion. Meanwhile, the American cavalry dashed forward. The legion cavalry were in advance of Mayham's, their front section led by Captain Armstrong. The planks sliding into the water, and the lighted portfire beyond, hanging above the howitzer, left no time for hesitation to a body of cavalry densely moving along the narrow causeway in its range. There was not a moment to be lost, and, driving his rowels into his steed, Armstrong dashed over the bridge, followed closely by his section, and drove the artillerists from the gun. Lieutenant Carrington followed with the second section, and the third advanced, but faltered. Mayham, with Marion's cavalry, feeling the halt, charged by it, but was arrested in his career by the death of his horse. Captain Macaulay, who led his front section, pressed over the bridge to the opposite causeway which was now crowded, hand to hand, with combatants. The British working party, snatching up their pieces, had fled, after delivering a single fire. Two of Lee's dragoons fell dead at the mouth of the howitzer, and several were severely wounded; but the leaders were unhurt, and, contending with Coates and his officers, who, covered by a wagon, were opposing them with their swords, while the British troops were pressing forward to a spot in which they might display. A fruitless and tedious endeavor, on the part of the Americans, to recover the floating planks, and repair the bridge for the detachment to cross, afforded to the enemy sufficient leisure for their objects; and when Armstrong, of the legion cavalry, and Macaulay, of Mayham's, looked about them, they found themselves almost isolated from their own people, while the British, formed in front, were ready for their destruction. It remained only to urge their way headlong through the fugitives along the causeway. Secure in the fact, that, while the British officers in the rear would save them from the fire of their troops in front, and pressing forward till a secure footing could be found in the woods on either side, they dashed to the right, and escaped by heading the stream. Prepared to receive a charge of cavalry, Coates renewed his labors upon the bridge, and succeeded in its destruction. He then pressed forward to the shelter of Shubrick's plantation, not daring to trust himself in the open field with such an active and powerful hostile cavalry about him. Here, in the cover of dwelling-houses, outhouses, and fences, he prepared to await the approach of Sumter's infantry. The latter, compelled to make a considerable circuit, did not reach the ground till three o'clock in the afternoon. It was Sumter's opinion, that if the wholesome audacity of the first sections of the cavalry had been sustained by the whole, the British must have been overwhelmed. "If the whole party had charged across the bridge, they would have come upon the enemy in such a state of confusion, while extricating themselves from the lane, that they must have laid down their arms."

Sumter found the British drawn up in a square, in front of the house, and prepared for his reception. He had few bayonets, and his policy was that of the brave fellows at King's mountain, where the rifle was made to baffle this weapon in the hands of the enemy. His infantry was divided into three bodies; his own brigade constituting one, and that of Marion the two other divisions. The first was ordered to advance and seek shelter under a line of negro-houses which they were to occupy. Marion's men, without any cover but the open worm fence of the country, were to approach on the right to the house of which the enemy were in possession. The cavalry, for which there was no present use, held a secure position sufficiently near to cover the infantry from pursuit. Sumter's men soon gained the negro-houses, whence they employed their rifles with effect. A fire from the fences on the British left, from a small detachment under Colonel Thomas Taylor, drew upon him a charge of the bayonet, which was not to be withstood. As they yielded, however, the men of Marion rushed to their assistance, and brought them off under a galling fire from the houses. Then, under the imperfect shelter of the fences, they continued to fire with fatal accuracy, so long as a charge of powder remained unexpended. They were then drawn off in perfect order, having been almost the only losers in the action. The battle was thus maintained from four o'clock, and while the day lasted, the enemy firing from the houses and within a picketed garden. The sun was down when the assailants retired, the combat having lasted three hours, to the exhaustion of all their ammunition. All that remained to them was a single wagon, captured at Dorchester, and that was with the artillery. Unfortunately, the powder, by some mismanagement, had been sent to headquarters, and it was not so certain that Captain Singleton, with the artillery, had anything to spare. Of pewter-bullets, Sumter was assured that there were plenty. The Americans were drawn off and encamped at a distance of three miles from the scene of action; the cavalry of Lee and Marion being employed to watch the enemy. The loss of the Americans fell almost entirely on Marion's men, and occasioned some bitter discontents among them. They alleged themselves to have been the victims of a partiality which had exposed them openly to the brunt of battle, while the troops of Sumter were carefully posted under shelter. The British lost more than seventy men under the deadly fire of the rifle. Their numbers were superior to those of Sumter, but they were without cavalry, and dared not advance from under cover.

The arrival of Sumter's artillery did not increase his strength. It brought with it no supply of ammunition. In the meantime, great discontents had arisen among the Americans. The several commanders were at issue in respect to the treatment they had severally received — the militia were withdrawing, and rumors reached the camp of the approach of Lord Rawdon, with all his force, from Orangeburg. Sumter was compelled to forego the prey almost within his grasp. But much had been done by the expedition, in exciting the fears of one class, the hopes of another, destroying the superior reputation of the enemy, and capturing stores and prisoners to a large amount and number. Among the captures of great importance was the paymaster's chest of Coates's army, containing seven hundred and twenty guineas, the largest sum ever seen in the American camp, which Sumter immediately divided among his soldiers. It was not the least grateful characteristic in this assault upon Coates, that it reassured the country on the subject of the spirit still remaining and ready in the state; that the troops by which it was made were almost exclusively South Carolina militia. The command was dissolved by the exigencies of the occasion — Sumter retiring across the Santee, and Marion into his brigade,

CHAPTER XIX.

The Camp of the Hills.—Greene's Army and his Labor.—The Capture and Execution of General Hayne.—Excitement of Greene and the Camp.—Retaliation threatened.—Stuart in Command of the British Army.—Successes of American Cavalry.—Greene's Army in Motion. —Retreat of Stuart.—Takes Post at Eutaw.—Greene approaches.

In failing to destroy or capture the detachment under Coates, the expedition, whose progress we have briefly pursued, failed in one of the chief objects for which it was undertaken. But something considerable was gained, not less in compelling the abandonment of the posts of Dorchester and Biggin, than in the lively effect which the incursion produced in the minds of friends and foes. There is no doubt that the party under Coates ought to have been brought to submission. Errors were committed, and openly charged against particular officers, by which the failure was produced. It does not belong to our narrative to inquire into this subject, which it might be difficult at this late day to analyze with any certainty. Though disappointed, in some degree, Greene was satisfied with the moral effect produced by the incursion, and longed for nothing so ardently as to follow it up with other enterprises which should confirm the wavering and the doubtful. Already had much been done to paralyze the zeal of the loyalists, and to awaken the enthusiasm of the whigs. The steady successes of the Americans, the gradual recovery of the country, and the animated spirit of the partisans, were all working to the most satisfactory results. The

British auxiliaries were deserting them, and their foreign troops, particularly the Irish, were either following the example, or exhibiting a more dangerous spirit of mutiny and disaffection. Could Greene have received the proper succors, from Congress or the contiguous states — men, money, horses, clothing — all of which were needed to success — enterprise would have been easy under the most grateful auguries, and success must have crowned endeavor with so many elements of favor as to sanction its impulses. But the whole system by which the conscript militia was brought into the field, was unprofitable and unwholesome. The natural strength of Virginia and North Carolina, to say nothing of Georgia and South Carolina, was frittered away by miserable expedients which led to nothing useful; and the American general soon discovered that, for the future, as hitherto, he must look chiefly to his own and the wretched resources of the country in which his operations were taken. We shall forbear, hereafter, the monotonous recurrence to these subjects of complaint, which, form the chief burden of his correspondence, and for which the necessities of every day afforded ample reason. One half of his cares seem to have arisen from the necessity of appealing constantly to those who would not hear, and of entreating those who, possibly, could not grant. His days and nights, when not actually in the face of his enemy, pursuing, or retreating before him, were consumed in labors at the desk, by the midnight lamp: suggesting schemes of organization for the militia of the states; devising plans for operating against the British in Virginia as well as in Carolina; now organizing an expedition against the enemy in Wilmington, and now preparing defences against the Indians along the frontier, or persuading them to treaties of peace and amity. For both purposes, Pickens had been employed with the native militia, and his efforts had been singularly successful. Of the cares of the commander of the southern army, in restoring civil government, we can employ general language only. It would be impossible, in the compass of a single volume, to depict the details of that terrible civil warfare which outraged humanity in the Carolinas, and moved the people, like the sons of Ishmael, to raise the hands of violence perpetually against their fellow-men. Greene, uniting his efforts with those of Governor Rutledge—a highly gifted man, upon whom South Carolina had conferred almost dictatorial powers, and who was now with the army at the High hills of Santee—contributed greatly to the restoration of civil authority for which the recent successful incursion below had greatly paved the way. But it was not easy to bring back the spirit of calm and peace, and subdue the domestic tempest, which still, though somewhat curbed, ran with too much riot through the land. Wrongs were remembered for retaliation only, and, but for the firmness of the American general, co-operating with Rutledge, the recent progresses of the partisans in the lower country would have covered the face of the land with carnage and desolation. Angry with defeat, and rendered querulous and unwise by disappointment, the British authorities gradually, with every new disaster gave to their policy a harsher character, which naturally increased the vindictive feeling with which they were regarded by the whigs. The train of events by which those feelings were illustrated, of cruelties on the one hand, and fierce retaliation on the other, must be sought in other histories. It will suffice, in this place, that we refer to one event, to which the domestic history has always assigned a conspicuous place over all others cf a like description. This was the wanton execution of

Colonel Isaac Hayne, by the British authorities, as a deserter and a spy.

This event followed the incursion of the partisans into the lower country. Their successful demonstration, at the very gates of Charleston, drew Lord Rawdon to the city, at the head of five hundred men. Colonel Stuart was left in command of Orangeburg. Rawdon was, no doubt, deeply mortified at the contraction of his sphere of power, and Lieutenant-Colonel Balfour, the commandant of Charleston, as greatly mortified by the insult offered to his authority when the flags of Taylor and Lee were flaunted in his sight with an insolent defiance which he lacked the ability to punish. Both of these dignitaries, no doubt, beheld the rapid approach of the hour when they should be expelled the country they had so much abused, and, from the bitterness of defeated pride, and an avarice which was arrested in the midst of its greatest gains, arose a darker passion, which brooded gloomily over its means of resentment. Unfortunately, the docile fates brought them a victim at the very moment which found this unholy passion most active in their bosoms.

Colonel Isaac Hayne was a gentleman of good character and family, a native of one of the parishes beyond the Edisto. He was a person equally amiable in his manners and above reproach in his morals. His offence may be summed up briefly in a few sentences. He came under the British authority, as a citizen, after the surrender of Charleston. A proclamation of Cornwallis required all persons, whether taken in arms or not, to receive a British protection. The requisition, as it might imply a voluntary recognition of British authority, was distasteful to Hayne, who consulted with his friends upon the subject. They gave it as their opinion that he might, without impropriety, receive the protection tendered him — that the state was in the hands of the enemy, — that he was in *duresse* accordingly, shadowed on all hands by their power, and that such an engagement implied nothing more than a forbearance, while under their protection, to demean himself as an enemy. He was the more ready to receive and recognise their arguments as, at the moment, his wife and children were suffering from smallpox, needing all his cares, and whom his affections and his duty equally denied that he should abandon. He took the required protection, and submitted to the power against which he could not contend.

But circumstances changed. Cornwallis disappeared. Rawdon was straitened, and forced to abandon his outposts. The sphere of British operations was contracted, and the partisans traversed the county in which Hayne resided, without meeting any enemy who had power to oppose them. The power to which he had submitted, had disappeared. It could no longer afford the protection which it promised. A new authority might propose new terms of obedience, and he was only too well pleased to find himself thus relieved from bonds which he had felt as irksome and humiliating. He followed the example of the partisans, drew the sword in the cause of his country, rallied a goodly troop of his neighbors, and took the field with spirit and success. With a detachment of Col. Harden's horse, he had succeeded, by a sudden dash in the vicinity of Charleston, in capturing a prisoner of peculiar consequence. This was General Williamson, who has been called the Arnold of South Carolina. Williamson was by birth a Scotchman, a man rude and unlettered, but of some popularity in the upper country. He had declared himself with the patriots in 1775, had been of service in quelling the movements of that region, but in the subsequent successes of the enemy had gone over to their side. Captured by Hayne, his fate seemed to be inevitable. He could scarcely hope for escape from the Americans, whose cause he had abandoned and betrayed. The commandant of Charleston was of course anxious to preserve him from this danger. In his solicitude to do so, he despatched in pursuit all the cavalry which could be found in and about Charleston. An unfortunate indiscretion, — such indiscretion as usually impairs the best qualities of the untrained militia officer — enabled them to overtake the American squadron, and in the conflict which ensued, Hayne in turn became a prisoner to the British.

He was conducted to Charleston, where, without a trial pursuant to civil or martial law, he was ordered to execution. Lord Rawdon only remained long enough in the city to witness the performance of the sanguinary deed, when he sailed for England. It was in vain that he had been petitioned by the inhabitants, without regard to class or party. All that could be obtained was a respite of forty-eight hours, "in consequence of the humane treatment shown by you to British prisoners who fell into your hands." The reason given for the indulgence sufficiently pronounces upon the crime of him who gave it.

It was while Greene lay at the High hills of Santee that he heard of this execution. His feelings were deeply roused by this event, the more particularly, perhaps, as it was tacitly assumed by the country that Hayne was selected as the victim to appease the *manes* of André. The hand of Greene had signed the death warrant of the latter, and the stroke of retaliation, if it were such, under which Hayne perished, was particularly designed to goad and sting the heart of the American general. He seemed to feel its purpose to be such, and gave way to one of those excessive bursts of indignation to which those men are especially liable in extreme provocation, who ordinarily keep their emotions under the greatest subjection. Like Washington, Greene was a man of strong feelings, and like him he had learned to humble them in obedience to his will and his necessities. At this time they burst their usual bounds, and he swore to revenge the wanton barbarity which had outraged all the wonted securities of war. It was while a cartel for the exchange of prisoners between the two armies was in progress, and at a time when numbers of American prisoners, under the same category with Hayne, were undergoing free release from British dungeons, that he was set aside for the sacrifice. And the matter with regard to himself was not only carefully withheld from Greene, but from Major Hyrne, his agent for the exchange, who was then temporarily residing within the city. He was suffered to leave the city with the belief that all of the prisoners were to be released, under the exchange which had been negotiated, *five* only excepted, one of whom Hayne was not.

The resolution of Greene to retaliate, was expressed in his correspondence in emphatic language. To Marion he writes: "I do not intend to retaliate upon the *tory* officers, but the *British*. It is my intention to demand the reasons of the colonel's [Hayne] being put to death; and if they are unsatisfactory, as I expect they will be, and if they refuse to make satisfaction, as I expect they will, to publish my intention of giving no quarters to British officers, of any rank, that fall into our hands." To General Washington he writes: "I am determined to retaliate, and as the enemy are indifferent about their militia officers, I mean to retaliate on the British, as the surest way to put a stop to a practice that can only serve to gratify private revenge." Simultaneously with this letter, he published a proclamation on this subject, which, after stating in emphatic language the case of Hayne went on to say that this proclamation had for its purpose to declare his intention "to make reprisals for all such inhuman insults as often as they take place"—and further that "it is my intention to take the officers of the regular forces, and not the inhabitants who have joined their army, for the objects of my reprisals." Letters, on the same day, were addressed to Lord Cornwallis and Lieutenant-colonel Balfour, under whom the execution of Hayne had taken place. To the former he writes firmly but respectfully, saying, among other things, "nor can I suppose your lordship can have a single doubt that a people who have gone thus far in support of their liberties, will hesitate a moment to retaliate for every violence offered to their adherents." His letter to Balfour was in a different tone, and reiterated his determination in the strongest language.

In all these proceedings, and this decision, he but reechoed the single sentiment of his army. Without a knowledge of what he had been doing, his officers met together and addressed him a memorial, recommending retaliation upon all British subjects in his power. "Permit us," concludes this document, "to add, that while we seriously lament the necessity of such a severe expedient, and commiserate the sufferings to which individuals will necessarily be exposed, we are not unmindful that such a measure may, in its consequences, involve our own lives in additional dangers; but we had rather forego temporary distinction, and commit ourselves to the most desperate situations, than prosecute this just and necessary war upon terms so dishonorable."

The list of signatures to this paper was headed by that of *Isaac Huger*, and closed by that of *William Washington*. There was but one known name of the army not upon it, that of Lee, and he was absent on the Congaree at the time of its preparation. These proceedings awakened the fears of the British officers

They were followed up by the commitment to the provost guard of several of their number, who had fallen into the hands of Marion. A meeting of the British officers in Charleston expressed their discontents to Balfour, in language which compelled that petty despot to open a negotiation with Greene on the subject of his complaints and threats. Captain Barry, his secretary, was appointed on the British side, by Balfour, with full powers to discuss and adjust the difficulties between the respective arms; but circumstances were now in progress which superseded the necessity even for retaliation, which the more deliberate second thought of Greene, in milder moments, made him anxious to escape. Could he have laid his hands upon either or both of the true offenders, Rawdon and Balfour, there would have been no relentings. Their crime had been such as to take from humanity all the sting and pain which still follows even upon the necessity of doing justice upon the criminal. The question was finally referred to Congress, and belongs to the many which were closed rather by the close of the war itself, than by any special consideration of the subject. We must return to the business of the campaign.

Stuart, left by Rawdon in charge of the British army at Orangeburg, was not for several weeks in a condition to move with his weary and discontented troops. Greene, meanwhile, uncertain of his future objects, but not doubting that the want of provisions would lead him to the banks of the Santee or Congaree, took measures for gleaning the resources of the country from before his path, and transferring his harvests to the northern side of both these rivers, thus increasing his own while cutting off the supplies of his enemy. The superiority of the Americans in cavalry, enabled them very successfully to perform this operation. At length, Stuart advanced on the route to M'Cord's ferry, taking post on the south side amid the hills near the confluence of the Congaree and Wateree. Here, with two large rivers running between, the two armies lay in sight of their opposing fires, sharpening their swords for future conflict. The intense heat of the weather prevented any present encounter, while the barriers offered by the rivers secured each from any danger of surprise. But the cavalry of the Americans were not inactive. Colonel Washington was detached down the country, across the Santee; the north bank of the Congaree was swept by Lee. The latter was sent to operate with Colonel Henderson, who had succeeded to the command of Sumter; the former to cooperate with Marion and Mayham, in covering the country on the Lower Santee, striking at the detachments, the convoys, and the posts of the enemy, between his camp and Charleston, whenever opportunity offered. Colonel Harden, meanwhile, with a body of mounted militia, gathered beyond the Edisto, had it in charge to traverse that region of country, and in like manner to strike at and straiten the operations of the enemy.

Speaking of the performances of these several detachments, at this period, Greene asserts that "their character for enterprise was never excelled." Washington soon succeeded in falling in with two parties of British horse, which he dispersed, making fifty prisoners. Lee, penetrating between the main body of the British and his post at Orangeburg, and in sight of the latter place, drove in, dispersed, and captured, several other parties. His communications constantly interrupted, and his supplies cut off, Stuart found himself in sight of provisions that he could not reach. He was compelled to draw his resources from below. To render this easy, he formed a line of posts—re-establishing that of Dorchester, and erecting a new one at Fairlawn, at the head of naviga tion on Cooper river. From this point the route of transportation to his headquarters was by land wholly; but with Marion, Washington, and Mayham, on the watch at all points, his means of subsistence became momently more and more precarious.

With his detachments thus engaged, Greene was anxiously looking on every hand for the recruits and reinforcements which had been promised him. His repeated disappointments, hitherto, had somewhat reconciled him to their recurrence. With the eight hundred Pennsylvanians, under Wayne, which he had been led to expect early in August, he must have overwhelmed his adversary, whose position left him entirely open to the American general, should his strength ever enable him to take advantage of the circumstance. But Wayne had been diverted from Carolina to Yorktown. Greene's North Carolina levies were sent to him without arms, and he had none with which to provide them. A corps of Georgians, one hundred and fifty in number, which had been raised by Colonel Jackson, were all of them seized with smallpox at the same time, fully one third of them perishing with the disorder. Of three thousand five hundred North-Carolinians which had been promised, less than five hundred made their appearance. Seven hundred mountaineers, under Shelby and Sevier, were to be with him by a certain day, and were already *en route* for the scene of action, when, hearing exaggerated accounts of the successes of Greene in the pursuit of Rawdon, they turned back, and wrote him, that they presumed he longer needed their assistance. Sumter, meanwhile, sick and offended, had retired from service, leaving his command to Henderson, few in number and grievously discontented.

But Greene's necessities were too pressing to permit him to brood long over his deficiencies. The state of affairs at the north left him no time to deliberate. "We must have victory or ruin," is the language of his impatience, addressed in one of his letters to Lee; and he adds, that to obtain the former he will spare nothing. Calling in his detachments, he broke up his camp at the High hills, on the 22d of August, a season when the heats are still quite too excessive, and the climate too sickly, to make active operations either grateful or successful. Great rains had swollen the swamps and water-courses, and an approach to his enemy required a tedious circuit to be made. He could only cross the Wateree by ascending to Camden. It was by this route that he reached Howell's ferry, on the Congaree, on the 28th. Here he was advised that Stuart, hearing of the movements of the American army, had fallen back upon his reinforcements, and taken post at the Eutaw springs. The British had moved by forced marches, and it was no longer in Greene's power to force him into action. Lee was instantly pushed forward to watch his movements, and Pickens, who had succeeded to the command of the troops of the state, was ordered to advance, leisurely, and take such a position as would enable him to keep an eye on the British garrison still at Orangeburg. These deliberate movements on the part of Greene, indicative, as it were, of a want of confidence in his own strength, had the desired effect on the British general. It had been the fear of the American, that his adversary, taking the alarm, would take his position too nearly to the garrison of the metropolis to be approached with safety—thus cutting off all the hope that he cherished of crippling him by a battle. Reassured by the cautious progress of Greene, Stuart came to a halt, and as Marion had recently disappeared from below, on one of his secret expeditions, he withdrew his garrison from Fairlawn, ordering the latter up to reinforce him for the conflict. Greene, meanwhile, continued his march, still very deliberately, and, encamped at Motte's, near the spot which the British had recently abandoned. This cautious progress served to disguise his real desires, and to dissipate the fears of his adversary. With the accession to Stuart's strength of the garrison at Fairlawn, that of Orangeburg being ordered to another, which was admirably chosen for supporting the main army, Greene perceived that his adversary was preparing for the chances of a struggle. But the American general had sufficiently concealed his real wishes, and lulled the British colonel into a false security. The former, accordingly, was permitted to approach within a few miles of his position, and Marion to form a junction with him, without any suspicion of the fact being entertained in the camp of the British. The order for Marion's junction with the main army is dated the 4th of September, and on the 5th we find him seventeen miles above the enemy, and in advance of his superior. On the afternoon of the 7th, the army had reached Burdell's tavern, on the Congaree road, seven miles from the Eutaw springs. Here, having effected a junction with all his detachments, Greene made his preparations for measuring swords, the next day, with his antagonist. His baggage, tents, and everything that might delay or embarrass his movements, had been left behind, at Motte's; and, with the exception of the tumbrils, the artillery, and two wagons containing hospital stores and rum, not a wheeled carriage accompanied the army. Greene's fare was that of the common soldier. That night, which was to precede a desperate struggle with his enemy for superiority, he slept beneath the shade of an ancient China-tree, the huge roots of which, bulging from the earth, yielded a natural pillow for his head.

CHAPTER XX.

Battle of Eutaw Springs.

THE memorable battle of Eutaw springs, by which British supremacy was fairly prostrated in South Carolina, was fought on the 8th day of September, 1781 The American force, as we have seen, lay the night before at Burdell's tavern, seven miles from the scene of battle. It consisted of about two thousand men, while that of the British, under Colonel Stuart, at Eutaw, was estimated at two thousand three hundred. The superiority of the Americans lay in their cavalry — a superiority more than counterbalanced by the position which the British occupied, which was that, measurably, of a fortified place; and by the quality of their troops, which were all well disciplined. Among their old regiments fought a large number of American tories and deserters, who added to the discipline of the regular service a rare skill as marksmen, and whose stubbornness in the conflict might safely be relied on, when the peculiar peril in which they stood is considered.

It was at four o'clock in the morning that the American army moved from its bivouac. It marched in four columns, in the following order: The South Carolina state troops and Lee's legion formed the advance, under the command of Colonel Henderson. The militia both of North and South Carolina, under the lead of Marion, followed next. Then came the regulars, under General Sumner: and the rear was brought up by Washington's cavalry and the Delawares of Kirkwood, under the command of the former. The artillery moved between the columns. The troops were thus arrayed, and marched in order of battle. The day was one of the most oppressive heat, and the progress of the army was necessarily slow. But, up to the moment of its movement, and, indeed, not until it was fairly in progress, did Stuart have any idea of its approach, so completely had the light detachments cut off the communication of the British with the country around them, capturing, on the night before the battle, the only party which Stuart seems to have sent out in the direction of his enemy's approach. The British colonel appears to have been remiss: but it is not improbable that, conscious of his superiority, in numbers no less than position, he was not unwilling to hazard everything on the chances of a general engagement. The moral of the British army, at this time, required support from victory; and the *prestige* of domestic authority was still more in need of its influence.

Whether prepared or indifferent, the advance of Greene seems to have operated as a surprise upon the British general. So entirely secure did he feel himself in his position, that, while the Americans were getting under arms at Burdell's, but seven miles distant, to march upon him, he was sending forth a foraging party of a hundred men, on the very road along which the former were approaching. This was called a *rooting* party. Its particular purpose was to root for supplies of the sweet potato, then growing, of which the crop was abundant throughout the state, and which, indeed, constituted the chief vegetable in the fields at this season of the year. Stuart was evidently thinking much more of feeding than of fighting.

His foragers were already abroad, and some three

miles from camp, when a couple of deserters from the North Carolina line made their appearance at Eutaw, and communicated the startling intelligence of Greene's approach. This was at six in the morning. Stuart immediately sent out a detachment of infantry and horse, two hundred in number, under Captain Coffin, to reconnoitre the American position, and to cover and bring in his foragers. The American advance had already passed the road which the potato-seekers had pursued, when they were encountered by Coffin. He, ignorant of the strength of this force, and not dreaming that it constituted the advance of the army, which he supposed to be still lying where it had been left by the deserters, charged it with a blind confidence which resulted in his defeat and dispersion. The report of firearms drew the foragers out of the fields, and the whole of this party fell into the hands of the Americans, with several slain and wounded, and fifty prisoners, of Coffin's detachment.

The audacity of Coffin, in thus boldly charging his advance, impressed Greene with the belief that the British army was at hand. The pursuit of Coffin, after the dispersion of his force, had been forborne for the same reason; and thus it was, that, while Stuart was pushing forward a detachment of infantry, a mile in advance of his position, with orders to engage and detain the Americans while he formed his men and prepared for battle, the latter were ordered to a halt upon the march. Greene was naturally desirous to secure as much time for his raw troops as possible, in order that they might form with coolness, and refresh themselves before the conflict. Had less caution been shown, the detachment of Coffin might have been entirely cut off, as the arrival of the fugitives at camp, had been so nearly simultaneous with that of their pursuers, as to have secured to the

Americans all the advantages, in the conflict which ensued, of a complete surprise.

The militia column of Greene, when displayed, formed his first line. The South-Carolinians, in equal divisions, occupied the right and left, with the North-Carolinians in the centre. Marion commanded the right, Pickens the left, and Colonel Malmedy the centre. Henderson, with the state troops, including Sumter's brigade, covered the left of this line, and Lee, with his legion, the right. The column of regulars also displayed in one line. The North-Carolinians, in three battalions, under the several commands of Colonel Ashe and Majors Armstrong and Blunt, occupied the right, and were marshalled by General Sumner. The Marylanders, under Colonel Williams, were on the left. They formed two battalions, commanded by Colonel Howard and Major Hardman. The Virginians, forming two battalions also, led by Major Sneed and Captain Edmonds, occupied the centre, and were commanded by Colonel Campbell. The artillery, consisting of four pieces, two *three* and two *six*-pounders, under Captain Gaines and Captain Brown, were divided equally between the columns, and moved severally with each. Colonel Washington, with his cavalry and the Delawares of Kirkwood, as a reserve, still marched in the rear, in column, with orders to maintain his cover in the woods. In this order the army moved steadily forward.

But the advance was necessarily slow. The country on each side, being mostly in woods, presented continual obstacles to the preservation of order. A cheerful constancy marked the progress of the troops. The day was clear and cloudless, and, but for the oppressive heat of the September sun, the rays of which, in the south, are perhaps more fatal to life than those of any other season, the progress might have appeared an advance rather to conquest than to conflict. The short but spirited rencontre with Coffin's detachment was encouraging, and full of pleasant auguries; and the halt and brief rest which they had taken, to say nothing of certain free draughts of the then popular beverage of rum and water, of which Greene had made sufficient provision, had given them new impulse to press forward in search of the enemy. The interval was not great between the parties. The delay in the approach of the Americans had afforded Stuart sufficient time for making all his preparations. His advance, as we have seen, consisting of a strong body of infantry and a field-piece, was thrown out a mile from his camp for the purpose of skirmishing with and retarding the American approach. This division was encountered spiritedly by the American first line, before which it gradually yielded. The opposing parties kept firing as the one advanced and the other retired, until the British party was received into its own line of battle, and the presence of their whole force, with their artillery in the main road, counselled the American skirmishers to disappear into their proper places in their own columns.

The position of the British, strong originally for defence, was rendered more so by the judicious arrangement which Stuart had made of his forces. His troops were drawn up in one line, the right of which was covered by the Eutaw creek. This lovely little streamlet, which issues from secret avenues of limestone, pursues a stealthy course beneath high banks and a dense umbrageous thicket. The ground on which the British line was drawn up was entirely in wood. Their left, which "was in air," employing the military language, was supported by Coffin's cavalry, and a strong detachment of infantry, which was held closely in reserve, but at a convenient distance, in the shelter of the wood. The only open grounds in the neighborhood, were those which formed the precincts of a plantation settlement and dwelling-house, the cleared fields of which lay immediately in the rear of the British position. The dwelling-house was of brick, two stories in height, with garret-rooms, the windows of which commanded all the open space around. This house was abundantly strong to resist the fire of infantry, and a garden in its rear, enclosed by a picket fence, increased its facilities for defence, and afforded an excellent temporary shelter in the event of disaster. A large barn, and various outhouses of wood, might also contribute to these objects. In the open ground, south and west of the house, the tents of the British encampment were left standing, while their line was formed for battle in the foreground. The rear was in great degree covered by the broken character of the country, deep thickets of the scrubby oak or blackjack, and occasional ravines. Where this was not the case, the land lay level, but in the original forest, pierced only by the single great avenue leading to the metropolis, and a narrow wagon track to Nelson's ferry, on the neighboring river. The British commander, in plain terms, had made the most of his position. The right of his line was composed of the third regiment, "the Buffs." The *debris* of several corps, led by Cruger, occupied the centre, and the left, having no natural advantage of position, was confided to two veteran regiments, the sixty-third and sixty-fourth. In the thickets by which Eutaw creek is bordered, a command of three hundred picked troops was given to Major Majoribanks, whose business it was to watch the American flank, while guarding his own, and to take advantage of any opening in the former, which should invite or justify attack. Major Sheridan, with a command of infantry, was ordered to seize upon and hold the dwelling-house at Eutaw, in the event of any misfortune, and from this point to cover the movements of the army. The artillery of the British occupied the main road. We have nothing now to delay our progress, in passing to the great struggle of the day.

The skirmishing parties driven in by the American advance) consisting chiefly of the Carolina militia, Henderson's state troops, and Lee's legion, forming the American first line), disappeared in the rear, leaving their pursuers opposed to the whole line of the British army. Stuart maintained his position, designing, as he found himself opposed only to militia, to repel the attack without advancing. His anxiety was only felt at the approach of the second or American line of regulars, for which he wished to hold his men steadily and with firmness. But the militia on this occasion were superior to that ordinary class with which he had been accustomed to deal. They might not be willing to stand the charge of the British bayonet, for which no weapons or training had prepared them, but they had long since learned in what manner to stand fire. They were the men of Marion and Pickens, leaders in whom they had perfect confidence, and who never failed to extract good service out of them. Their behavior this day was that of veterans; and as the field-pieces of Gaines were wheeled forward to answer the bellowing thunders of those which confronted them from the British line, along the road, the steady fire and keen aim of the southern marksmen, continued to tell, with fearful effect, upon their serried infantry, whose regular volleys of musketry, with louder echoes, were yet very far from doing the fearful execution which followed the sharp crack of the deadly rifle. Stuart soon found that he should vainly contend with such enemies, while he occupied his original position. At the long arm, they were more than a match, this first line of militia, for all his army. It was with surprise and delight that Greene beheld them advance with shouts of defiance into the very blaze of the enemy's fire, unaffected by the fall of comrades, and only seeking, with cool and resolute purpose, in what manner to avenge them. But the artillery of Gaines, by this time, had been demolished; one of the enemy's four-pounders had shared the same fate. The carnage on both sides was great, and the militia, though counting their bullets, were receiving the unremitted fire of a line more than twice the number of their own. A forward movement of the enemy at length forced them to retire, but not until seventeen rounds had been delivered.

General Sumner, with his three battalions of North-Carolinians, was then ordered up to the support of the militia. This corps was composed of new levies, but they had been under discipline, and behaved handsomely. The battle was resumed with all its former fury, and, with the appearance of Sumner's division, Stuart was compelled to order into line on his left the infantry of his reserve. The struggle was thus continued by fresh troops on both sides — without, however, relieving some of those who had been at work from the commencement of the action. Such was the case with the infantry of the American covering parties, both on the right and left of the line. The legion infantry was engaged on the right with the sixty-third; while Henderson, on the left, with the troops of the state, had been thrown into the most exposed situation of the whole field, in consequence of the American left falling short of the British right, and subjecting it to the oblique fire of a large proportion of this wing of the enemy, together with that of the battalion under Majoribanks, which was also in cover of the woods. These were new troops, and their constancy was severely tried. Henderson entreated to be permitted to charge the enemy opposed to him, and in this way extricate himself from a fire with which he could not contend equally; but any such movement must have periled the flanks of the militia, and exposed the artillery: and the brave colonel held his position, sustained with unflinching fortitude by all his command, until he was disabled by a wound. With the appearance of Sumner, and the resumption of the battle, order was restored in his detachment, now under the command of Colonel Wade Hampton, sustained by Colonels Polk and Middleton, and they continued in the fight until Sumner's brigade, after a noble contest, yielded in turn to the fire of numbers much greater than their own. The British had gained the advantage, but it was only by bringing their reserve into action. All their strength was now engaged in the *melée*, while the greater part of the second line of the Americans, with the whole of their reserve and cavalry, hitherto unemployed, were wholly fresh for action. Of this fact, warmly engaged in the excitement of the struggle, the British line knew nothing. With the yielding of the American centre before them, they concluded the victory to be won, and, exulting in the prospect, they darted forth as if to secure the prey. This was the very moment for which Greene had been watching. Pressing forward with loud shouts, the British line became disordered, and, seeing his moment, the American general gave the order to the commander of the second line—"Let Williams advance and sweep the field with his bayonets!" The rival regiments of Maryland and Virginia, the one led by Williams, the other by Campbell, rushed forward with trailed arms to obey it. Reserving their fire, they hurried on with shouts of exultation, and preserving their order, while exhibiting the highest degree of emulation, they moved to the fatal charge. Within forty yards of the enemy, the Virginians poured in a destructive fire, when the whole line pressed forward to finish the work with naked steel. With their advance the British line showed symptoms of disquiet, and began to retrograde in some disorder. At this lucky moment, the legion infantry of Lee, on the extreme left, availing itself of the exposure of the British flank, delivered a heavy enfilading volley, and followed it up with a charge of bayonets. This confirmed the apprehensions of the enemy, and their left was thrown into irretrievable disorder. But their right and centre still appeared immoveable. It was now for the Marylanders to do what the Virginians had rather precipitately done before. They threw in a fatal fire of their whole brigade, and the panic which already pervaded the British left extended to the remaining divisions. No troops ever came nearer to the actual crossing of the bayonet: so nigh were they, indeed, that the opposing officers sprang at each other with their swords. But the appearance of a conflict so desperate was only for an instant. "The Buffs" alone stood firm against the shock, and, for a while, the mutual thrust of the bayonet transfixed the opposing combatants in their several ranks. But the fire of the Marylanders, followed up by their desperate charge, swept away all opposition. The whole line of the enemy gave way. The rout was complete, the fugitives hurrying away to seek the shelter of the post already designated for this purpose, in the event of disaster, while many, with a nameless terror, sped forward to carry the tidings of defeat and dismay to the very gates of Charleston.

The victory was now considered certain, but fortune was about to exhibit one of those caprices which are supposed to prove her blindness. Many, who already joined in the shouts of victory, were yet decreed to bleed. The carnage had only commenced. The Americans pursued the fugitive enemy to their camp. Here, however, the British officers had made their stand. Here, as previously concerted, the dwelling-house had been converted by Major Sheridan into a fortress, which he occupied with a strong body of infantry; while others were busy in arresting the fugitives in their flight and subduing them to order under the cover of the fences and pickets. Majoribanks, with his detachment of three hundred, still stood firm under cover, in the thickets which border the Eutaw, and where the extreme of the British right, stretching considerably beyond the American left, still betrayed a reluctance to give way. They felt the protection afforded them by his command, and were not insensible to the superiority which they yet possessed over their enemy. The two armies meanwhile—the American right pressing the British left, which no longer offered resistance—were now performing together "a half wheel which brought them into the open ground in front of the house." Greene now saw that unless Majoribanks was dislodged, the Maryland flank would be traversed by his fire. Orders were given to Washington to pass the American left and charge the British right. Colonel Hampton was despatched to co-operate with Washington. The latter, however, had already proceeded in his charge; and, sweeping through the woods with his mounted men only, was endeavoring to break through the dense and almost impervious thicket in which Majoribanks found shelter. While engaged in this endeavor, the fire of Majoribanks was delivered with destructive effect, which emptied a score of saddles, and brought down every officer but two. Washington himself fell, his horse being shot under him, and, while struggling to extricate himself, was bayoneted and taken prisoner. Hampton with his command appeared at this moment, and, collecting the scattered fractions of Washington's, renewed the desperate attempt, but with similar disappointment. His attempt was followed up with more perseverance by Kirkwood's infantry, before whose bayonets the detachment of Majoribanks slowly yielded, still holding their cover in the thicket, and making for a new position, in closer neighborhood with the main army, with their rear protected by Eutaw creek, and sheltered by the pickets of the garden. At this moment the whole British line was flying before the bayonets of the Americans. Their right had imbibed the panic which had seized the left, and were in full flight. Their course lay through their encampment. The Americans were pressing closely at their heels, making prisoners at every step; and the sole hope of the British lay in the possession which Sheridan had taken of the brick dwelling-house which commanded the field —in the compact front which Majoribanks still presented—and in the fact that some of the routed companies, from the left, had made good their retreat into the picketed garden, from which, under a partial cover, they could fire with effect. Even these positions were not gained but with great difficulty. So keen and close had been the pursuit, that detached bodies of the Americans had reached the house before it was yet fairly occupied by the men of Sheridan. An attempt to enter along with them, brought on a severe struggle at the entrance, in which, had the American party been sustained by the appearance of their horse, as they should have been, even this last resort of the British must have been taken from them. The latter prevailed, however, succeeding in effecting their own entrance and excluding their assailants, while their sharp-shooters from the upper windows effectually repelled the audacity of their pursuers. So short was the time allowed them—so narrow was their escape—that they could only secure the dwelling against the Americans by shutting the door in the faces of some of their own officers. These were made prisoners by the former. One of them was a dapper little gallant of the British army, a great ladies' man, a wit, and some thing of a Brummell. This was Major Barry, the secre tary of Balfour, the commandant of Charleston. Barry fell into the hands of Lieutenant Manning, of Lee's legion. Manning, finding the upper windows to be full of British musketeers, about to measure his person with their muzzles, did not scruple to seize Barry, and, before the astonished Briton could conceive his purpose, to hoist him upon his shoulders. Thus covered with the scarlet of a British uniform, with the person of one of their officers completely covering his own, the lieutenant reasonably calculated that he should interpose a sufficient physical as well as moral reason why he should not incur the penalty of a shower of British bullets. It was in vain that Barry interposed in the language of offended dignity: "Sir!" said he, "sir, I am Henry Barry; I am deputy-adjutant of the British army; captain in his majesty's fifty-second regiment; secretary to the commandant of Charleston, &c.; major of," &c. "The very man I was in search of," answered Manning; "I am delighted to make your acquaintance! Fear nothing, Adjutant Barry, fear nothing. It is my policy to take care of you, and I am determined you shall take care of me: we must, in times like these, take care of each other." The Virginian succeeded in carrying off his captive upon his back in safety.

It was at this moment that the fruits of the victory were lost to the Americans. When the pursuing army made their way to the British encampment, and found their tents all standing, filled with "creature comforts" of a character too tempting for a famished soldiery, the business of pursuit was forgotten; the object of strife, the new perils which attended their position. They were unequal to the temptation, and fell to, with fiercest appetite, upon the unwonted luxuries of the British commissariat. They scattered themselves among the tents, and eagerly seizing upon the food and liquor which they contained, became in a short time utterly unmanageable. Irretrievable was the confusion which followed in the ranks of the American army. It was in vain that their officers, exposing themselves to the British marksmen firing from the windows, strove to extricate them from their wretched predicament. But a few corps escaped the pernicious attraction, from the baneful effects of which, upon the army, it was difficult to perceive a remedy. The tents were covered by the fire from the house. This was fast thinning the American officers, whose sense of duty prompting the sacrifice, passed from tent to tent in the hope of bringing the soldiers to their duty. These were fast becoming indifferent to the consequences of their error. Greene was soon conscious of his danger. He saw that, while the fire from the house swept the encampment, Majoribanks, supported by Coffin's cavalry, was watching his moment to engage in the performance. His orders were extended for the legion cavalry to fall upon and disperse the command of Coffin; while the artillery of the second line of the Americans, which had not been dismounted in the conflict, together with a couple of six-pounders which the enemy had abandoned in their flight, were brought forward to batter the house in which Sheridan had taken shelter. Unfortunately, the very ardor of those to whom this duty was intrusted was fatal to its object. They had run the pieces so nearly to the house as to leave them commanded by its musketry. The consequence was, that the artillerists had scarcely opened their fire, which must have compelled the surrender of the garrison, if properly directed, when they were all swept away by the destructive storm of bullets which responded from the house. The guns were left unmanned, utterly abandoned, and, very soon after, a movement of the detachment of Majoribanks threw them into his possession. The orders sent by Greene to Lee, for the dispersion of Coffin's cavalry, did not find the former officer, who was with his infantry. They were delivered to Major Eggleston, with a detachment. He made the charge with promptness and decision, but lacked the force to make the proper impression on the command of Coffin. The latter drove forward, and, but for the timely arrival of Hampton, with his own and the remains of Washington's cavalry, that of Eggleston would have been scattered like chaff before the wind. An obstinate struggle followed, hand to hand, in which the British horse were finally driven back to the shelter of the infantry under Majoribanks. These lay *perdu;* and the eager pursuit of Coffin brought the cavalry of Hampton once more within reach of their destructive fire. The American cavalry recoiled beneath it, were again repulsed and broken, and, availing himself of the moment when they were seeking shelter in the woods, Majoribanks dashed out from his covert, seized the artillery, and dragging it off in triumph, proceeded to feel with his bayonets the tents where still lingered that remnant of the American soldiers who were too inebriate for escape. Greene, with the failure of his artillery, had called off his forces. His army was soon rallied in the cover of the woods; and, though Stuart had now succeeded in forming his line anew, he was in too crippled a condition to venture beyond the cover of the house.

CHAPTER XXI.

The American Army retires to the Hills of the Santee.—Its Condition and that of the British.—The Movements of the Partisans.—Stuart at Wantoot.—The Fall of Cornwallis.—The Hopes it inspired.—Their Disappointment.—Greene marches for the Edisto.—Rapid Approach to Dorchester.—Flight of the Garrison.—Stuart retreats.—Alarm in the British Army.—The Americans take Post on the Round O.

THUS ended this obstinate conflict, in which both sides claimed the victory: the Americans, because the enemy had been driven from the field, and pursued to their encampment; the British, because, in the second struggle, at the encampment, all the advantages lay with them—the Americans being repulsed with the loss of their artillery. Thus far, the claims of both parties may be regarded as very nearly equal. If, with a superior force, the British deserve reproach for being driven from the field, still greater is it to the discredit of the Americans that they should have suffered the victory already in their possession to be lost by misconduct or mismanagement. Unquestionably the affair was mismanaged by the Americans, and there was great misconduct. It is not within the compass of a work like ours to discuss the degree of censure which should apply to those having in charge the duties which were slurred in performance, and the mistakes which led to the disaster. It is enough, in regard to our subject, to say that Greene succeeded in drawing off his several corps in most respects entire. He might still have renewed the battle with advantage, and probably would have done so, but for the excessive heat of the weather, the intensity of which was such that the soldiery might be seen to plunge, for water to quench their intolerable thirst, into puddles which were deeply discolored with the blood of their comrades. Content with having driven his enemy from the field, and so crippled him as to make his further flight to the metropolis essential to his safety, Greene retired for the present to the place where he had spent the previous night, seven miles from the field of battle. He halted on the ground only long enough to collect and bring off his wounded, and make arrangements for burying his dead; and leaving Colonel Hampton with a strong picket to watch the enemy, he withdrew to Burdell's, the only place in which water could be found adequate to the wants of the army.

The losses of the American army, chiefly the result of the second conflict in the open grounds, were very heavy. Their returns exhibited a loss of one hundred and fourteen rank and file killed, three hundred wounded, and forty missing—the aggregate exceeding one fourth of all who marched into battle. The British acknowledged a loss of three commissioned officers killed, sixteen wounded, and ten missing; of rank and file, eighty-two killed, three hundred and thirty-five wounded, and two hundred and forty-seven missing. And yet Greene brought off from the field of battle four hundred and thirty prisoners, not including seventy wounded which Stuart left behind him when, the next day, he abandoned the Eutaws. The American loss had been particularly severe in officers: sixty-one of these had been killed or wounded; of these, twenty-one had died upon the field of battle—the gallant Campbell, of Virginia, among them, dying in the arms of victory—declaring himself "contented," when told that the enemy were flying. The condition of Washington's command particularly provoked the regrets and sorrows of the American general. Their almost desperate charge upon the thickets which covered the detachment of Majoribanks was a proof of the most chivalrous self-devotion. Visiting the hovel where their wounded lay, the evening after the battle, his full heart forced from his lips the apology — "It was a trying duty, but unavoidable. I could not help it."

Feeble as he was, scarcely less crippled than his enemy, and exceedingly deficient in officers, of which he had never been provided with an adequate complement, Greene was by no means insensible to the necessity of grasping all the advantages which must ensue from the bloody struggle which was just ended. He reasonably conjectured that the necessities of his condition would compel the British commander to abandon his position and seek security in Charleston, or be compelled to call up reinforcements from that place for the maintenance of his ground. In order to baffle either purpose, Lee and Marion were despatched, with instructions to cover the avenues between, and cut off the retreat, or arrest the reinforcements; while Greene himself, in the event of Stuart's flight, should press the pursuit, and try the issue of another conflict. But Stuart was even more crippled than the Americans had imagined. His exigencies admitted of no delay. Calling up the garrison at Fairlawn to cover his retreat, he broke up his encampment the day after the battle, destroying his stores, a thousand stand of arms, leaving his dead unburied, and seventy of his wounded to the mercy and care of the Americans. His flight was so rapid as to elude the attempt of Lee and Marion to cast themselves across his path — at least before his junction had been effected with the reinforcement from Fairlawn, which left them too inferior in force to attempt to retard his progress. Greene, himself, at once joined in the pursuit, which was continued for a day, but without overtaking his enemy. Finding the chase fruitless, he determined to give his army a necessary rest, and, after a short halt at the Eutaws, he returned once more to the salubrious hills of the Santee.

Never was respite from toil more necessary. Critical and embarrassing as had been his frequent situations, it was never more so than immediately after the battle at Eutaw. His militia had left or were about to leave him. Of the North-Carolinians there remained but a hundred men, and their term of service was at its close. The South Carolina militia, under Marion, Pickens, Hampton, and others, were necessarily detached for the purpose of covering the country; and the army, now consisting of continentals alone, was burdened with the duty of attending upon nearly six hundred wounded, one half of whom were British: and this at the worst period of the year—when the heat was most excessive, when the acute fevers of the climate were most prevalent, and when exposure by night or day, however slight, was eminently full of peril. Yet his wounded and prisoners were to be conveyed by water through a region of malaria. They were taken in boats up the Wateree, inhaling the fatal miasma of the swamps through which they passed, and suffering accordingly from their subtle and poisonous influences. A muster at the American army at headquarters, ten days after the battle of Eutaw, could not have shown a thousand soldiers fit for duty. Greene has been reproached for moving from the "Hills," and attempting the enemy's post, at so early a period in the season. But we can not, at this late day, do full justice to his motives and necessities. The movement was probably necessary for the encouragement of his militia, and with the view to drive the enemy from a region in which the now rapidly maturing harvests enabled him to supply his exhausted granaries. It was probably taken with the advice of Governor Rutledge, at this time in the American camp, a gentleman admirably informed in the condition of the country, and to whose judgment Greene habitually deferred in most local matters. Nor, indeed, when we regard the consequences of the movement, have we any reason to be dissatisfied. If the American army was enfeebled by the enterprise, its results were far more hurtful to the enemy. If the regulars were prostrated by sickness from taking the field in September, the militia had been busy the whole summer, under Marion and Pickens, exposed to still worse hazards. In all probability the main army suffered rather by its previous repose, than by its subsequent activity; since all experience has served to show that, in a southern climate like that of Carolina, the powers for physical resistance to the approaches of disease are far less easily sustained by a languid mode of life than by that which duly exercises the body and maintains a proper vitality in the skin. Greene's army needed numbers rather than health, not snffering in this latter respect more than is ordinarily the case with armies in midsummer, whether in action or in camp. It was the militia system which kept him feeble, rather than the climate, and, at this very moment we find him complaining only of his numerical weakness, which forbade the efforts which his military judgment rendered him anxiously inclined to make.

His eye was still fixed with yearning upon the career of Cornwallis in Virginia. The very day on which the battle of Eutaw was fought, he received intelligence of the operations of the northern army against his ancient adversary, with the suggestion that, in the exigency of the latter, he would endeavor, by a forced march through North Carolina, to make his escape to Charleston. In this event, how could Greene, with the skeleton regiments of the southern army, arrest his retreat? It was this force which alone would be relied upon for the attempt, yet with what hope or prospect of success could it be used? Still it was necessary to prepare for the event; and, feeble as he was, Greene was well aware of the disastrous consequences which would result to the American cause, should Cornwallis with his division succeed once more in making his way into South Carolina. While mourning, accordingly, over his shattered columns, he yet meditated to throw himself across the path of the British general at all hazards, holding him at bay, if possible, until the army from Virginia could assist him in compassing the game. From his camp at the hills he could dart at any moment in the required direction, and this was a principal motive in resuming his position at this point. Here he once more resumed those toilsome and seemingly little-profitable labors by which he hoped to arouse the contiguous country to a sense of their duties and his necessities. The governors, lawyers, and chief men, of the neighboring states, were addressed with the thrice-told tale of privation, and urged, with strenuous arguments and entreaties, in behalf of new and energetic movements for the relief and increase of the army proper. Again was the prayer for reinforcements almost desperately urged in quarters which had but too frequently listened with dull ear before; and thus passed the months of September and October, with little relief to the monotony of labors which were compelled by a sense of duty; but he was too often mortified by repulse not to feel in the performance much more weariness than hope.

Meanwhile, Stuart had recovered from his panic. The report of the probability of Cornwallis's approach had reached him also, and had prompted him to a demonstration, which was perhaps quite as much intended for the recovery of public opinion, as with the view to any more important advantages. Collecting reinforcements from below, and strengthening his cavalry, he pushed the

American detachments from before his path, and once more advanced upon the Eutaws. Marion and Hampton were both compelled to retire across the rivers; and the apprehension was felt that, should he cross the Santee, his power might be re-established. But he was probably too feeble to venture so boldly, and the conjectures with regard to Cornwallis gradually gave way to other conclusions. Active measures were adopted by the governors of Virginia and North Carolina to arrest his flight to the south; and a movement of the loyalists in North Carolina, which had probably been inspirited by the reports in relation to Cornwallis, had been suppressed; while the subsequent evacuation of Wilmington lessened the apprehensions of the whigs of that neighborhood in relation to the future. The British army, meanwhile, in South Carolina, had taken post at Fludd's plantation near Nelson's ferry. Its strength at this place, increased by reinforcements, consisted of more than two thousand men, not including a detachment of three hundred at Fairlawn under M'Arthur. In addition to this, the loyalists from the upper country had been enrolled, either independently or with the British regiments, and formed a considerable addition to their active infantry. Their cavalry had now become superior to that of the Americans, in consequence of the severe handling which the latter had received recently; and it was not until that of Sumter's brigade could be again brought together, with the wounded infantry of Marion, Horry, and Mayham, that the superiority of Greene in this arm could be restored. For a brief period, accordingly, Major Doyle, who had succeeded temporarily to the command of the British force on the Santee — Stuart still suffering from a wound received at Eutaw — exercised undivided authority over the country south of the Santee and Congaree, and west of the Edisto. He made hay during his brief period of sunshine, sweeping off with greedy hands every negro young and old, that he could possibly gather into his clutches in this extensive territory. The presence of Marion, guarding every accessible point along the river, alone arrested him in his paternal desire to extend the same covering arms over the opposite region. To protect the country as well as he could with his light troops, was all that Greene could do. He had no force with which to confront that of the enemy. We have shown his condition ten days after the battle of Eutaw.

The approach of winter found it still more hazardous and discouraging. His troops were wanting the absolute necessaries of life — medicines were wanting — salt had failed. For two years, the southern army had received no pay — no clothing — were often short in the usual allowance of meat and bread, and commonly subsisted without ardent spirits. Symptoms of mutiny were actually beginning to show themselves in camp, and a victim expiated upon the gallows his impatience under sufferings which had strictly followed the failure of the government to comply with its contracts. Greene could only sympathize and weep over misfortunes that he could not prevent. He strove to soothe the sufferings of his people — shared those sufferings — was early and late engaged in the work of tendance and watching — now in the ranks, now at the hospitals, encouraging by kind offices, entreating with gentle arguments, and, with a thousand anxieties moving him to querulousness and impatience, subduing his own discontents that he might soften theirs. The superior care of strengthening his army against the enemy, and in becoming employment, was necessarily his worst anxiety. Yet, in this work, he was constantly thwarted by others who were more considerate of the objects under their immediate eyes, than of those which were remote, however vital to the cause. We have seen how small had been the regard shown by Congress and the north to the army of the south. Greene was destined, in his moment of greatest necessity, to suffer from another proof of this selfish partiality. It was at the very moment when the time of service of the Virginia line was about to expire, with not a single recruit from that state on the march to supply its place, when he was advised that his reinforcements from Maryland and Delaware, seven hundred in number, had been arrested and embodied with the army against Cornwallis. Yet these had been regarded as absolutely necessary to enable him to keep the field. He had voluntarily abandoned to Virginia and Lafayette all other reinforcements. Yet, at this very time, the New England states had a countless multitude of troops on paper, myriads if we may believe the chronicles, and there was actually a force of six thousand Frenchmen operating with the army of Washington and Lafayette against this very force of Lord Cornwallis. Well might the officers and soldiers of the southern army feel themselves abandoned, if not sacrificed. "Why struggle longer—they have abandoned us—let us yield the contest—let us retire." "Never," cried Greene with a noble constancy of purpose, as the murmur reached his ears:—"I will deliver this country or perish!" He was willing to meet all the peril, to make all the sacrifice, to continue the almost hopeless-seeming struggle to the last, unsupported, unassisted, if the struggle and the endurance were necessary for the safety of the country, and if that country could do nothing better for the cause. And yet he is compelled to remark in a letter to Washington—"I am told your force in Virginia amounts to little less than fifteen thousand men; if so the Maryland troops will be of little or no consequence." His officers and men were not equally patient with himself, and one of his chief labors was to quiet them. Fortunately, one of his subjects of anxiety was soon to cease.

On the 9th of November, the grateful intelligence reached the camp of the fall of Yorktown and the capture of Cornwallis, an event which had taken place fully twenty days before. The day was observed as a jubilee. All punishments were remitted, all prisoners discharged, and the few luxuries that were to be found in camp were distributed with liberal hand, that no countenance might remain darkened at a moment when the occasion was so full of joy. It was now the hope of Greene that the French fleet and army might co-operate with him in an attempt on Charleston, and that the army which had captured Cornwallis might be set in motion for the south. But the co-operation of the French commander could not be secured; and, in respect to the northern army, those who knew with what difficulty the New England troops could be persuaded to approach Yorktown, could have but little expectation of persuading them still further south. They constituted about one third of Washington's army; and the detachments sent to Greene were drawn entirely from the contingents of Maryland and Pennsylvania. These were confided to the command of General St. Clair and Wayne. They were now compelled, in midwinter, to traverse a weary extent of territory, and when they reached the camp of Greene, which they did not until the 4th of January, 1782, their number was less by one half than when it crossed the Potomac.

Advised, however, of this promised reinforcement, upon which he was taught to build largely, Greene felt the necessity, at an early period in October, of resuming active operations. He was able, during this month, to replace the six-pounders which he had lost at the Eutaws, and was joined about this time by Colonels Shelby and Seviere with five hundred mountaineers; a detachment of one hundred and sixty North-Carolina recruits was also added to his infantry; his wounded were recovering and able to take their place in the ranks, and the harvest being in and the cool weather beginning to prevail, the several commands of Sumter, Marion, and the other parti sans, had been collecting around their favorite leaders. The army once more began to assume that appearance of strength and order which promised usefulness and demanded employment. Seviere and Shelby, with Horry and Mayham, were placed under Marion, whose scene of operations was the country between the Santee and Charleston. Together they formed a very efficient command of cavalry, mounted infantry, and riflemen. Sumter, with his brigade of state troops, and some companies from his own, and the militia brigades of Pickens, was ordered to take post at Orangeburg, and to cover the country from the forays of the loyalists assembled in Charleston. Pickens, with two regiments, traversed the mountain frontiers, checking at all points the civil war, which ever and anon flamed up in that quarter; and overawing the hostile Indians who were always in readiness to rise.

These several parties soon found employment and were kept watchful. Sumter's command was soon tasked to arrest the upward progress of General Cunningham, with a strong body of seven hundred loyalists, whose aim was to regain position in the upper country, and who, gaining some advantages over one of Sumter's detachments, compelled the later to fall back to a position of greater security. The force of the two parties being nearly equal, they were employed for awhile as checks upon each other. Marion was also brought to a halt by encountering Colonel Stuart at Wantoot with a force of nearly two thousand men, a force quite too great to be attempted by a command so inferior as that of our partisan. Stuart's object was provisions and plunder. Anticipating the siege of Charleston, naturally, as the result of the fall of Yorktown, and the leisure which that event must afford to the army and the navy of the French, he was diligently accumulating supplies; including, in this category, thousands of slaves, who were useful in the laborious work of fortifying the place, and, in the event of its fall, profitable as plunder in the West India markets. The British were still superior to the Americans in number; but the moral of their army had been greatly impaired by recent events. The affair at the Eutaws, had grievously lessened their enterprise, while it had shown in the native militia an audacity and hardihood, which greatly encouraged their own, and the hopes of their leaders. With an ample commissariat, Greene could have attempted boldly; but the very shifts to which his necessities reduced him were of a kind to impair the virtues of his soldiers and to lessen their efficiency in all respects. In the ordnance and quartermaster's departments everything was wanting. There was no ammunition — half of the troops were without tents — there were no axes, few camp-kettles, and, until this period, no canteens. Mere valor, courage, and constancy, in the soldiers, were of little avail under these deficiencies. The moral sufficed to encourage their general in a bold demonstration, and his reliance was rather upon this moral, and upon its inferiority in the enemy, than upon any of the substantial resources by which an army's victories are won. But it was useless to repine at wants which no complaining could supply; and it was Greene's hope to remedy, by energy and skill, the defects of fortune. On the 18th of November, the camp on the hills was again broken up and the army set in motion for below. The line of march led by Simons' and M'Cord's ferries, through Orangeburg to Riddlespurgers, and thence by the Indian Field road where that road crosses the Edisto to Ferguson's mill. The design of Greene was to take post on the Four Holes, for the twofold purpose of covering the country beyond him and controlling the operations of the enemy on his right. To secure the army in this progress, Marion, supported by Captain Eggleston with the legion, strengthened by a detachment of the Virginia line, was ordered to keep in check the force under Stuart. Without this security on his left, Greene would scarcely have ventured upon a position so much exposed to an attack from Charleston. But Marion was suddenly stripped of a large portion of his detachment by the desertion of his mountaineers, to whom, at this moment, the employment was not sufficiently active, and who, becoming discontented, had gone off in a body. This was a loss of five hundred men at a moment's warning, and after a service of three weeks, in which Fairlawn was captured, and the tributary posts on Cooper river disquieted by frequent demonstration, to which the disappearance of the mountaineers put a sudden finish. But for the vast proportion on the sick list of the British troops under Stuart, the flight of the mountaineers would have seriously compromised the safety of Marion, operating as he did in the neighborhood of the post which the former occupied.

Fortunately for Greene and Marion, the movement of the former across the Congaree, had alarmed the British general for his own safety. He seems not to have suspected the feebleness of the one or the difficulties and deficiencies of the other, and no doubt still apprehended from the appearance of a French fleet upon the coast. He was prompted to strike his tents and draw off toward Charleston. This movement, evincing a complete ignorance of the condition of the Americans, and a consciousness of his own weakness, encouraged Greene to an enterprise which was calculated to confirm all the false impressions of the enemy, and, by forcing him within the walls of Charleston, to secure possession of the whole country without striking a blow. This was an important object, as, at this very juncture, Governor Rutledge was about to re-establish the American authority by calling the legislature into existence. Proclamations were already issued for the general election of members.

Confiding the army, still on its march, to the care of Colonel Williams, Greene moved briskly forward on the route to Dorchester at the head of four hundred men, cavalry and infantry. The cavalry consisted of Lee's and Washington's commands, and a hundred men from Sumter's. The infantry, including detachments from the lines of Maryland and Virginia, was that of the legion. Greene flattered himself with the hope that, in addition to his other objects, he should surprise Dorchester. For this purpose he scattered his cavalry abroad with the view to cut off intelligence, covering as large a space in his front as possible. With the same object he pursued difficult and obscure routes, by swamp and unsuspected paths, wherever these could be found. But, in spite of these precautions and the celerity of his movements, the garrison at Dorchester was apprized of his coming. There were too many lurking tories in the swamp thickets, too many outlying negroes, who knew the value of such intelligence, not to seek for its reward. The tidings of his approach reached the British twelve hours in advance of himself. They lay on their arms at Dorchester all night, and, on the next morning, despatched a reconnoitring party of fifty loyalists which fell into the hands of Colonel Hampton's horse, who suffered few to escape. The report of the fugitives, brought out the whole body of the British cavalry at the post. These were accompanied by a strong detachment of infantry. Hampton soon appeared and darted upon this force consisting chiefly of loyalists. They shrunk from the encounter and succeeded in making their way back into the garrison; but not without losing, killed, wounded, and taken, some thirty of their number. The presence of the commander of the American army at once inspired the garrison with a belief that his whole force was approaching. With this conviction, they destroyed their stores that night, flung their cannon into the Ashley, and commenced their retreat for Charleston. Destroying a contiguous bridge in their flight, they arrested the pursuit of Greene, who, indeed, was by no means inclined to press it, since the infantry of the enemy, alone, exceeded five hundred in number. They halted at the Quarter-house, less than six miles from Charleston, where they were joined by Colonel Stuart with his command. Here, active preparations were begun for the purpose of resisting the advance of the Americans. Rumor had so magnified the strength of Greene, that, in addition to the regiments which could be spared from the garrison at Charleston, the British general Leslie proceeded to the desperate measure of enrolling and arming the negroes. They were stripped of their uniforms as soon as the panic was at rest.

Greene had attained his object. No demonstration could have been more brilliant or more successful. His *ruse* had completely deceived the enemy. At this moment when Stuart was flying before him, when Leslie was marshalling into line, in very desperation, his sable regiments, the American general had not in camp eight hundred men, and, after supplying with ammunition his different detachments, the army had not four rounds left to a man. Well had he deserved the applauses which this enterprise procured him. Williams writes: "Your success at Dorchester would make your enemies hate themselves, if all circumstances were generally known· and the same knowledge would make your friends admire the adventure even more than they do." This was the sentiment of the army. General Washington, writing to Laurens of the affair, remarks: "This brilliant manœuvre is another proof of the singular abilities which that officer [Greene] possesses."

On the 7th of December, Greene rejoined his army which had taken post at Saunders' plantation on the Round O. He now made his arrangements for keeping the ground which he had won. Marion, advancing still nearer to Charleston, kept the right of the enemy in check; Sumter, occupied Orangeburg and the Four-Hole bridge; W. Hampton with a detachment of state cavalry kept open the communication with Marion; Colonels Harden and Wilkinson watched the movements of the enemy along the tract of country lying between Charleston and Savannah; while Lee, in command of the light detachment, posted in advance, kept him from prying into the real weakness of the American army. To watch and wait was all that could be done at present, and while the ammunition of the army did not suffice to fill the cartouch-boxes of the soldiers. It was a redeeming circumstance that Greene was now encamped in a fertile region where rice was in abundance, and where the ranges for cattle were excellent. Here he had room and time for meditation. His thoughts, those excepted which belonged to a consciousness of cares firmly borne and duties faithfully performed, were not of the most grateful description. His reinforcements under St. Clair and Wayne had not yet made their appearance, and advices were received of a British fleet from Ireland, with three thousand troops on board, within two days' sail of Charleston, to be followed by another force of two thousand from New York. There was no reason to discredit this intelligence; and Greene at once felt that any such force in his present circumstances, would expel him from the country. His labor seemed to have been taken in vain. Again the necessity rose before his imagination, for the renewal of all those toilsome marches and countermarches, those anxious days and nights, and weeks, and months, of watch, and vigilance, exposure, trial, suffering; the defeat of hope, the mockery of expectation; the constant disappointment of cherished anticipations, and the as frequent defeat of well-laid schemes; which had followed from the miserable system which had decreed him to the manufacture of bricks without an adequate supply of straw. The British were at work restoring their fortifications, collecting provisions, organizing the loyalists, incorporating the slaves into their ranks, preparing, in short, for a desperate and final struggle, which, in the event of their expulsion from the other states, would leave them secure in the possession of Georgia and Carolina. In the presence of these facts, Greene conceived the idea of recruiting his regiments with negroes also. He had witnessed their fidelity to their masters, their patient docility, and, with a knowledge of their capacity for physical endurance, as well of the climate as of ordinary labor, he assumed that discipline would do the rest in converting them into valuable soldiers. His proposition was submitted to the governor and council and through them to the legislature. It was rejected by that body, and the American general was forced to cast about him for other means of encountering his enemy. Fortunately, his mind was soon relieved in regard to these reported reinforcements. The formidable body of three thousand troops from Ireland was diminished to some sixty artillerists; while the force from New York, consisted of two regiments with a squadron of dragoons one hundred and fifty in number. Greene took heart. Though disquieted at any addition to the enemy's strength, while his own remained as feeble as before, he was determined to maintain his ground against the present army of the British. He declared himself in his letters resolved to fight, and so to fight, as, if beaten, to "make the wounds of the enemy sufficient to prevent his pursuit.'

CHAPTER XXII.

American Attempt on the British Post at John's Island.—Its Failure.—Second Attempt.—Withdrawal of the Garrison.—The Legislature assembles at Jacksonborough.—Its Character.—Governor Rutledge.—His Speech.—Compliments Greene.—Address of the Senate and House of Representatives to Greene.—The latter Body votes him Ten Thousand Guineas.—Liberality of Georgia and North Carolina.

THE drawn battle at Eutaw, in spite of all the subsequent struggles of the British, was really fatal to their power in Carolina. It broke down their spirit, diminished their resources, discouraged their friends, and, in due degree, increased the energy and enthusiasm of their enemies. From this period the real endeavors of the British leaders and their tory allies seem to have been addressed to the acquisition of spoils. Anticipating the approaching necessity which should compel them to abandon the pleasant places in which they had luxuriated so long, they proceeded to "borrow from the Egyptians" in a style less courteous than that which the Israelites employed. The movement of Stuart toward the Santee and that of the loyalists about the same time toward the upper country, were designed for like objects, and hence the importance of the demonstration made by the American general, in his rapid progress toward Dorchester. The effect of that progress was to arrest the spoiler in his employment; to force him to forego the further hope of plunder in the region which he then occupied, and to hurry below with his sick and woundod, crowding them into the already crowded limits of the city. The forces of the British were now cooped up within the narrow limits of "the Neck"—the suburb of the city lying between the rivers Cooper and Ashley, and extending some six miles only into the country—and the islands which lie adjacent to the metropolis. Their whole army had really become only a garrison for Charleston.

To diminish this area by all possible means, Greene conceived the plan of expelling them from John's island, where they still maintained a considerable detachment under Craig. This measure was conceived to be necessary, in order to give proper security to the legislature, now about to assemble at Jacksonborough. This little village lies on the Edisto, and within easy striking distance from the island in question. John's island, in addition to the detachment under Craig, was guarded at every accessible point by galleys carrying guns of heavy calibre. It was ascertained that there was one point of approach to the island, which, at certain periods of the tide, was accessible. Here, at low water, the passage might be forded; and, to cover this point, two well-manned galleys had been stationed within four hundred yards of each other. It was also ascertained that the passage was not watched with any great degree of vigilance, and the attempt upon the island was confided to Colonels Lee and Laurens. The enterprise was one of difficulty and peril, and the movements of the assailing party were required to be made at night. To divert the attention of the enemy from the real point of attack, the main army moved on the 12th of January, 1782, on the route to Wallace's bridge. Two light detachments, meanwhile, under Laurens, crossing the country from Ashley river, headed the north branch of the Stono on the night of the 13th, and advanced to "New-Cut," which is at the head of the south branch. The main army, which had halted on the night of the 12th, as if for the purpose of encampment, was, however, once more put in motion, soon after dark, and, following the route of the light detachments, with the view to supporting them, reached the New-Cut before the hour of low water, at which period only is the ford passable. Here Greene found his attacking party in a state of embarrassment. This select body of troops had been separated into two columns on the march, Lee's column being in advance, and Laurens in person accompanying it. The other column was confided to Major Hamilton, and, not moving at the same time with the former, a guide had been left with it to show the route. No mistake was apprehended, but the guide disappeared while on the march, having probably lost his way, and being ashamed or afraid of the consequences of his error. The column under Laurens was passed over to the island, in the meanwhile, in perfect safety, and there awaited the approach of that under Hamilton. It was not in sufficient strength to attempt the assault without the support of its associate, Craig's force being well posted, numbering five hundred men, and covered by the galleys, which, in the event of an alarm, could effectually cut off the retreat of the assailants and prevent them from receiving help by the only avenue of approach. And this avenue was about to be closed. The tide was now rising, and nothing had been done. It became necessary to recall the detachment of Laurens, before its retreat should be cut off, and the order to this effect, delayed to the last possible moment, was at length reluctantly given. The tide was now running breast high, and a few minutes' longer pause would have compromised the safety of the party. They recrossed, vexed and disappointed, just as day was breaking, and had scarcely regained the main when they discovered the lost column straggling into sight, having been wandering about all night in the vain effort to resume the road from which it had igno rantly gone astray. The annoyance was equally great to all parties. It was one of those mischances, however, which occasion no reproach. The best zeal and courage are thus sometimes thrown away, through ignorance or want of fidelity in inferior agents.

But the object was quite too important to be abandoned without another effort. The garrison might be destroyed; it was necessary that it should be removed, and there were spoils of value to be acquired. Here the British had their pastures, and a large number of cattle had been accumulated, which would be quite as useful to an American as a British commissariat. Greene resolved on forcing his passage to the island. A boat was brought on wagons, and, while his artillery drove the galleys from the station which they occupied, was launched by a party under Colonel Laurens, who passed over to the island. He penetrated to Craig's encampment, but the bird had flown. The British had become acquainted with the narrowness of their escape the night before, and had fled, but so precipitately as to leave several stragglers; while the schooner which they had laden with their baggage, and a hundred invalids, had nearly fallen into Laurens's hands. Their cattle had been driven across the river to the opposite island, or were scattered in the woods. The enterprise had been only in part successful. Carried out as it had been planned, the affair would have been equally brilliant and profitable. Still, the purpose of Greene had been attained: the post had been wrested from the enemy, their field of operations circumscribed, and all chances of peril to the legislature, during its proposed session, from any sudden enterprise of the British, were fairly at an end.

The assembly at Jacksonborough convened on the 18th of January. The civil authority of the state was established under the protection of the army. For that matter, it was as much a military as a civil body, the members, in the majority of cases, being those who had carried and still continued to carry arms, in defence of the country. Greene took post with the army at Skirving's plantation, six miles in advance of Jacksonborough, on the road leading to Charleston. This was on the 16th, two days before the opening of the session. He had, a few days before, been joined by the long-expected detachments under St. Clair and Wayne. The Virginia line had been dismissed, and the reinforcements did little more than supply their place. Believing, however, that the war was virtually at an end in South Carolina, and that its close would be a simple act of withdrawal, at an early period, of the remains of the British power from the country—assured, at all events, that, with the force which he possessed, and the partisan militia, he should be quite able to maintain his ground against the present strength of the British within the state—Greene determined to direct his attention to the recovery of Georgia. The enemy at this time possessed no foothold in the interior of Georgia. His possessions, after the fall of Augusta, had been chiefly confined to the seaboard. His vessels swept the coast from Charleston and Savannah to St. Augustine, without impediment; but his only garrisoned posts in the country, besides Savannah, were at Ebenezer and Ogeechee. Of these he was soon dispossessed by the partisan militia under Twiggs and Jackson; but the country was still traversed by armed bands of tories, and parties from Florida, mixed savages and whites. To strike at Savannah, which was the centre of strength and energy to these wandering parties, and to disperse these parties also, Greene despatched General Wayne, soon after his arrival in camp, with a force consisting of the third regiment of dragoons and a detachment of artillery. He was to assume command of the American army in Georgia.

Hampton's cavalry was also placed at his disposal, and the militia of Carolina along the Savannah river, under General Barnwell, were ordered to co-operate with him whenever called upon. It was impossible, with the inferiority of his own army, to do more for the sister state than he had done. He was considered as perilling himself and the legislature, by stripping himself of these detachments; the more particularly, as the assembling of this body, within hearing of his posts, had given great offence to the British general, who only waited for reinforcements "to resent the insult of convening the legislature to sit and deliberate within hearing of his *reveillé.*"

It is not within our province to review the legislation of this assembly, at this renewal of its civil obligations, under the peculiar circumstances in which we find it placed. That the members should have legislated in all respects temperately and wisely is scarcely to be expected at this juncture, laboring as they did under a thousand excitements and provocations, and fresh from the army without venturing to unbrace the sabre from the side. The convocation of this body had become necessary for the restoration of civil order, for the raising of supplies, the organization of the militia, the very safety of the army. It was necessary, also, with regard to the anticipated evacuation of the city, for the prevention of waste and plunder. For two years the government of the state, where the country was not in the grasp of the enemy, had been solely confided to the individual will and judgment of John Rutledge, its governor. Powers had been conferred upon him to see that the republic sustained no harm. The large discretion thus confided to this remarkable man, were in no instance abused or suffered to rust from non-user. He had traversed the country at all periods, in all difficulties, shared the perils and fortunes of the army for many months, and exercised an equal constancy and ingenuity in enduring privation and providing against emergency. He brought to the necessities of the army the sanction of the civil power, and reconciled to many of the extremities of martial service the high-spirited and impatient volunteers, who are but too apt to suspect the military arm of tyranny and injustice. To restore the power which he had swayed to the people from whom it was obtaiued—to render an account of his administration—to recall the exiles to their homes—to encourage them with hopes of peace and independence—to organize the links of society once more—to bring back obedience to the laws, and reconcile with prosperity and order those liberties for which all the struggle had been taken—was, equally with Greene and Rutledge, a duty and desire. Their responsibilities had been no less heavy than their distinctions had been high; and it was with feelings of equal pride and relief that they welcomed to the halls of council the citizens who had been so long scattered abroad in dismay and apprehension.

The long interval between the fall of Charleston, in 1780, and the present moment, had been one of terrible vicissitudes and the most humiliating necessities. The state had been overborne in the conflict; their regular troops cut up in frequent conflict, and finally made captive; their partisan militia still maintaining the unequal conflict whenever the odds of the combat would allow, and, under favorite leaders, preserving the spirit of liberty and a determined resistance, without other motive than the love of country; and this without pay, or provisions, or clothing, or any supplies needful to the spirit as well as the strength of a soldiery. They had seen their brethren in exile and captivity—wandering as fugitives in swamp and thicket, seeking to elude the bloodhounds set upon their path by the conqueror, or crowded by thousands into the narrow hold of the prison-ship, sweltering with heat and pestilence, and perishing of the most loathsome diseases. Armies furnished by their sister states of the south had been cut off by the rashness of their generals; other armies had been barely kept alive and in safety by a prudence that dared venture nothing in the inferiority of their numbers, and in the neglect of those authorities which failed to provide for the necessities of their starving and naked regiments. But courage and perseverance, constancy and patriotism, had at length succeeded in enduring and in triumphing over all. The bow of promise was arched above the land, and the billows of invasion were slowly but certainly receding from the shores on every side. Well might the noble partisan lift his forehead as he passed from the camp to the council-board, with the gratified sense of a duty well performed and a peril nobly defied and undergone. Nor were the soldiers who met on this occasion, to restore to South Carolina the ægis of law and order, merely men of arms and blood, stern and resolute, with wills made stubborn by habitual authority, and souls set only on its retention and maintenance. The body which assembled at Jacksonborough were men singularly distinguished for talent and moderation; they were citizens first and last — soldiers only under the exigency which denied that they should be citizens of a free state. No people could have assembled in better spirit or temper, more disposed to be considerate of the claims of others, or more indulgent even to their enemies. That they erred in one respect seems to be admitted; but we are scarcely in the situation now to determine of the necessities which at that period compelled men to put on the severe aspects of resentment and indignation, particularly as the enemy still threatened from his fortresses, and still the outlawed tory, leagued with the hireling sav age to desolate the frontier. If the legislature of Jacksonborough seemed to be vindictive in one of its measures, we are not to forget the extent of its provocation, and the dangers which still beset the country, and rendered severity to some the source of security to others, who might otherwise have provoked punishment by presuming on indulgence.

The governor, in his opening address — a masterly performance, which reviewed the history of the interim with a comprehensive and impartial judgment — concluded with a high eulogium upon the conduct of Greene and the troops under him. "I can now," said he, "congratulate you, and I do so cordially, in the pleasing change of affairs, which, under the blessing of God, the wisdom, prudence, address, and bravery, of the great and gallant General Greene, and the intrepidity of the officers and men under his command, has been happily effected." He urged the claims of Greene "to honorable and singular marks of our approbation and gratitude." — "His successes," continued the orator, "have been more rapid and complete than the most sanguine could have expected. The enemy, compelled to surrender or evacuate every post which they held in the country, frequently defeated and driven from place to place, are obliged now to seek refuge under the walls of Charleston and on the islands in its vicinity. We have now full and absolute possession of every part of the state; and the legislative, judicial, and executive powers are in the free exercise of their respective authorities."

The tone and spirit of the governor's eulogy on Greene were met by a corresponding sentiment on the part of both houses of the legislature. They expressed themselves in terms of equal praise and gratitude. The senate declared itself "impressed with a high sense of the eminent services" which he had rendered to the country, and unanimously voted him their thanks, in behalf of the state, "for the distinguished zeal and generalship which he had displayed on every occasion, particularly during the last campaign." They expressed themselves sensible of the many disadvantages under which he took command of the army; and that it was to his "superior military genius and enterprising spirit *were* to be attributed the blessings" which their people now enjoyed — the restoration of their country, and the securities of a free constitution. The house expressed itself in like manner, but gave an additional proof of its gratitude by originating a bill "for vesting in General Nathanael Greene, in consideration of his important services, the sum of ten thousand guineas." This liberality was of great importance to Greene. He was poor. He had left the smithy for the camp. His paternal property, originally small, had not improved in value during his absence, and, in fact, his private resources had been consumed by the exigencies of his public station. He was probably, when this grant was made, not worth a copper in the world. The gift of South Carolina, the spontaneous acknowledgment of her gratitude for his services and sacrifices in her cause, came to him at a seasonable moment, to lighten his heart of its anxieties, and relieve him of the harassing doubts which prompted him continually to inquire of himself, from what quarter, the war being over, should he find the means to support a large and growing family. But the liberality of South Carolina was fruitful of other and similar results. It furnished the proper example to Georgia and North Carolina. These states were not to be outdone, though anticipated, in generosity. The former voted to him five thousand guineas, and the latter twenty-four thousand acres of land.

CHAPTER XXIII.

The State of the Army.—Wayne's Victories in Georgia.—Discontents among the Troops of Greene.—Treachery of Soldiers of the Pennsylvania Line.—Their Detection and Punishment.—Continued Distress and Sickness of the Army.—Movements of the British.—Marion defeats Fraser.—Affair on the Combahee.—Death of Laurens.—Pickens punishes the Tories and the Indians.

LEAVING the legislature free to pursue its deliberations, and heedful only to make it secure while doing so, Greene continued to watch his enemy with a patient anxiety that suffered nothing of consequence to escape his attention. The British afforded him very few opportunities for enterprise. His resources were quite too small to suffer him to attempt anything of magnitude, and they gave him but few provocations to activity in minor matters. They no longer exhibited that impatient desire for performance which had marked their character in the previous campaign, and their endeavors were confined to small predatory incursions, for the collection of plunder or provisions. The war was really transferred to Georgia. Here Wayne was acquiring laurels daily, pressing the enemy on every hand, cutting off his supplies, and sweeping the loyalists from before his face with an unsparing besom. In a little while the British were confined entirely within the precincts of Savannah; and the Georgians, following the example of South Carolina, reorganized their legislative assembly at Ebenezer, within hearing of the British *reveillé* at Savannah, and under the protection of the American army. The result of Wayne's activity was shortly to compel the evacuation of Savannah, an event which increased the number of Greene's enemies in Charleston, since the garrison of the former city, nearly a thousand men, was transferred to the latter. This event rendered necessary the return of Wayne's troops to South Carolina, where, during the progress of events in Georgia, affairs had begun to assume a less encouraging aspect. A variety of unfortunate incidents, which may all be traced to the positive weakness of the army in Carolina, had subjected Marion's command, in the absence of that general at headquarters, or in attending on the legislature, to some vexatious reverses; the result of which was, to lay open the whole country from the Edisto to the Santee to the incursions of the enemy. This region of country had been confided to the keeping of Marion's brigade. In Marion's absence, the brigade was under the command of Horry. A question of rank between this gentleman and Colonel Mayham, who was ranked by Horry, led to the absence of that cordial co-operation between the two which alone could insure the usefulness of the command. Before this quarrel could be settled, the British had obtained several slight successes over some of the parties of the brigade, and finally in Mayham's absence with his horse, the brigade itself was surprised and dispersed at Wambaw, by a sudden movement from Charleston, up Cooper river, of a strong detachment of horse, foot, and artillery, under Colonel Thomson, afterward the celebrated Count Rumford. A subsequent attempt upon the cavalry of this detachment, made by Mayham's horse, under the lead of Marion, was wholly unsuccessful, arising from an unhappy error of the officer who led his column to the charge. Marion's force was thus temporarily dispersed, with a serious loss in arms and horses. His presence, however, sufficed to bring them once more around him in considerable numbers, and to restore confidence among them. The approach of Colonel Laurens to his assistance, with a detachment from the army, soon compelled the British to retire, with the stock and provisions which they had been able to procure, and which, quite as much as the attempt on the brigade, had been the object of the expedition. General Leslie, indeed, had begun to be exceedingly straitened in Charleston by the *cordon* which had separated him from the country. He had been already compelled to butcher the horses of a large portion of his cavalry, which he was no longer in the condition to feed ; and his enterprises were scarcely prompted by any object more inspiring than that of a present necessity. There was no longer, indeed, a motive for enterprise, beyond the support of the garrison. The British ministry were evidently about to forego a contest of which their people were heartily tired. The approach of peace was scarcely to be doubted, and it is not improbable that Leslie's instructions were to economize his strength and resources, and peril nothing further in a conflict in which the hope of triumph was at an end. An occasional foraging party issued from the garrison of Charleston, and, having snatched up its prey, hurried back to the shelter of their lines with a rapidity which mostly mocked pursuit.

The winter wore away in this manner. The legislature of South Carolina, meanwhile, had adjourned. John Mathews had been elected a governor in place of Rutledge, who retired. Mathews was friendly to Greene and to the army; and so, indeed, were most of the members composing the assembly. It was not, therefore, with any wish to embarrass the operations of the army, that a law was passed prohibiting impressments. This put an end to foraging. To provide the army with all necessary supplies, the governor was empowered to take order. A law was enacted requiring that he should, from time to time, appoint a sufficient number of fit and proper persons, in different parts of the state, as agents or commissioners, to procure their supplies. All other persons were strictly forbidden to do so. It was no doubt necessary to arrest the unlicensed foraging, which but too much prevailed, under the alleged necessities of the army, to the distress and impoverishment of the country. But the support of the army was thus made to depend upon commissioners appointed by another authority than that which could determine upon its wants, and who, if incompetent to perform their duties, could only be removed by the appointing power. Meanwhile, the soldiers had no means of procuring supplies. If the commissioner failed them, they must starve and suffer. The commissioner did fail them. In a little time the army was in great distress. The troops were frequently without provisions. Greene remonstrated with the governor, but could not shake his confidence in the person he employed. The army continued to suffer, soothed by entreaties and occasional full supplies, or subdued by severities, which their impatient discontents seemed to provoke. They could plead, in mitigation of their offences, the extremity of their wants. Their nakedness and wretchedness might well excuse their excitements. A very large proportion of them were actually without clothes. The tattered fragments were kept together by thorns of the locust, their substitute for pins and needles; and happy was the wretch who could piece his rags with the refuse of others, better clad, which his better fortune threw in his way. The old troops of Greene bore up bravely under their privations, but the additions to his army, brought by St. Clair, were not calculated to improve its *morale*. The Pennsylvania line was composed of the very mutineers who had triumphed over government in the Jersey insurrection. There was in it, indeed, one of the sergeants who had been put in command of the regiments in that mutiny, with a number of others of like character who had deserted from the British while he had possession of Philadelphia. These wretches were ripe for any mischief, and they were sufficiently practised to refine upon it. The soldiers, brought to the verge of mutiny before their arrival, by their distress and misery, were not helped by their connexion. We shall shortly see the fruits of it.

With the adjournment of the legislature, the army of Greene moved from Skirving's down to Bacon's bridge, on Ashley river. Here he was within twenty miles of the enemy, within striking distance, and accessible by land and water. His securities from any enterprise of the British lay in the latter's sluggishness and his own caution rather than Greene's strength. He was yet to appreciate the element of mischief, within his own camp, of which he had certainly made no calculation while estimating his securities. But, with the opening of spring, it became obvious that a new life was beginning to prevail in the Charleston garrison. Greene was well provided with spies in that city, some of whom, indeed, were persons of no small notoriety. The vigilance of Marion had made this provision, and his judgment of character had secured him against deception. These were now busier than ever, since there was much to report, the secret of which they could not wholly fathom. A new spirit was evidently at work in the British army, significant of objects of importance which could not yet be conjectured. Designs were on foot upon which large calculations were founded. There was an organization of troops, mostly picked men, under select officers. The note of preparation was sounded keenly, though in subdued accents, and all things betokened an enterprise on foot which showed that, if compelled to give up their conquests, the British were not unwilling to crown the humiliating necessity by some redeeming and brilliant performance.

These movements were all conveyed to Greene. He readily conjectured their import. He was sensible equally of the condition of his army, and of the demoralizing influence which had been at work, for some time, to impair its usefulness and increase its discontents. He was by no means ignorant of the *refuse* character of a considerable portion of his late reinforcements. Besides, he was no longer surrounded by those veteran troops who had traversed with him, in weary march and countermarch, the wildernesses of North Carolina — who had fought with him at Guilford, at Hobkirk's, and at Eutaw. His well-tried officers were with him no longer. Williams had returned to Maryland; Howard still suffered from his wounds; Wayne was still gathering laurels in Georgia; St. Clair had obtained leave of absence; the partisans were all operating in detachments; Marion on the left; Pickens among the Indians, while Sumter had retired in disgust. The legion of Lee was almost stripped of its officers, Lee himself having retired, like Sumter, in disgust and dissatisfaction.

Greene felt his danger from his deficiencies. These, at once, led him to suspect the source and secret of his danger, and of the enemy's projected enterprise. His fears were still more enlivened by the discontents and bickerings among many of his remaining officers. Reviewing his condition, the materials of his army, its necessities and discontents, and the various signs which could not entirely escape him, his quick instincts associated the designs of the British with the discontents among his troops. But how these were to operate, he had no knowledge. He could only renew his diligence, his watch, his circumspection, and put in exercise all the agents upon which he could rely for security against mishap. Meanwhile, treason was busy in his camp. His Pennsylvania mutineers, such as had been conspicuous in Jersey, had opened a communication with the enemy. Their discontents were known to the British, and their promises and demands were heard with greedy attention. They were to sell Greene and his army — what the price and what the process, have never been accurately known — and the object was quite too important to the desperate cause of the invader to make him scruple at the scheme, or the conditions upon which it was to be prosecuted. Sergeant Gornell was at the head of the conspiracy. He had entered upon it with equal skill and secrecy. He seems to have been an adept in the business, and his plans were almost matured for execution. A day was fixed upon when a mutinous demonstration of the Pennsylvanians was to be covered and countenanced by the sudden appearance, in force, of the British army. We have seen that the preparations of the latter were of a nature to render the scheme successful, should it once be permitted to attain full ripeness in the American camp.

Fortunately, it was destined that such should not be the case. The conspirators had grown insolent from impunity, and, in degree as they became confident of success, they grew careless of the means of security. Their mutinous language reached the ears of their superiors, and increased their vigilance. An attempt to work upon the fidelity of the Maryland line, was the first clue to their secret machinations, and the keen ears of a woman, one of the followers of the camp, arrived at other clues, which conducted to the conspiracy. This was all that was required to enable justice to decide upon her victims. The vigilant eyes of Greene had already fastened upon the doubtful persons, and his prompt decision and becoming rigor strangled the treason on the eve of execution. Putting his most trusted troops in order for the enemy, he sent a despatch to Marion to hasten to the camp with all the force that he could muster, and, at the same moment, the hand of arrest was laid upon the conspirators. Gornell, and several others, were brought before a court-martial and tried for their crimes. The former was condemned and executed. Four other sergeants of the same line were sent under a strong guard into the interior, and twelve soldiers broke away that night, apprehending arrest, and made their escape to the enemy. Almost simultaneously with these events, the British horse made their appearance, hovering about the outposts of the American camp. They succeeded in capturing ten of the legion cavalry, which unexpectedly encountered them; but they failed utterly in securing the contemplated and more important prey. The great preparations of General Leslie came to nought, and his detachment sunk back once more under cover of the metropolis. Nothing accrued to him from this deep and well-planned conspiracy, which was effectually crushed by the blow which fell upon the offender at the proper moment. The mutinous temper ceased among the troops, though their causes for complaint were by no means lessened. Their wants were still of a kind which we must suppose could only have been borne by those whose crude virtues were sustained by a spirit very far superior to that which belongs to fear. Still were they compelled to suffer the want of adequate food and clothing, and as the sultry heats of summer began to prevail, their distress was aggravated by the diseases of the climate which now rapidly began to spread through the camp. This was unavoidably transferred to a sickly region. As the necessities of the service required, Greene gradually drew nigher to the metropolis. In April he nad moved from Bacon's bridge to Beach Hill, a distance of but seventeen miles from Charleston. In July we find the army at Ashley hill, and still nearer to the British garrison. This position, which favored the objects of the campaign, was yet in the very heart of the malaria influence. Here the rich swamps and teeming fields in which the rice crop flourished, assailed with deadly enmity the more delicate organization of the white man, and with every breath he imbibed the subtle poison of an atmosphere in which the African alone could luxuriate in safety. Yet here, amid severest suffering, the army remained throughout the summer. The camp became a hospital. Greene himself was prostrated by the fever, as well as most of his officers and men in turn, and all of them agreed that a conflict with thrice the number of their foes, in open field, under the worst circumstances, was infinitely preferable at any time to the humiliating and exhausting struggle with a danger to which no courage or strength could offer itself without discomfiture, and which no degree of caution could escape.

But the partisan militia were not allowed to remain with Greene during this season of sickness and prostration. Marion, about the middle of July, having consolidated his regiments, was enabled to cross the Santee, and take post on the Wassamasaw, another region equally liable to the pernicious malaria influences of the low country. Here, his employment was to cover the country, and cooperate, when necessary, with the main army. But the increase of strength which General Leslie had acquired by the transfer of the garrison of Georgia to the metropolis, now enabled the latter to assume an aspect of greater activity. He proceeded to arm a numerous fleet of small vessels, with a strong body of troops. These, convoyed by galleys and brigs-of-war, issued from Charleston, destined, as it was thought, to operate against Georgetown

To this place Marion was accordingly ordered. But the enterprise of the enemy took another direction. Their object was plunder and provisions. They penetrated the south Santee with this object, and gleaned largely from the rice along the banks of that river. Marion, meanwhile, had rapidly thrown his cavalry across the Sampit, so as to intercept them in their anticipated march to Georgetown, the public stores and provisions of which he proceeded to place in security. He had left behind him a small body of infantry at Watboo, which, as his absence with the cavalry was known, attracted the attention of the British. But the famous partisan was not unmindful of his flock. The enemy did not make sufficient allowance for the rapidity of his movements. He was back among his infantry, in waiting for their approach, while they thought him busy on the Santee. Attacked by Major Frazier, early on the 29th of August, at Watboo, he totally discomfited him in a brief conflict, in which the British suffered severely. They were only saved from the rapid pursuit of Marion's horse, by the timely appearance of a strong detachment of infantry, before which Marion himself was compelled to retire.

Another detachment of the British foraging fleet was sent to penetrate the Combahee. General Gist, with his light brigade, was ordered to cover the plantations in this quarter. It was while in command of a detachment of this brigade, that the gallant Colonel Laurens, one of the most remarkable and highly endowed of the young men of the Revolution, met his death. Hearing of the British movement, and of the duties assigned to the light brigade to which he was attached, he rose from a sick bed, on which he was scarcely convalescent, and hurrying away to the southward, succeeded in overtaking the brigade which was already on the north bank of the Combahee river. At the head of a command which he had eagerly solicited, he fell at the first fire, while charging a superior force of the enemy, in a skirmish which took place at Chehaw point; an event which could not have happened had the despatch which Gist sent to apprize him of the unexpected superiority of the British detachment, not failed to reach him in proper season. Greene deeply lamented the fall of this brave young man, who has received the title of the "Bayard of the Revolution." He writes to General Williams: "Laurens has fallen in a paltry little skirmish. You knew his temper, and I predicted his fate. The love of military glory made him seek it upon occasions unworthy his rank. This state will feel his loss."

This precious life might have been saved. The petty skirmish in which he fell was the closing of the struggle. The evacuation of the state was already determined upon by the invader. A convoying fleet had already arrived in Charleston for the purpose of covering the evacuation and receiving their troops. The expedition to Combahee had for its sole object the accumulation of the provisions necessary for the voyage; and these, but for an unwise rigor on the part of the civil authorities, might have been sold to the invader, at a fair price, instead of being yielded to him only at the price of blood. General Leslie had made overtures to this effect, and public virtue did not require that his application should have been rejected. It was clear that the enemy should be fed, and equally certain that, if not allowed to traffic peacefully for the provisions which they required, they would seize them by violence. The alternative was urged by the British general, and was unwisely disregarded by the local authorities.

A few small events conclude the history of the war. The enemy left the Combahee, losing one of their galleys, which fell into the hands of the Americans, and was employed in purging the river of their stragglers. The American horse, under Kosciusko, darted upon their convoys at James' island, and succeeded in recovering a number of very fine horses, belonging to citizens of the state. Several bold enterprises on John's and James' island, by Captain Wilmot, resulted finally in his falling into an ambush, in which he perished. This was the last blood shed in the war of the Revolution. While these events were in progress along the seaboard, General Pickens, recovered from the wounds received at Eutaw, had been employed in the upper country against the tories and the Indians. He was particularly successful against both. He carried the war into the heart of the savage nations along the borders, compelled them to yield at discretion, and exacted a heavy forfeiture in lands, as a penalty for their treacheries. The territory thus conquered includes all that fine country which lies between the upper waters of the Savannah and Chatahoochie. Pickens was the first to employ mounted gun men in the war against the Indian nations.

GREENE'S NECESSITIES

CHAPTER XXIV.

Greene's Necessities.—He resorts to Impressment.—The British prepare to Evacuate Charleston.—That Event takes place on the 14th of December, 1782.—The American Army enter the City.—Their Reception.—The Joy of the Inhabitants.—Condition of Public Affairs in Carolina.—Discontents and Difficulties.—Sufferings of the Army.—Mutiny.—Army Disbanded.—Greene Revisits the North.—His Reception by Congress.—His Monetary Difficulties.—Greene returns to Carolina.

THE summer had worn away, the winter had set in, and still the British were in possession of the metropolis. The season through which he had just passed, had been to Greene one of the most painful weariness and anxiety. The distress of his troops from want of food and from sickness—his own sufferings of body—and the mortifying feeling of a feebleness which forbids performance, at the very time when the public service cries for it most, had kept the mind of the American general in a continued fever of chagrin and disappointment. Yet his watch, patient and vigilant, though inactive, was nothing in its humiliations to the constant struggle which he was compelled to maintain with the local authorities to procure the necessary provisions for the army. The officer appointed by government to furnish supplies, at length totally failed in his duty, and Greene was compelled to resume, however much against his desire, the practice of impressing, wherever he could, for the public service. He had forborne this necessity as long as possible. He had entreated, and counselled, and expostulated, and warned, but all in vain; and to avoid the worse dangers of a mutiny, he was compelled to do as the enemy had done, seize upon the means of life for those who, devoted to the defence of the country, were left without all other means of support. But the necessities of the soldier are seldom acknowledged, when his service appears no longer necessary; and the measures taken by Greene, however essential to the maintenance of his troops, and to their good behavior, was greatly offensive to the citizens. Public feeling on this subject, however, was not likely to assume a very decided hostility as long as the enemy still held possession of the city, and the exultation and joy which followed his evacuation of it, were calculated, naturally, to make the people forgetful of all minor sources of annoyance. General Leslie's proceedings for evacuating Charleston were conducted with a politic ostentation which had its objects. His preparations for his departure all complete, he opened negotiations with Greene in order that it should be peaceful. There was no reason that such should not be the case, as any blow struck while the invader was about to withdraw wholly from the conflict, would have attested rather a revengeful spirit than the wisdom of one who never thwarted the objects of humanity.

The 14th of December was the day fixed for the evacuation of Charleston. With the sound of the morning gun, the rear-guard abandoned their advanced redoubts. With the same signal, the Americans marched in, and took possession of them. This duty was assigned to Wayne, at the head of three hundred infantry, the cavalry of the legion, and a detachment of artillery. Closely did the eager Americans press upon the heels of their retiring foes. A distance of two hundred yards between the rear of the one and the advance of the other had been agreed upon; but the anxiety of the Americans, resuming possession of their ancient city, beholding once more the old familiar walks and the old familiar faces, from which they had been so long separated, made them trespass upon this limit, and the cry from the British officers, at such moments — "You are pressing upon us — you march too fast for us" — would check momentarily the progress, and compel a halt which the troops found it exceedingly difficult to observe. The lines passed, the enemy filed off to Gadsden's wharf, and by eleven o'clock, A. M., the embarkation was complete. Wayne marched forward, and halted at the intersection of the two principal streets, Meeting and Broad, taking up his position in front of the statehouse. His detachment was followed by the calvacade which attended Greene in person — an imposing assemblage, consisting of the first persons of the state, the governor, and his suite and the public authorities. These were preceded by a detachment of dragoons. They were followed by Major-Generals Moultrie and Gist, by a long cavalcade of officers and citizens, by the governor's council, and by another body of cavalry. It was a glad day for the city. Its long-banished citizens were restored — the brave hearts that refused to succumb, or to despair — preferring to make sacrifice of property and hope itself, for the maintenance of principle. Fond and touching was the welcome they received. The doors were thrown wide for their reception, while balconies and windows, crowded with joyous faces, looked the delight which was throbbing in every heart. Mute, for a while, was the voice of pleasure, in the eagerness of curiosity, and the novelty of those emotions which were yet to find a voice. The feeling, at first, could express itself in tears alone. Aged women might be seen upon their knees, thankful but dumb, entreating in their hearts for the blessings of that Benign Father, to whom they felt how deep was their debt of gratitude. But when the procession had reached the centre of the city

— when every eye had feasted upon the hitherto unknown face of that brave and prudent commander to whose firmness and policy the country was so great a debtor — when they had recalled all the well-known features of their own gallant and faithful sons — and the heart could receive nothing more, and needed relief from its own deep overflow — then rose from earth to heaven the fervent cry of delight and gratitude. Then gratitude found its voice, and joy its shout of exultation. Voices rose wild in gratulation and applause; and fervently did the soul of prayer declare itself in blessings and benedictions. "God bless you all!" was the cry from thousands. "God bless you, brave men — and welcome! welcome! all, to your homes and to ours!"

The work upon which Greene had been sent to the south was thus accomplished. The war was at an end. He had found the country covered with its foes, and in two years they had disappeared from its face. He had found them fortified in numerous posts of strength, from all of which they had been expelled. The two Carolinas and Georgia were once more restored to their original possessors; and all these results had been obtained in the face of every disadvantage. With inferior troops, inferior appliances and implements, without money, without clothes for his troops, and frequently without provisions and ammunition, we find him steadily waging the conflict — evading the foe whom he could not confidently meet, but ever hanging about his path, watchful to take advantage of all his mistakes, and to dart upon his moments of unwariness and inaction. And the consequences had not been partial. The recovery of the country was complete, and the negotiations were already in progress which promised that the peace of the states should be followed by their independence.

But Greene's troubles were not yet over. The absence of the enemy brought no peace to his threshold. His cares were destined to continue to the end of his life, to harass his mind to the last, and so to embitter his days as in all probability to shorten their duration, and give force to the disease by which he prematurely perished. He still held command in South Carolina, and had the misfortune to be embroiled in a struggle between the civil authorities and the army. Hitherto, his progress, directly beneath the eye of John Rutledge, had received the sanction of that noble patriot, and of his successor, in the chair of state. The legislature, also, themselves mostly sensible of his great services, the purity of his heart, and the integrity of his character, had shown him, as we have seen, that they could do justice to his merits. In their proceedings they justly represented the sentiments of the people. But, with the departure of the British, the support and presence of an army became equally unnecessary and irksome to the civil authorities. We have seen, already, with what difficulty and constant struggle, Greene succeeded in procuring food for his troops after the legislature had determined that this provision should be made only through their own agents. The difficulty naturally increased with the absence of that foreign enemy in whose presence alone that of a defensive army found the popular sanction. Frequent bickerings ensued between the conflicting authorities of the state and the army. Questions of paramount authority continued to arise between the one, insisting upon its independence, and the other, claiming to represent a central power to which all were required to submit. Greene took strong ground upon this subject, and in behalf of the latter, which, perhaps, would not have been taken but for the fact that the domestic authority was not yet so thoroughly restored as to place its assumptions beyond dispute. The confederacy had been formed in respect to the war—to the pressing exigency arising from foreign invasion—and the rights of the central government, in the season of returning peace, were yet to be the subject of new discussions and new leagues. But, with his army not yet disbanded, with the country still infested with outlawed bands that defied the civil arm, and with the foreign enemy not yet withdrawn from the coast, the American general naturally demeaned himself as if the war was still in progress. This he might reasonably assume, as no treaty of peace had yet been ratified. He, accordingly, engaged in the discussion with the state authorities, on subjects over which they claimed exclusive control, and mortally offended some of the officers of the state government, the executive among them, by this alleged interference. The payment of the state contribution—the treatment of the tories—subjects which seemed to be at once popular and domestic—were among those vexing questions, in the discussion of which it was Greene's misfortune to give offence to the people he had so lately served with so much zeal and success. It is not necessary that we should take part in this discussion, nor is it necessary that we should inquire in how far he was right in desiring to increase the strength of the central establishment at the expense of the individual states.

The army, meanwhile, continued to suffer in consequence of this difficulty between the civil authorities and representatives of Congress and the state. Congress, the creature of the states, had no means of supporting the troops unless by the state subsidies. The states withheld their subsidies from the support of an army for which they no longer had any use. South Carolina claimed to have already contributed a far greater amount than her quota. Indeed, she had supported the army during the last three years of the war in the south, almost exclusively, and at the close of the war was the largest creditor state in the Union. With this fact before them, a large party in the state opposed resolutely every appropriation which could have supplied the wants and met the necessities of the soldiery. Greene's efforts to obtain the necessary supplies were only construed into an offensive effort at dictation, and was denounced as an arrogant presumption. We need not pursue this subject, or go into the numerous petty and vexatious details which might display the mutual errors and mistakes of the conflicting parties. But a single instance of collision between the civil authorities and the army occurred, and in this instance the governor of the state receded from a position which he had unwarily taken. Greene behaved with equal moderation and firmness, and no evil consequences ensued.

The long and painful history which followed upon the individual attempts of the American general to sustain the army on his own credit, is one that must be greatly condensed for this narrative. In the failure of the Congress and of the state to provide for his troops, it was attempted to supply the deficiency by contract. The transaction was one which was naturally considered exceedingly hazardous, since it was very doubtful in what quarter the contracting party could finally look for payment. The only offer was made by a person named Banks, and after an interval of nearly three months, in the absence of all other proposals, his were accepted. But Banks seems to have been a needy man, and was already much involved. He was just such an adventurer as such times were calculated to produce. His creditors, becoming apprehensive at what he had done, as endangering their securities, threatened to foreclose the mortgage which they held upon his property, and thus deprive him of the credit upon which, alone, could he be able to meet his contracts. In this predicament, Banks shrunk from the responsibilities he had undertaken; the army was again neglected—its patience was exhausted—and its discontents soon rose to such a height, that, apprehensive of a mutiny among the most insubordinate, Greene was compelled to call out a select body, drawn from such troops as he supposed faithful, in order to overawe the residue. His detachment was actually put under arms, with cannon loaded and matches lighted, so near was the anticipated trial of his strength and firmness. In this exigency, with the evil still at work, and the danger still present and threatening, Greene was persuaded that his personal security would suffice to extricate Banks from the immediate danger of his creditors, and enable him to fulfil his contract for supplying the army. There seemed to be no other alternative by which to avoid a crisis, and Greene unhesitatingly pledged himself as the security for Banks. We need not describe the details. The result was that Banks became a bankrupt, and the whole burden of his indebtedness fell on the American general. But this information reached him only after the army was dissolved. That event followed upon the arrival of the long-expected news of peace. This intelligence reached Charleston on the 16th of April, 1783; and was received by the southern army, stationed on James' island, with as much joy and exultation as could well be shown by soldiers whose only food at the time consisted of meat, without the accompaniment of a single breadstuff. The troops were soon furloughed to their respective states, the last act of their commander, in connexion with them, consisting in an earnest appeal to the governor of the states within his command, entreating their attention and justice to the brave fellows who had so long been suffering in the common cause. The close of August found Greene himself, on his way homeward, respited, after a seven years' apprenticeship to war, to the enjoyment of the sweets of home and its endearing relations. His journey was taken by land, a journey of many fatigues, and at the worst season of the year. But he had too frequently traversed the same weary path in the prosecution of duty—should he feel its privations now when the promised end before him was repose and happiness? His route was cheered by the congratulations of the authorities and of the people in all the states through which he travelled, all of whom vied in the desire to acknowledge his great service to the country. Congress was in session at Princeton, and thither he repaired to surrender up his trusts in person. To that body he made the simple request that he should be permitted to return to Rhode Island—"that it was now going on nine years since he had had an opportunity to visit his family and friends, or pay the least attention to his private fortune." This request was answered by a compliment. A committee was appointed "to report a suitable expression of the approbation of Congress," and the result was a resolution—"That two pieces of field ordnance taken from the British army at the Cowpens, Augusta, or Eutaw, be presented by the commander-in-chief of the armies of the United States to Major-General Greene, as a public testimonial of the wisdom, fortitude, and military skill, which distinguished his command in the southern department, and of the eminent services, which, amidst complicated difficulties and dangers, and against an enemy greatly superior in numbers, he has successfully performed for his country:—and that a memorandum be engraved on the said pieces of ordnance expressive of the substance of this resolution."

A further resolve gave him the required permission to visit Rhode Island, for which the consent of the commander-in-chief had already been obtained. Washington, on this occasion, met with Greene for the last time. Perhaps, there was no general of the American army whose particular genius so much resembled that of Washington as the commander of the southern army. It is certain that he modeled himself after the former, whom he had chosen for his study, and whom he ever regarded with the profoundest admiration and respect. It was among the subjects which vexed the enemies of Washington that he had singled out Greene as the favorite general, upon whose counsels he always most preferred to rely.

It was while at Philadelphia, that Greene first heard of the failure of Banks, the contractor for the army, for whom he had unwisely become security. The full force of the blow was scarcely felt by him at this moment. There was still some reason to believe that the affairs of Banks were not wholly desperate, and though his conduct was in the last degree suspicious, he having withdrawn from the hands of a third person the bills which had been pledged for Greene's indemnity, the sanguine temperament of the latter refused to acknowledge the full extent of the evil which he had every cause to fear. At this moment, too, when released, for the first time for many years, from the heavy and various duties of a station full of the most exciting and vital responsibilities — free from a load of care — and about to revisit the scenes of his youth and early manhood, and take to his embraces the precious children whom, for so long a season, he had not been permitted to see: — his mind naturally refused to burden itself with apprehensions which might lessen the enjoyments which his affections and his hopes now promised him. Discarding all his doubts, yielding himself only to hope, he hurried away to Rhode Island, cheered on his route by the same demonstrations of public approbation which had awaited him on his journey from the south. His arrival in Rhode Island, was something of a triumph. The voice of his native state declared its approval of his conduct by the warmest testimonies, and his home, under the earnest welcome of old friends and neighbors, seemed, for a time, to have realized all his anticipations. Here, honored by all, beloved by many — with an ample circle of friends and associates — with a precious homestead full of dear objects of equal interest and affection — with leisure for books and thought, and with just that degree of occupation in the cultivation of farm and garden, in which the man of taste combines equally recreation and employment — nothing was wanting to the happiness of Greene but escape from his cruel pecuniary entanglements. These haunted him in the sacred retreats of home, and embittered all its pleasures. His residence in Rhode Island was for a time only. His resolution had been taken to remove to the south, where he might enjoy with more profit to his interest, the estates which the liberality of Georgia and the Carolinas had enabled him to procure. In the month of June, 1784, he returned to South Carolina to complete his preparations for the final removal of his family. But his evil destiny pursued him. The cloud which hung about his fortunes, with the feeling it produced, may be gathered from a letter to one of his brothers, written from Charleston. "My heart is too full," he writes, "and my situation too distressing, to write much. . . You may remember, I told you last winter of some heavy embarrassments, which hung over me from becoming security for Banks, Hunter, & Co. They being public contractors, and the feeding of the army depending upon supporting their credit, I was obliged to guaranty sundry of their debts. But that I might be secure, they engaged that all the contract money should go to the discharge of my guaranty bonds. This they have found means to avoid; their affairs have grown desperate, and I am and shall be involved in heavy and unavoidable losses. . . . It will oblige me to sell a considerable part of my estate. My situation is truly afflicting! To be reduced from independence to want, and from the power of obliging my friends, to a situation claiming their aid. . . . My heart faints within me when I think of my family. I have only one consolation—it is not the fruits of extravagance."

Banks, the miserable insolvent dared not encounter the man he had ruined. He fled from Charleston the moment he heard of Greene's arrival in that city. Believing that he still possessed the means of indemnity, Greene resolved to pursue him, and compel restoration. Mounting his horse, though at the most sickly season of the year, taking with him a single servant, and provided only with his pistols and a change of garments in his saddle-bags, he at once set forth in pursuit. His route was taken over the same region which he had formerly traversed at the head of an army. At every step forward some recollection of mingled pain and pleasure, started up before him. What had been his situation then? One of peril surely, of many privations, but none of such humiliating involvements as now vexed his heart, and drove peace and quiet from his mind. If he was then, the soldier of fortune only, having nothing but his sword, he was still the soldier of freedom whose only cares were such honorable ones as belong to his country. But with peace, he had been cheered with a promise of independence for himself, and plenty for his children, vouchsafed him only, as it would seem, to mortify and mock. His feelings and fears were a terrible goad to his endeavors. Under the burning sun of that season and region, he pressed his pursuit; and in a chase of 400 miles he at length overtook the wretched bankrupt. But

Banks had been already overtaken by a more fatal, if less angry creditor. Greene found him dying, the victim to a malignant fever which had seized upon him even before he fled from Charleston. The excitement of fear — the intense desire to escape from his pursuer — had sustained him on this long and painful route; and believing himself secure from the man he had wronged, he laid himself down to die. He does not seem to have fled with any spoils. His flight appears to have been prompted only by an earnest anxiety to escape the eyes of his creditor. His conscience had been the goad to the fugitive; and Greene gained nothing from the pursuit but a confirmation of all his fears. He had but to retrace the path in disappointment which he had lately trod in eagerness and hope. He writes — "My distresses are sufficient already to sink me under water. A little more, and I am gone." From this sentence his mental agony may be inferred. That one who had borne so many vicissitudes, and had passed so manfully through such a career of peril, defeat, and disappointments, should have expressed himself in language so desponding, is sufficient to understand his situation, and the extremity of his apprehensions. These were mostly realized. He was compelled, at a time of peculiar pressure in the moneyed condition of the country, to sell the lands which he had bought in Carolina, at an enormous sacrifice. His slaves were removed to his estate in Georgia. To this estate — a beautiful place called Mulberry Grove, on the Savannah, which had been presented him by the state of Georgia — he at length retired in the spring of 1785. A memorial to Congress which was presented in August, of this year, giving a simple history of his relations with Banks, and the losses sustained by him, amply showed that these losses had been sustained entirely for the country, and were unavoidable from his situation. His state ments, made when all the facts were fresh in the public mind, proved him to be equally patriotic and unfortunate, and, without preferring a claim to the immediate interference of Congress, left it to their sense of right to determine, whether the losses incurred in their cause, should not be met by their justice and liberality. This was his last official communication to his government. It presents the spectacle, at once noble and painful, of a man who has faithfully served his country, modestly preferring a claim, which, however humbled by misfortune, he yet disdains to solicit.

CHAPTER XXV.

His Removal to Georgia.—Challenged by Captain Gunn.—He declines the Challenge.—The Extent, Prospect, Peace and Beauty of his Remains.—His Sickness and Death.—Public Sorrow and Honors on the Event.—His Character.—Conclusion.

GREENE'S annoyances from the failure of Banks, continued to the end of his life. But these were not all. Scarcely had he reached his new abode in Georgia, when a personal difficulty assailed him which he had no reason to anticipate. He was waited on by Colonel Jackson, as the friend of Captain Gunn, who demanded redress for a supposed injury done to himself by Greene, while the latter was in command of the southern army. The offence arose from a habit which but too much prevailed among the dragoons, of seizing and keeping the horses of the public or of their own troopers. By the constitution of the corps each officer was required to provide his own horse, and an allowance was made him, in money, to enable him to do so. But, as the government finally failed altogether in making payment to the troops, the officers of cavalry, when they lost their own horses, did not scruple to dismount their troopers at pleasure, or appropriated such horses as were procured for the public service. Abuses still more gross had resulted from this license, and there were very few officers who did not keep from one to three horses. Captain Gunn, whose challenge to the field of personal combat, awaited Greene on his arrival in Georgia, had improved upon the system,

He had exchanged a public horse with a brother officer, for which he had received two other horses and a slave. Greene brought him to trial for this offence, and he was compelled to make restitution for the horse. His present demand was based upon Greene's proceedings in the case.

Greene had been brought up in a school which did not tolerate duelling. Fortunately for his reputation as a man of personal courage, that was sufficiently well-known, to render necessary any resort to this means, for securing him in the respect of his neighbors. But he placed his refusal to meet with Gunn, on other grounds, and, after a clear and correct narrative of the whole affair, which he gave to Colonel Jackson, he concluded with declaring his resolution never to sanction the call of an inferior officer upon his superior, for supposed injuries done in the course of command. Jackson, upon understanding the history of the case, withdrew from all connexion with it: but Gunn, not to be pacified, procured another agent, in the person of Major Fishburne, who renewed for him his requisition upon Greene. The latter refused any answer, and was accordingly threatened by Gunn with a personal assault, for which he gave the challenger to understand he always went prepared. The parties do not seem to have sought or shunned each other. By good fortune they never met, and the affair was soon blown over. But Greene seems to have been troubled with some misgivings in relation to the course which he had pursued. His career as a soldier had grievously shaken the foundations of his quaker philosophy. He had become sensible in the army, of the extreme delicacy which belongs to a military reputation, and the exceeding readiness with which the youthful salamander learns to question the courage of the more sedate and scrupulous. He accordingly addressed to

Washington a private letter on the subject, entreating his opinion. "If," said he, "I thought my honor or reputation would suffer in the opinion of the world, and more especially with the military gentlemen, I value life too little to hesitate a moment to answer the challenge."

The reply of Washington affirmed the propriety of Greene's judgment in the matter. He says—"I give it as my decided opinion that your honor and reputation will stand not only perfectly acquitted for the non-acceptance of his [Gunn's] challenge, but that your prudence and judgment would have been condemned for accepting it; because, if a commanding officer is amenable to private calls for the discharge of his public duty, he has a dagger always at his heart; and can turn neither to the right hand nor to the left without meeting its point. In a word, he is no longer a free agent in office, as there are few military decisions which are not offen sive to one party or another."

With this affair the annoyances of Greene appear to cease. His mind began to recover its tone; his spirits are more fresh and buoyant. He had brought on his family to Georgia in the latter part of 1785, and he indulges in all those dreams of happiness, in his own grounds, which the public man is apt to feel after a long and trying service, when he finds himself apart from the busy world, and respited from all its troubles. He has found a refuge. The seclusion of his plantation is no solitude. His wife and children are about him. He is solaced with their sympathies, and gladdened by their sight. He is honored by his neighbors, and finds their society grateful. His duties are no longer burdensome. His cares involve no humiliations. To cultivate his fields, to clear and beautify his grounds, to multiply the produce of the earth, and watch the growth of plants and flowers, which his own hands have set out, provides him with employments at once grateful to his tastes, and in unison with his duties. It is evident, from his correspondence at this period, that Greene had shaken off his despondency, and was beginning to see the world once more through the rose-colored medium of youth. His escape from the drudgery of public service was like that of a boy released from school, and rioting with his comrades in the broad fields and in the blessed sunshine. His residence was a delightful one, and it awakened all his enthusiasm. His letters at this period are full of his grounds and garden—his shrubbery—the pigeon-house and poultry-yard. He had fairly surrendered himself to the luxury of domestic life. What a contrast, its calm, its peaceful solitudes, its mild enjoyments, to the continued turmoil, the fierce excitements, the anxieties and dangers of the camp. In April, a bit of a letter shows us how happily he lords it in his little empire. "This is a busy time with us, and I can afford but a small portion of time to write. We are planting. We have got upward of sixty acres of corn planted, and expect to plant one hundred and thirty of rice. The garden is delightful. The fruit-trees and flowering shrubs form a pleasing variety. We have green peas almost fit to eat, and as fine lettuce as you ever saw. The mocking-birds surround us evening and morning. The weather is mild and the vegetable world progressing to perfection. We have in the same orchard, apples, pears, peaches, apricots, nectarines, plums of various kinds, figs, pomegranate, and oranges. And we have strawberries which measure three inches round."

He has evidently forgotten the demands of Gunn, and the failure of Banks. He has delivered himself to the present, and to the lovely empire of fruit and flower with which he has environed himself in his retreat. But, it was Heaven's will that he should not behold the ripening of the fruits which his hands had set to grow; it was the will of the same Divine Providence that the wretched entanglement with Banks should still be the means, in some degree, for cutting him off in his felicity. His presence was required in Savannah, on Monday the 12th of June, 1786, for the purpose of settling with one of Bank's creditors. In returning from that city, he spent the day at the house of Mr. William Gibbons. Greene had become a rice-planter, and a natural curiosity to see the progress of Mr. Gibbons' crop, led them after breakfast into the rice-field together. The sun was intensely hot, as it usually is during this month in the south, but Greene had too frequently endured his fiercest rays in Carolina, to apprehend danger from them now. The exposure was followed by a sharp pain in the head, which he felt while going home, and which continued throughout the ensuing day. But it occasioned no alarm, and was supposed to be nothing but an ordinary headache. On Thursday, however, the pain had increased greatly, over the eyes in particular, and the forehead appeared swollen and inflamed. In the evening, Major Pendleton, late his aid, paid him a visit, and was immediately impressed with the unfavorable change in his appearance. His apprehensions were excited, and early on Friday, a physician was summoned, who opened a vein, and administered some ordinary remedies. But the inflammation continued to increase. Another physician was summoned; more active medicines were employed; more blood was taken, and blisters were put upon the temples. But the remedies were applied too late. The head had now swollen greatly—the unfavorable symptoms rapidly increased. Greene sank into a complete torpor from which he never recovered, and early on Monday, the 19th of June, he expired.

This mournful event, which cut off a citizen so distinguished, in the midst of his hopes, in the prime of his manhood — for he was but forty-four years old when he died — was doubly felt as it was so totally unexpected. In the south the grief was at once deep and general. In the city of Savannah, the tidings produced a suspension of all business, public and private. The shops were shut, the public places were wrapped in mourning, and a spontaneous movement of the people, prepared for the mournful duty of committing the remains of one so honored to their final resting-place. On the morning after his death, the body was brought down by water to the city. It was met on the banks of the river by the municipality and the military of the place. The citizens turned out as one man to follow in the melancholy procession to the grave, and in the absence of a regular minister of the gospel — for Savannah had not yet recovered from the devastating influences of war — the funeral service, according to the rites of the church of England, was read by the Honorable William Stevens. Deposited in an unknown vault, the coffin of Nathanael Greene was distinguished only by a small metallic plate, which, in the usual manner, bears the name and age of the occupant. Upon this plate rests the only hope of identifying the remains of our subject, the search for which, partially urged, perhaps, has hitherto proved fruitless.

Congress, immediately after his death, decreed a monument to his memory, to be erected at the seat of the federal government — nay — went a step farther and even composed the inscription — but to this day nothing has been done toward the work; neither bust nor stone, nor trophied monument, has been raised to do justice to a memory which history can not fail to honor.

We have no need to dwell upon the services which deserve this memorial. The public career of Nathanael Greene is on record. His virtues, talents, courage, and eminent prudence, will always secure for him the unquestioning gratitude of those who read thoughtfully and feelingly the history of our revolutionary struggles. Brave without rashness, prudent without fear, bold without temerity, temperate without phlegm, firm without obstinacy, strict without harshness, indulgent without partiality, thoughtful without tardiness, sanguine without impulse, and endowed with a constancy that never lost sight of its object in its incidents,—Greene presented us one of the happiest specimens of a mind well balanced, a heart matured, and a judgment ripe for all the exigencies that distinguished his career.

His conduct during the progress of the struggle was frequently the subject of cavil and complaint. Slander and defamation strove to fasten upon his skirts; but, like his great exemplar, Washington, he shook off the reptile as easily as Paul, the viper, after his shipwreck on the barbarous island of Melita. His reputation, freed wholly from stain, or imputation of offence, has been steadily rising to the first rank among the military men of the Revolution. His talents, as a soldier, are supposed to resemble those of the commander-in-chief, and, of all our major-generals of the Revolution, he is universally admitted to be the one who stands nearest to Washington.

APPENDIX.

SOUTHERN ARMY.

A NARRATIVE OF THE CAMPAIGN OF 1780,

BY COLONEL OTHO HOLLAND WILLIAMS, ADJUTANT-GENERAL.

THE city of Charleston, South Carolina, was invested by a British army, commanded by General Sir Henry Clinton, on the first day of April, 1780. Major-General Lincoln of the American army, who commanded the garrison, made the best possible defence his situation and circumstances would admit of; but, finding his garrison inadequate, and the resources of the country cut off or exhausted, he applied to the commander-in-chief of the American army for a reinforcement.

On the 16th day of April, 1780, the quotas of Maryland and Delaware troops, about fourteen hundred infantry, marched under the orders of Major-General the baron De Kalb, from cantonments near Morristown in New Jersey, for the head of the Chesapeake bay. They embarked the 3d day of May, at the head of Elk river, and arrived at Petersburg in Virginia early in June.

Here the unwelcome news of the surrender of Charleston (on the 12th of May) was first communicated to the detachment, the principal object of whose destination was lost; but the country was not yet conquered; and it was presumed that the countenance of a body of regular troops, however small, would contribute more than anything else to sustain the fortitude of the militia. Every exertion, therefore, was made in Virginia to expedite the march of the baron's detachment, which here received a small reinforcement of artillery. It proceeded with some celerity and in fine spirits as far as Wilcox's iron works, on Deep river, in the state of North Carolina; but here, on the 6th day of July, the baron found himself under the necessity of halting for want of provisions.

The state of North Carolina had made no provision for the troops of the Union; she was solely occupied with her own militia, a great portion of which, being disaffected, were obliged to be dragooned into the service. All the baron's applications and remonstrances to the executive were without effect; he was obliged to send small detachments, under discreet officers, to collect provisions from the inhabitants, who at that season of the year had but little to spare. Many of them were subsisting themselves upon the last of the preceding crop of grain, and the new, although it promised plenty, was not yet mature; consequently some of the inhabitants must have suffered, notwithstanding the strict orders to the officers to impress only a proportion of what was found on the farms. In this dilemma the troops remained several days, but the resources failing in the vicinity of the camp, it became necessary to draw supplies from a greater distance, or to march to where there was greater plenty. The former was impracticable, as the means of transportation were not in the baron's power. He consequently determined on the latter, previously extending the excursions of his foraging parties, with directions to form a small magazine at Cox's (or Wilcox's) mill, on Deep river, where the troops arrived on the — day of July, and encamped near Buffalo ford.

Still, however, the supplies of grain were scarcely sufficient, even for the present subsistence of the troops; and the only meat ration that could be procured was lean beef, daily driven out of the woods and the canebrakes, where the cattle had wintered themselves. Inaction, bad fare, and the difficulty of preserving discipline, when there is no apprehension of danger, have often proved fatal to troops and ruined whole armies. But here, the activity of the officers, and the persevering patience of the privates, preserved order, harmony, and even a passion for the service.

The baron did not fail to represent his situation to Congress, and to repeat his remonstrances to the executive of the state of North Carolina. He had been flattered with a promise of a plentiful supply of provisions and a respectable reinforcement of the militia of North Carolina, which about that time took the field, under the command of Mr. Caswell, who was appointed a major-general. The supplies, however, did not arrive; and the commandant of the militia, ambitious of signalizing himself, employed his men in detachments against small parties of disaffected inhabitants, who, to avoid being drafted into the service of their country, retired among the swamps and other cover with which that country abounds.

It was in vain that the baron required General Caswell to join his command; and it was equally fruitless to expect much longer to find subsistence for his soldiers in a country where marauding parties of militia swept all before them. The baron therefore hesitated whether he had better march to join the militia, in hopes to find that Caswell's complaints of a want of provisions for himself were fictitious, or to move up the country and gain the fertile banks of the Yadkin river. But, before any resolution was taken, the approach of Major-General Gates was announced, by the arrival of his aid-de-camp, Major Armstrong, who was to have acted as deputy adjutant-general, but was prevented by sickness.

General Gates, who had so fortunately terminated the career of General Burgoyne in the north, was appointed to command the southern army immediately after the reduction of Charleston. His arrival, on the 25th of July, was a relief to De Kalb, who condescendingly took command of the Maryland division, which included the regiment of Delaware. Besides these two corps, the army consisted only of a small legionary corps, which formed a junction with them a few days before, under the command of Colonel Armand, being about sixty cavalry and as many infantry; and Lieutenant-Colonel Carrington's detachment of three companies of artillery, which had joined in Virginia.

General Gates was received with respectful ceremony. The baron ordered a continental salute from the little park of artillery, which was performed on the entrance into camp of his successor, who made his acknowledgments to the baron for his great politeness; approved his standing orders; and, as if actuated by a spirit of great activity and enterprise, ordered the troops to hold themselves in readiness *to march at a moment's warning*. The latter order was a matter of great astonishment to those who knew the real situation of the troops. But all difficulties were removed by the general's assurances that plentiful supplies of *rum* and *rations* were on the route, and would overtake them in a day or two—assurances that certainly were too fallacious, and that never were verified. All were in motion, however, early in the morning of the 27th of July, and the general took the route over Buffalo ford, leading toward the enemy's advanced post on Lynch's creek, on the road to Camden, leaving two brass field-pieces and some baggage for want of horses. Colonel Williams, presuming on the friendship of the general, ventured to expostulate with him upon the seeming precipitate and inconsiderate step he was taking. He represented that the country through which he was about to march was by nature barren, abounding with sandy plains, intersected by swamps, and very thinly inhabited; that the little provisions and forage which were produced on the banks of its few small streams were exhausted, or taken away by the enemy, and by the hordes of banditti (called tories), which had retired from what they called the persecution of the rebels, and who would certainly distress his army, small as it was, by removing what little might remain out of his way. On the other hand, the colonel represented that a route about northwest would cross the Pedee river somewhere about where it loses the name of Yadkin, and would lead to the little town of Salisbury, in the midst of a fertile country, and inhabited by a people zealous in the cause of America; that the most active and intelligent officers had contemplated this route with pleasure, not only as it promised a more plentiful supply of provisions, but because the sick, the women and children, and the wounded, in case of disaster, might have an asylum provided for them at Salisbury or Charlotte, where they would remain in security, because the militia of the counties of Mecklenburg and Roan, in which these villages stand, were stanch friends. The idea of establishing a laboratory for the repair of arms at a secure place, was also suggested as necessary; the security of convoys of stores from the northward, by the upper route; the advantage of turning the left of the enemy's outposts, even by a circuitous route; that of approaching the most considerable of those posts (Camden) with the river Wateree on our right, and our friends on our backs; and some other considerations—were suggested. And, that they might the more forcibly impress the general's mind, a short note was presented to him, concisely intimating the same opinion, and referring to the best-informed gentlemen under his command. General Gates said he would confer with the *general officers* when the troops should halt at noon. Whether any conference took place or not the writer does not know. After a short halt at noon, when the men were refreshed upon the *scraps* in their *knapsacks*, the march was resumed. The country exceeded the representation that had been made of it: scarcely had it emerged from a state of sterile nature; the few rude attempts at improvement that were to be found were most of them abandoned by the owners and plundered by the neighbors. Every one, in this uncivilized part of the country, was flying from his home, and joining in parties, under adventurers, who pretended to yield them protection, until the British army should appear, which they seemed confidently to expect. The distresses of the soldiery daily increased. They were told that the banks of the Pedee river were extremely fertile—and so, indeed, they were; but the preceding crop of corn (the principal article of produce) was exhausted, and the new grain, although luxuriant and fine, was unfit for use. Many of the soldiery, urged by necessity, plucked the green ears and boiled them with the lean beef, which was collected in the woods, made for themselves a repast, not unpalatable to be sure, but which was attended with painful effects. Green peaches also were substituted for bread, and had similar consequences. Some of the officers, aware of the risk of eating such vegetables, and in such a state, with poor fresh beef, and without salt, restrained themselves from taking anything but the beef itself, boiled or roasted. It occurred to some that the hair-powder, which remained in their bags, would thicken soup, and it was actually applied.*

The troops, notwithstanding their disappointment in not being overtaken by a supply of *rum* and provisions, were again amused with promises, and gave early proofs of that patient submission, inflexible fortitude, and undeviating integrity, which they afterward more eminently displayed.

On the 3d day of August the little army crossed Pedee river, in batteaux, at Mask's ferry, and were met on the southern bank by Lieutenant-Colonel Porterfield, an officer of merit, who, after the disaster at Charleston, retired with a small detachment, and found means of subsisting himself and his men in Carolina until the present time.

Colonel Marion, a gentleman of South Carolina, had been with the

* Captain W. D. Beale, &c

army a few days, attended by a very few followers, distinguished by small black leather caps and the wretchedness of their attire. Their number did not exceed twenty men and boys, some white, some black, and all mounted, but most of them miserably equipped; their appearance was in fact so burlesque, that it was with much difficulty the diversion of the regular soldiery was restrained by the officers; and the general himself was glad of an opportunity of detaching Colonel Marion, at his own instance, toward the interior of South Carolina, with orders to watch the motions of the enemy, and furnish intelligence.

These trifling circumstances are remembered in these notes, to show from what contemptible beginnings a good capacity will rise to distinction. The history of the war in South Carolina will recognise Marion as a brave partisan, if only the actions of the last two years' campaigns are recorded.

The expectation, founded on assurances of finding a plentiful supply of provisions at May's mill, induced the troops again to obey the order to march with cheerfulness; but being again disappointed, fatigued, and almost famished, their patience began to forsake them. Their looks began to be vindictive, mutiny was ready to manifest itself, and the most unhappy consequences were to be apprehended—when the regimental officers, by mixing among the men and remonstrating wlth them, appeased murmurs, for which unhappily there was too much cause. The officers, however, by appealing to their own empty canteens and mess-cases, satisfied the privates that all suffered alike; and, exhorting them to exercise the same fortitude of which the officers gave them the example, assured them that the best means of extricating them from the present distress should be immediately adopted; that if the supplies expected by the general did not arrive very soon, detachments should go from each corps, in all directions, to pick up what grain might possibly be found in the country, and bring it to the mill.

Fortunately, a small quantity of Indian corn was immediately brought into camp; the mill was set to work, and as soon as a mess of meal was ground it was delivered to the men; and so, in rotation, they were all served in the course of a few hours. More poor cattle were sacrificed, the camp-kettles were all engaged, the men were busy, but silent, until they had each taken his repast; and then all was again content, cheerfulness, and mirth. It was as astonishing as it was pleasing to observe the transition.

The general and field officers were not the first served upon this occasion, nor were they generally the most satisfied; but, as no one could point out the means of immediate redress, no remonstrances took place with the commanding officer. The commanding officer, however, was well informed of what was passing in the camp, and of the critical disposition of the troops. Impressed by a sense of difficulties, and perhaps conceiving himself in some degree accountable to the army for the steps he had taken, he told Colonel Williams, who acted as deputy adjutant-general to the southern army, that he had, in a measure, been forced to take the route he had done; that General Caswell had evaded every order which had been sent to him, as well by the baron De Kalb as himself, to form a junction of the militia with the regular corps; that it appeared to him that Caswell's vanity was gratified by having a separate command; that probably he contemplated some enterprise to distinguish himself and gratify his ambition, "which," said he, "I should not be sorry to see checked by a rap over the knuckles, if it were not that the militia would disperse, and leave this handful of brave men without even nominal assistance." He urged further that it was the more necessary to counteract the indiscretion of Caswell, and save him from disaster, as he then commanded the only corps of militia that were embodied in the Carolinas; that the assurances he had received from the executive of North Carolina gave him cause to suspect that supplies of provisions had been forwarded and used in profusion in Caswell's camp, notwithstanding intimations had been communicated to him that the militia were in as bad a situation in that respect as the regular corps; that, moreover, having marched thus far directly toward the enemy, a retrograde or indirect movement would not only dispirit the troops, but intimidate the people of the country, many of whom had come in with their arms, or sent their submissions to the general—promising, upon his engagement to indemnify them for what had passed, to assemble themselves under their own leaders and follow the colors of the Union. The *poverty* of the country and the *perfidy* of the people were in vain opposed to these agreements, and in fact the troops had penetrated so far, as to make it even as hazardous to return or file off for the upper country as to advance.

Dangerous as deceptions had been, it was still thought expedient to flatter the expectation of the soldiery with an abundance of provisions so soon as a junction could be formed with the militia. Therefore, after collecting all the corn which was to be found in the neighborhood of May's mill, and huckstering all the meal that could be spared from our present necessities, the march was resumed toward Camden.

On the 5th day of August, in the afternoon, General Gates received a letter, informing him that General Caswell meditated an attack upon a fortified post of the enemy on Lynch's creek, about fourteen miles from the militia encampment. More anxious than ever, General Gates urged on the march of the regulars. Whatever the men suffered, and whatever they thought, the example of the officers, who shared with them every inconvenience, repressed the murmurs which were hourly expected to break forth. The next morning orders were issued for the army to march with the utmost expedition to join the militia, under the idea that it was the only expedient to gain a supply of provisions; but another and more vexatious cause to General Gates was, a letter from General Caswell, advising him that he had every reason to apprehend an attack on his camp by the garrison from Lynch's creek (the very garrison which he, the day before, had determined to assault, for there was no possibility of surprising troops so situated), and requesting General Gates to reinforce him with all possible despatch.

One of Caswell's letters began—"*Sir, General W———, my aid-de-camp.*" The ostentation of this address weakened the little confidence which the general-in-chief might have had in the major-general's capacity for command, and increased his desire to have all the forces under his immediate direction. Such evasions of orders, such pretences to enterprise, and such sudden signs of intimidation, in the militia general, determined Gates to reach his camp in person that same day, although it was impracticable, without retreating the militia, for a junction to be formed until the next. The deputy adjutant-general had the honor of attending the general commandant to the headquarters of the commandant of the militia. The reception was gracious, and the general and his suite were regaled with wine and other novelties, exquisitely grateful and pleasingly exhilarating; but a man must have been intoxicated, not to perceive the confusion which prevailed in the camp: tables, chairs, bedsteads, benches, and many other articles of heavy and cumbrous household stuff, were scattered before the tent doors in great disorder.

It was understood that General Caswell had discovered, upon the last alarm, that, by the death of horses and breaking down of carriages, he was rendered unable to move, and was making an effort to divest himself then of his heavy baggage. (If, in these notes, a tenor, censorious of General Caswell's conduct, appears to the reader, the writer begs that it may not, as it ought not to be, imputed to any personal prejudice or malicious motive. He never had the honor of seeing the general until this time, and all that he had ever heard of him was extremely favorable to his character as a gentleman and a patriot. A regard to facts, to which the writer thinks he may possibly hereafter be called to testify on oath, obliges him to state them faithfully as they occurred, or were communicated to him—preserving the memory of authorities, as well as incidents, in order to a correct statement of the circumstances about which he may be interrogated.)

On the 17th of August, the wished-for junction took place at the cross roads, about fifteen miles east of the enemy's post on Lynch's creek.

This event enlivened the countenances of all parties: the militia were relieved from their apprehensions of an attack, and the regulars, forgetting their fatigues, and disdaining to betray the least appearance of discontent, exulted in the confidence with which they inspired their new comrades; a good understanding prevailed among the officers of all ranks, and General Caswell seemed satisfied with the honor of being the third in command.

The baron De Kalb commanded the right wing of the army, composed of the regular troops, and General Caswell the left, of militia.

After the junction, which happened about noon, the army marched a few miles toward the enemy's post on Lynch's creek, and encamped in order.

The deputy adjutant-general, who had as much anxiety as if he had been personally responsible for the fate of the army, in order to observe what guards were established for the safety of the left wing, went with Lieutenant-Colonel Ford (officer of the day), at an unusual hour, to inspect the lines. The guards and sentinels of the right wing were, as usual, attentive, and hailed the visiting rounds with that alacrity and spirit which inspired a confidence of security in that quarter; but in the left wing all was tranquil. The officers patrolled around the encampment without being hailed once; and then rode into the lines, and among the tents, and even approached the marquees of some of the general and field officers—one of whom complained of being disturbed, and intimated that it was an unseasonable hour for *gentlemen to call.* The officers of the preceding day were sent for, and guards and patrols sent out to secure the encampment from surprise.

The morning of the 8th of August dawned without revealing any appearance of an enemy.

Under the judicious mask of offensive operations, the commanding officer of the post on Lynch's creek evacuated it and retired unmolested and at leisure to a much stronger position on Little Lynch's creek, within a day's march of Camden—which last was strongly fortified, and had a considerable garrison under the command of Lord Rawdon.

The small posts which the enemy had advanced into the country were calculated to cover the parties which were sent in all directions to collect the forage and provisions that might be found on the waters of Lynch's creek and Black rivers; and this business having been already effected, the posts were no longer an object to them.

General Gates saw himself master of the field, but it was a barren one. The troops still subsisted upon precarious supplies of corn meal and lean beef, of which they often did not receive half a ration per day, and no possibility existed of doing better, without departing from the route which the general had all along pertinaciously persisted in. To have descended among the fertile fields of Black river, would have been leaving the garrison of Camden between the army and the expected reinforcements from Virginia. Besides, the refugees of North Carolina repeated their assurances of joining in considerable numbers in a few days.

On the other hand, the Waxhaw settlement offered the greatest prospect of a comfortable supply of provisions, but it could not be gained under two or three days' march; it lay too much out of the way; the movement would look like retreating from the enemy, and the *swampers*, as the expected volunteers were called, would surely desert the cause. There was no deciding—there was no delaying: the army marched unconscious what step was next to be taken. General Gates, however, began to perceive the danger of approaching an enemy of whose numbers he had no certain intelligence, encumbered as he was with an enormous train of heavy baggage, a multitude of women, and not a few children. An effort was therefore formed under Major Dean, and a number of wagons were appointed to convey to Charlotte all the heavy baggage, and as many of the women as could be driven from the line; many of the latter, however, preferred sharing every toil and every danger with the soldiery, to the security and provisions that were promised them. The army advanced, but, approaching the enemy's post on Little Lynch's creek, it was discovered by good intelligence to be situated on the south side of the water, on commanding ground; that the way leading to it was over a causeway on the north side to a wooden bridge, which stood on very steep banks; and that the creek lay in a deep, muddy channel, bounded on the north by an extensive swamp, and passable nowhere for several miles but in the face of the enemy's work. The enemy was not disposed to abandon these advantages, without feeling the pulse of the approaching army; and General Gates observed that, to attack him in front, "would be taking the bull by the horns." It was necessary, for once, to depart from the shortest route to the enemy's principal outpost, Camden. The army defiled by the right, and Colonel Hall, of Maryland, with a detachment of about three hundred men, covered the left flank until it was out of danger from surprise, and then formed the rear-guard. This manœuvre, on the 11th of August, induced the garrison to retire with some precipitation to Camden, and about the same time the British garrison which had occupied Clermont (or Rugley's mills), on the north road, retired to the same place.

Lord Rawdon, who commanded the advanced corps of the British army, wisely collected his whole force at Camden, which, besides being flanked by the river Wateree and Pinetree creek, was considerably strengthened by a number of redoubts.

As his lordship's emissaries were in all parts of the country, he could not fail to be informed that General Gates was in his neighborhood with a brigade of regular troops and two brigades of militia, besides some small corps of artillery and cavalry; that Brigadier-General Stevens was on the same route with a brigade of Virginia militia; that Colonel Marion below, and Colonel Sumter above Camden, were stimulating their countrymen to reassume their arms; and that, in short, the whole country were ready to revolt from the allegiance which had been extorted from them but a few weeks before. He therefore permitted General Gates to march unmolested to Clermont (where the Americans encamped on the 13th), and employed his men in strengthening his post for defence, until reinforrements might arrive from Charleston, where Lord Cornwallis was left in command, Sir Henry Clinton having returned to New York soon after the reduction of the former city.

Brigadier-General Stevens arrived with his Virginians at Clermont on the 14th, and encamped with the rest of the army. On the same day (or the 15th) an inhabitant of Camden came, as if by accident, into the American encampment, and was conducted to headquarters. He affected ignorance of the approach of the Americans, pretended very great friendship for his countrymen the Marylanders, and promised the general to be out again in a few days with all the information the general wished to obtain. The information which he then gave was the truth, but not all the truth, which events afterward revealed; yet, so plausible was his manner, that General Gates dismissed him, with many promises if he would faithfully observe his engagements. Suspicions arose in the breasts of some of the officers about headquarters that this man's errand was easily accomplished; the credulity of the general was not arraigned, but it was conceived that it would have been prudent to have detained the man for further acquaintance.

Colonel Sumter, of the South-Carolina militia, had intelligence that an escort with clothing, ammunition, and other stores, for the troops at Camden, was on the road from Charleston, by way of M'Cord's ferry on the Congaree, and that it would necessarily pass the Wateree at a ferry about a mile from the town, under cover of a redoubt on the opposite side of the river. This intelligence he communicated to the general, requesting a small reinforcement of infantry and two small pieces of artillery to join his volunteers, promising to intercept the convoy. The colonel's accurate knowledge of the geography of the country, and the qualities of the men who were his followers, favored the execution of this enterprise. The general ordered a detachment of one hundred regular infantry, and a party of artillery with two brass field-pieces, under Lieutenant-Colonel Woolford, to join Colonel Sumter, and act under his command.

To attract the attention of the garrison in Camden, if they did not choose to retire—which seemed to be but too confidently expected—and to facilitate the execution of the little expedition under Sumter, all other objects seemed to be suspended.

The only stores which were forwarded to the army by General Stevens were a few articles of West-India produce, the principal of which was molasses. No supply of provisions of any sort was collected more than to serve from day to day. The obscure route the army had marched actually kept their friends ignorant of their movements; and the arrival of General Gates at Clermont was, when known, a subject of more surprise to the patriots than to the enemies of the country. It is probable, and in the opinion of many a matter of no doubt whatever, that if General Gates had taken a secure position with his army, and waited only a few days, abundance of provisions would have flowed into his camp; and that, by the addition of volunteers from the Carolinas, he would have acquired such a superiority over the British army, which did not much exceed four thousand men, that he would have found no difficulty in recovering the country as far as Charleston: but opinions are fruitless. On the 15th of August, 1780, General Gates issued the following:—

After General Orders.—"The sick, the extra artillery stores, the heavy baggage, and such quartermaster's stores as are not immediately wanted, to march this evening, under a guard, to Waxhaws.

"To this order the general requests the brigadier-generals to see that those under their command pay the most exact and scrupulous obedience.

"Lieutenant-Colonel Edmonds, with the remaining guns of the park, will take post and march with the Virginia brigade, under General Stevens; he will direct, as any deficiency happens in the artillery affixed to the other brigades, to supply it immediately; his military staff and a proportion of his officers, with forty of his men, are to attend him and await his orders.

"The troops will be ready to march precisely at ten o'clock, in the following order, viz.:—

"Colonel Armand's advance; cavalry commanded by Colonel Armand; Colonel Porterfield's light infantry upon the right flank of Colonel Armand, in Indian file, two hundred yards from the road; Major Armstrong's light infantry in the same order as Colonel Porterfield's, upon the left flank of the legion.

"Advance guard of foot, composed of the advanced pickets, first brigade of Maryland, second brigade of Maryland, division of North Carolina, Virginia division; rear-guard, volunteer cavalry, upon the flank of the baggage, equally divided.

"In this order the troops will proceed on their march this night.

"In case of an attack by the enemy's cavalry in front, the light infantry upon each flank will instantly move up, and give and continue the most galling fire upon the enemy's horse. This will enable Colonel Armand not only to support the shock of the enemy's charge, but finally to rout them; the colonel will therefore consider the order to stand the attack of the enemy's cavalry, be their numbers what they may, as positive.

"General Stevens will immediately order one captain, two lieutenants, one ensign, three sergeants, one drum, and sixty rank and file, to join Colonel Porterfield's infantry; these are to be taken from the most experienced woodsmen, and men every way the fittest for the service.

"General Caswell will likewise complete Major Armstrong's light infantry to their original number. These must be immediately marched to the advanced posts of the army.

"The troops will observe the profoundest silence upon the march; and any soldier who offers to fire without the command of his officer, must be instantly put to death.

"When the ground will admit of it, and the near approach of the enemy renders it necessary, the army will (when ordered) march in columns.

"The artillery at the head of their respective brigades, and the baggage in the rear.

"The guard of the heavy baggage will be composed of the remaining officers and soldiers of the artillery, one captain, two subalterns, four sergeants, one drum, and sixty rank and file; and no person whatever is to presume to send any other soldier upon that service.

"All bat-men, waiters, &c., who are soldiers taken from the line, are forthwith to join their regiments, and act with their masters while they are upon duty.

"The tents of the whole army are to be struck at tattoo."

After writing this order, the general communicated it to the deputy adjutant-general, showing him, at the same time, a rough estimate of the forces under his command, making them upward of seven thousand. That this calculation was exaggerated the deputy adjutant-general could not but suspect, from his own observation. He therefore availed himself of the general's orders, to call all the general officers in the army to a council to be held in Rugley's barn—to call also upon the commanding officers of corps for a field return, in making which they were to be as exact as possible; and, as he was not required to attend the council, he busied himself in collecting these returns and forming an abstract for the general's better information. This abstract was presented to the general just as the council broke up, and immediately upon his coming out of the door. He cast his eyes upon the numbers of rank and file present fit for duty, which was exactly *three thousand and fifty-two*. He said there were no less than *thirteen* general officers in council; and intimated something about the disproportion between the numbers of officers and privates. It was replied, "Sir, the number of the latter is certainly much below the estimate formed this morning."—"But," said the general, "these are enough for our purpose." What that was, was not communicated to the deputy adjutant-general. The general only added, "There was no dissenting voice in the council, where the orders have just been read"—and then gave them to be published to the army.

Although there had been no dissenting voice in the council, the orders were no sooner promulgated than they became the subject of animadversion. Even those who had been dumb in council, said that there had been no consultation; that the orders were read to them, and all opinion seemed suppressed by the very positive and decisive terms in which they were expressed. Others could not imagine how it could be conceived that an army, consisting of more than two thirds militia, and which had never been once exercised in arms together, could form columns, and perform other manœuvres in the night, and in the face of an enemy. But, of all the officers, Colonel Armand took the greatest exception. He seemed to think the *positive* orders respecting himself implied a doubt of his courage; declared that cavalry had never before been put in the front of a line of battle in the dark; and that the disposition, as it respected his corps, proceeded from resentment in the general, on account of a previous altercation between them about horses, which the general had ordered to be taken from the officers of the army to expedite the movement of the artillery through the wilderness. A great deal was said upon the occasion; but the time was short, and the officers and soldiers generally not knowing or believing, any more than the general, that any considerable body of the enemy were to be met with out of Camden, acquiesced with their usual cheerfulness, and were ready to march at the hour appointed.

As there were no spirits yet arrived in camp, and as until lately it was unusual for troops to make a forced march, or prepare to meet an enemy, without some extraordinary allowance, it was unluckily conceived that molasses would, for once, be an acceptable substitute: accordingly the hospital stores were broached, and one gill of molasses per man, and a full ration of corn-meal and meat, were issued to the army previous to their march, which commenced, according to orders, at about ten o'clock at night of the 15th. (But I must arrest the progress of the narrative to apologize for introducing a remark seemingly so trivial. Nothing ought to be considered as trivial in an army which in any degree affects the health or spirits of the troops; upon which often, more than upon numbers, the fate of battles depends. The troops of General Gates's army had frequently felt the bad consequences of eating bad provision; but at this time, a hasty meal of quick-baked bread and fresh beef, with a dessert of molasses mixed with mush or dumplings, operated so cathartically as to disorder very many of the men, who were breaking the ranks all night, and were certainly much debilitated before the action commenced in the morning.)

It has been observed that the direct march of the American army toward Camden, and the prospect of considerable reinforcements of militia, had induced the commanding officer, Lord Rawdon, to collect there all the forces under his direction; and it is certain that the seeming confidence of the American general had inspired him with apprehensions for his principal post. Lord Cornwallis, at Charleston, was constantly advised of the posture of affairs in the interior of the country; and, confident that Lord Rawdon could not long resist the forces that might and probably would be opposed to him in a very short time, resolved to march himself, with a considerable reinforcement, to Camden. He arrived there on the 14th, and had the discernment at once to perceive that delay would render that situation dangerous, even to his whole force—the disaffection from his late assumed, arbitrary, and vindictive power, having become general through all the country above General Gates's line of march, as well as to the eastward of Santee and to the westward of Wateree rivers. He therefore took the resolution of attacking the newly-constituted American army in their open, irregular encampment at Clermont. Both armies, ignorant of each other's intentions, moved about the same hour of the same night, and approaching each other, met about half way between their respective encampments at midnight.

The first revelation of this new and unexpected scene was occasioned by a smart mutual salutation of small-arms between the advanced guards. Some of the cavalry of Armand's legion were wounded, retreated, and threw the whole corps into disorder—which, recoiling suddenly on the front of the column of infantry, disordered the first Maryland brigade, and occasioned a general consternation through the whole line of the army. The light infantry under Porterfield, however, executed their orders gallantly; and the enemy, no less astonished than ourselves, seemed to acquiesce in a sudden suspension of hostilities. Some prisoners were taken on both sides. From one of these the deputy adjutant-general of the American army extorted information respecting the situation and numbers of the enemy. He informed that Lord Cornwallis commanded in person about three thousand regular British troops, which were in line of march about five or six hundred yards in front. Order was soon restored in the corps of infantry in the American army, and the officers were employed in forming a front line of battle, when the deputy adjutant-general communicated to General Gates the information which he had from the prisoner. The general's astonishment could not be concealed. He ordered the deputy adjutant-general to call another council of war. All the general officers immediately assembled in the rear of the line. The unwelcome news was communicated to them. General Gates said, "Gentlemen, what is best to be done?" All were mute for a few moments, when the gallant Stevens exclaimed, "Gentlemen, is it not too late *now* to do anything but fight?" No other advice was offered, and the general desired that the gentlemen would repair to their respective commands.

The baron De Kalb's opinion may be inferred from the following fact. When the deputy adjutant-general went to call him to council, he first told him what had been discovered. "Well," said the baron, "and has the general given you orders to retreat the army?" The baron, however, did not oppose the suggestion of General Stevens, and every measure that ensued was preparatory for action.

Lieutenant-Colonel Porterfield, in whose bravery and judicious conduct great dependence was placed, received in the first rencontre a mortal wound (as it long afterward proved), and was obliged to retire. His infantry bravely kept the ground in front, and the American army was formed in the following order: the Maryland division, including the Delawares, on the right; the North-Carolina militia in the centre; and the Virginia militia on the left. It happened that each flank was covered by a marsh, so near as to admit the removing of the first Maryland brigade to form a second line, about two hundred yards in the rear of the first. The artillery was removed from the centre of the brigades, and placed in the centre of the front line; and the North-Carolina militia (light infantry), under Major Armstrong, which had retreated at the first rencontre, was ordered to cover a small interval between the left wing and the swampy grounds on that quarter.

Frequent skirmishes happened during the night between the advanced parties, which served to discover the relative situations of the two armies, and as a prelude to what was to take place in the morning

At dawn of day (on the morning of the 16th of August) the enemy appeared in front, advancing in column. Captain Singleton, who commanded some pieces of artillery, observed to Colonel Williams that he plainly perceived the ground of the British uniform at about two hundred yards in front. The deputy adjutant-general immediately ordered Captain Singleton to open his battery, and then rode to the general, who was in the rear of the second line, and informed him of the cause of the firing which he heard. He also observed to the general that the enemy seemed to be displaying their column by the right; the nature of the ground favored this conjecture, for yet nothing was clear.

The general seemed disposed to wait events; he gave no orders. The deputy adjutant-general observed that if the enemy, in the act of displaying, were briskly attacked by General Stevens's brigade, which was already in line of battle, the effect might be fortunate, and first impressions were important. "Sir," said the general, "that's right—let it be done." This was the last order that the deputy adjutant-general received. He hastened to General Stevens, who instantly advanced with his brigade, apparently in fine spirits. The right wing of the enemy was soon discovered *in line;* it was too late to attack them displaying; nevertheless, the business of the day could no longer be deferred. The deputy adjutant-general requested General Stevens to let him have forty or fifty privates, volunteers, who would run forward of the brigade and commence the attack. They were led forward within forty or fifty yards of the enemy, and ordered to take trees and keep up as brisk a fire as possible. The desired effect of this expedient—to extort the enemy's fire at some distance, in order to the rendering it less terrible to the militia—was not gained. General Stevens, observing the enemy to rush on, put his men in mind of their bayonets; but the impetuosity with which they advanced, firing and huzzaing, threw the whole body of the militia into such a panic, that they generally threw down their *loaded* arms and fled in the utmost consternation! The unworthy example of the Virginians was almost instantly followed by the North-Carolinians; only a small part of the brigade, commanded by Brigadier-General Gregory, made a short pause. A part of Dixon's regiment, of that brigade, next in the line to the second Maryland brigade, fired two or three rounds of cartridge. But a great majority of the militia (at least two thirds of the army) fled without firing a shot. The writer avers it of his own knowledge, having seen and observed every part of the army, from left to right, during the action. He who has never seen the effect of a panic upon a multitude, can have but an imperfect idea of such a thing. The best disciplined troops have been enervated and made cowards by it. Armies have been routed by it, even where no enemy appeared to furnish an excuse. Like electricity, it operates instantaneously—like sympathy, it is irresistible where it touches.

But, in the present instance, its action was not universal. The regular troops, who had the keen edge of sensibility rubbed off by strict discipline and hard service, saw the confusion with but little emotion.

They engaged seriously in the affair; and, notwithstanding some irregularity, which was created by the militia breaking pell-mell through the second line, order was restored there time enough to give the enemy a severe check, which abated the fury of their assault, and obliged them to assume a more deliberate manner of acting. The second Maryland brigade, including the battalion of Delawares, on the right, were engaged with the enemy's left, which they opposed with very great firmness. They even advanced upon them, and had taken a number of prisoners, when their companions of the first brigade (which formed the second line), being greatly outflanked, and charged by superior numbers, were obliged to give ground. At this critical moment the regimental officers of the latter brigade, reluctant to leave the field without orders, inquired for their commanding officer (Brigadier-General Smallwood), who, however, was not to be found; notwithstanding, Colonel Gunby, Major Anderson, and a number of other brave officers, assisted by the deputy adjutant-general, and Major Jones, one of Smallwood's aids, rallied the brigade, and renewed the contest. Again they were obliged to give way, and were again rallied; the second brigade were still warmly engaged; the distance between the two brigades did not exceed two hundred yards, their opposite flanks being nearly upon a line perpendicular to their front. At this eventful juncture the deputy adjutant-general, anxious that the communication between them should be preserved, and wishing that, in the almost certain event of a retreat, some order might be sustained by them, hastened from the first to the second brigade, which he found precisely in the same circumstances. He called upon his own regiment (the sixth Maryland) not to fly, and was answered by the lieutenant-colonel, Ford, who said—"They have done all that can be expected of them; we are outnumbered and outflanked. See, the enemy charge with bayonets." The enemy, having collected their corps, and directing their whole force against these two devoted brigades, a tremendous fire of musketry was for some time kept up on both sides, with equal perseverance and obstinacy, until Lord Cornwallis, perceiving that there was no cavalry opposed to him, pushed forward his dragoons—and his infantry charging at the same moment with fixed bayonets, put an end to the contest. His victory was complete. All the artillery and a very great number of prisoners fell into his hands; many fine fellows lay on the field, and the rout of the remainder was entire. Not even a company retired in any order; every one escaped as he could.

If, in this affair, the militia fled too soon, the regulars may be thought almost as blamable for remaining too long on the field, especially after all hope of victory must have been despaired of. Let the commandants of the brigades answer for themselves. Allow the same privilege to the officers of the corps comprising those brigades, and they will say that they never received orders to retreat, nor any order from any *general* officer, from the commencement of the action until it became desperate. The brave major-general, the baron De Kalb, fought on foot, with the second brigade, and fell, mortally wounded, into the hands of the enemy, who stripped him even of his shirt—a fate which probably was avoided by other generals only by an opportune retreat.

The torrent of unarmed militia bore away with it Generals Gates, Caswell, and a number of others, who *soon* saw that all was lost. General Gates at first conceived a hope that he might rally at Clermont a sufficient number to cover the retreat of the regulars; but, the farther they fled, the more they were dispersed, and the generals soon found themselves abandoned by all but their aids.

Lieutenant-Colonel Senf, who had been on the expedition with Colonel Sumter, returned, and overtaking General Gates, informed him of their complete success; that the enemy's redoubt on the Wateree, opposite to Camden, was first reduced, and the convoy of stores, &c., from Charleston, was decoyed and became a prize to the American party almost without resistance; that upward of one hundred prisoners and forty loaded wagons were in the hands of the party, who had sustained very little loss. But the general could avail himself nothing of this trifling advantage. The detachment under Sumter was on the opposite side of the Wateree, marching off as speedily as might be, to secure their booty, for the course of the firing in the morning indicated unfavorable news from the army.

The militia, the general saw, were in air; and the regulars, he feared, were no more. The dreadful thunder of artillery and musketry had ceased, and none of his friends appeared. There was no existing corps with which the victorious detachment might unite, and the Americans had no post in the rear. He therefore sent orders to Sumter to retire in the best manner he could, and proceeded himself with General Caswell toward Charlotte, an open village on a plain, about sixty miles from the fatal scene of action. The Virginians, who knew nothing of the country they were in, involuntarily reversed the route they came, and fled, most of them, to Hillsborough. General Stevens followed them, and halted there as many as were not sufficiently refreshed, before his arrival, to pursue their way home. Their terms of service, however, being very short, and no prospect presenting itself to afford another proof of their courage, General Stevens soon afterward discharged them.

The North-Carolina militia fled different ways, as their hopes led or their fears drove them. Most of them preferring the shortest way home, scattered through the wilderness which lies between the Wateree and Pedee rivers, and thence toward Roanoke. Whatever these might have suffered from the disaffected, they were probably not worse off than those who retired the way they came—wherein they met many of their friends, armed, and advancing to join the American army; but, learning its fate from the refugees, they acted decidedly in concert with the victors—and capturing some, plundering others, and maltreating all the fugitives they met, returned exultingly home. They even added taunts to their perfidy: one of a party, who robbed Brigadier-

General Butler of his sword, consoled him by saying, "You'll have no further use for it."

The regular troops, it has been observed, were the last to quit the field. Every corps was broken and dispersed; even the bogs and brush, which in some measure served to screen them from their furious pursuers, separated them from one another. Major Anderson was the only officer who fortunately rallied, as he retreated, a few men of different companies, and whose prudence and firmness afforded protection to those who joined his party on the route.

Colonel Gunby, Lieutenant-Colonel Howard, Captain Kirkwood, and Captain Dobson, with a few other officers, and fifty or sixty men, formed a junction on the route, and proceeded together.

The general order for moving off the heavy baggage, &c., to Waxhaws, was not put in execution, as directed to be done, on the preceding evening. The whole of it consequently fell into the hands of the enemy, as well as all that which followed the army, except the wagons of General Gates and De Kalb, which, being furnished with the stoutest horses, fortunately escaped, under the protection of a small quarter-guard. Other wagons also had got out of danger from the enemy; but the cries of the women and the wounded in the rear, and the consternation of the flying troops, so alarmed some of the wagoners, that they cut out their teams, and taking each a horse, left the rest for the next that should come. Others were obliged to give up their horses to assist in carrying off the wounded; and the whole road for many miles was strewed with signals of distress, confusion, and dismay.

What added not a little to this calamitous scene was the conduct of Armand's legion. They were principally foreigners, and some of them probably not unaccustomed to such scenes. Whether it was owing to the disgust of the colonel at general orders, or the cowardice of his men, is not with the writer to determine; but certain it is that the legion did not take any part in the action of the 16th; they retired early and in disorder, and were seen plundering the baggage of the army on their retreat. One of them cut Captain Lemar, of the Maryland infantry, over the hand, for attempting to reclaim his own portmanteau, which the fellow was taking out of the wagon. Captain Lemar was unarmed, having broken his sword in action, and was obliged to submit both to the loss and to the insult. The tent-covers were thrown off the wagons generally, and the baggage exposed, so that one might take what suited him to carry off. General Caswell's mess-wagon afforded the best refreshment: very unexpectedly to the writer, he there found a pipe of good Madeira, broached and surrounded by a number of soldiers, whose appearance led him to inquire what engaged their attention. He acknowledges that in this instance he shared the booty, and took a draught of wine, which was the only refreshment he had received that day.

But the catastrophe being over, before we pursue a detail of all its distressing consequences, it may be excusable to consider whether the measures which led to the necessity of fighting a general battle were justifiable, and whether such an event might not have been avoided at almost any time before the two armies were actually opposed.

If General Gates *intended* to risk a general action, conscious of all circumstances, he certainly made that risk under every possible disadvantage; and a contemplation of those circumstances would seem to justify Colonel Armand's assertion, made in the afternoon of the day in which the battle was fought: "I will not," said he, "say that we have been betrayed; but if it had been the purpose of the general to sacrifice his army, what could he have done more effectually to have answered that purpose?"

General Gates, however, notwithstanding his after order of the 15th, had, in the opinion of most of his officers, and particularly of the writer, no more apprehension of meeting the enemy in force than the least-informed man of his army. The circuitous route, first recommended to him, would certainly have been the safest and best. Magazines, an armory, a hospital, and even fortified posts, might have been established, without halting the effective force of the army—posts to which they might, in case of disaster, have retired under protection of the patriotic militia of Mecklenburg and Roan counties, who only wanted time to join the army in respectable numbers. Such at least were their subsequent declarations, and such their subsequent conduct rendered most probable.

But, even on the route the army had marched, the danger of meeting an enemy of equal or superior force was passed when they got into the vicinity of the Wateree, and in the neighborhood of their friends. It was only necessary for General Gates to have been informed of the march of Lord Cornwallis from Charleston, to have avoided, almost as long as he pleased, a conflict between the two armies.

In the opinion of the writer it was not too late, even after Lord Cornwallis reached Camden. If, instead of meeting him involuntarily, General Gates had been informed of his intended movement, and quietly in the afternoon of the 15th have followed with his whole army the detachment under Woolford, over the Wateree, it would have been impossible for the armies to have met until the next day, and after the success of Sumter's expedition. If his lordship should then have thought of forcing a passage over the Wateree, General Gates would have had the alternative of opposing him under that disadvantage, or of retiring to any position he might prefer higher up the river. Lord Cornwallis could not have adventured the passage of the river much above Gates's army, because, the river being fordable in many places, his garrison and magazines at Camden would have been jeoparded: the forces he could afford to leave for its defence would have been insufficient for half a day; and, if the *post* and its *stores* had been gained by the Americans, the British army, destitute of supplies, would have been obliged to retire toward Charleston. On the other hand, if his lordship should keep his post in his rear, he must consequently leave the communication open between the American army and their friends in the uppe country, which would have rendered more practicable the avoiding of a general engagement. But these are subsequent reflections on measures, the idea of which perhaps never occurred nor was suggested to the general. Involved as he was in the necessity of fighting, the disposition which was made for battle, after the alarm, was perhaps unexceptionable, and as well adapted to the situation as if the ground had been reconnoitred and chosen by the ablest officer in the army of the United States. (It was afterward approved by the judicious and gallant General GREENE, to whom the writer had the solemn pleasure of showing the field of battle, and with whom he had the additional mortification of participating the danger and disgrace of a repulse near the same place, the very next campaign.)

The only apology that General Gates condescended to make to the army for the loss of the battle was, "A man *may* pit a cock, but he can't *make* him fight; the fate of battle is uncontrollable"—and such other common maxims as admit of no contradiction.

It is, however, morally certain, considering the disposition of the citizens generally, and the respectable body of militia that had already joined the army, that *time* was, of all things, the most important to the success of General Gates's army.

Lord Cornwallis, conscious of this truth, and of the disadvantage which the least lapse would prove to him, seized the first moment to hasten the decision of an experiment which was to gain or lose the country, for that season at least—perhaps for ever.

Generals Gates and Caswell arrived at Charlotte on the night of the action. The ensuing morning presented nothing to them but an open village, with but few inhabitants, and the remains of a temporary hospital, containing a few maimed soldiers of Colonel Buford's unfortunate corps, which had been cut to pieces on the retreat, after the surrender of Charleston.

General Caswell was requested to remain there, to encourage the militia of the country, who were to rendezvous there in three days (as it was first intended), to countenance the reassembling of the American army. General Gates perceived no effectual succor short of Hillsborough, where the general assembly of North Carolina were about to convene; thither he repaired with all possible expedition, and was followed the next day by General Caswell, who despaired of the meeting of the militia—probably because he thought that their first object, the army, was annihilated.

On the two days succeeding the fatal action, Brigadier-General Gist, who commanded the second brigade of Maryland troops previous to its misfortune at Charlotte, arrived with only two or three attendants, who had fallen into his route. Several field officers and many officers of the line also arrived, similarly circumstanced; and, although not more than about a dozen men of different corps arrived in irregular squads from time to time, not less than one hundred infantry were collected in the village within that time, besides Armand's cavalry, which was very little reduced, and a small corps of mounted militia, which retired from the Waxhaw settlement, under the command of Major Davy, an enterprising and gallant young man who had been raising volunteer cavalry to join the army. Very few of the fugitive militia resorted to this place.

Fortunately, there was a small supply of provisions in the town; the inhabitants did all they could to refresh both men and officers; and by the provident care of Colonel Hall, of Maryland, a quantity of flour was sent back on the route of the retreating troops.

Brigadier-General Smallwood, who had the honor of the second line, or *corps de reserve*, assigned him in the late action, deliberately came in on the morning (or about noon) of the 18th, escorted by one of his aids-de-camp, two or three other gentlemen, and about as many soldiers, all mounted. His route was by way of the Wateree.

The small squads assembled by Major Anderson and the other officers already mentioned were on the direct route. The latter were not yet arrived, but were hourly expected; and afforded, in addition to those already collected and those with Colonel Sumter, a prospect of forming such a body as might still encourage the militia to form at least the semblance of an army, which might keep up some appearance of opposition until the resources of the Union could be called forth by Congress or by the states most immediately interested.

An incident which occasioned great distress the next day must be here related. It has been observed that many of the wagoners and retreating troops accelerated their flight by taking horses from the wagons which were left on the route. In this way many wounded officers and soldiers made their escape, and bore with astonishing fortitude the pains incident to their situation. They gave, indeed (some of them), proofs of the utmost pain and fatigue that the human constitution can bear; others sank under their accumulated distresses. Those who arrived at Charlotte were taken the best possible care of; the horses were turned out to graze in the adjacent fields, no forage being provided. It should have been remarked that the tribe of Catawba Indians, good friends to the Americans, quitted their villages on the Wateree, and followed the remnant of the army toward the town of Charlotte, where many of them had already arrived. Some of them, in their irregular way, fired a number of guns after nightfall on the 18th, which gave a very general alarm, and many of the people fled in the night, taking as many of the horses as they could find or had occasion for.

Another incident, much more consequential! The morning of the 19th was fair, and the officers were assembling about the public square and encouraging one another with hopes of a more favorable course of affairs than had been current for some time past, when they received unquestionable information that Colonel Sumter, whose arrival they looked for every moment, was completely surprised the preceding day and the whole party killed, captured, or dispersed! Dead or alive, he was censured for suffering *a surprise.*

No organization nor order had yet been attempted to be restored among the few troops that had arrived in Charlotte; the privates were therefore hastily formed into ranks, and the officers were among themselves adjusting the commands to be taken by them respectively, when the number of supernumerary officers was discovered to be very considerable. Every one, however, took some charge upon himself. The care of the wounded, the collection of provisions, the transportation of the heavy baggage (preserved by Major Dean's small guard), and other matters which might in any way alleviate the general distress, engaged the attention of those who had no division of the men.

There was no council, nor regular opinion taken respecting this irksome situation. The general idea was that Charlotte, an open, wooded village, without magazines of any sort, without a second cartridge per man, and without a second ration, was not tenable for an hour against superior numbers which might enter at every quarter. Moreover, it was estimated by those who knew the geography of the country, that even the victorious enemy might be in the vicinity of the place. It was admitted by every one that no place could be more defenceless.

Only one officer, who was of the legion, proposed a temporary defence, by pulling down the houses and forming a redoubt, which might induce the enemy to grant a capitulation. No respect was paid to this destructive proposition, and the first suggestion prevailed.

Difficulties almost innumerable presented themselves to obstruct a march. Several officers with small parties were known to be on the route from Camden; some refugees might possibly escape from Sumter's detachment; many of the wounded were obliged to be left in the old hospital, dependent probably on the enemy or on a few of the inhabitants who were unable to retire; and even some who might have have got off on horseback were deprived of the means by the alarming incident of the preceding night. Were all these to be abandoned?

Time was never more important to a set of wretches than now; but how to take it—whether "by the forelock," as the adage is, or wait its more propitious moments—none of us could decisively resolve. Brigadier-General Smallwood, who quartered himself at a farmhouse a little way from town, appeared at this crisis approaching the parade in his usual slow pace. As senior officer, his orders would have been obeyed, even to setting about fortifying the village; but being informed of what has just been related, and concurring in the general sentiment, he leisurely put himself at the head of the party and moved off toward Salisbury. The deputy adjutant-general and Brigade-Major Davidson took the route to Camden, in order to direct all they might meet to file off toward Salisbury. The small parties that had attached themselves to Colonel Gunby and Colonel Howard were met near town, and an express was sent to Major Anderson, who had, to no purpose, spent some time in endeavors to bring off some wagons which had escaped beyond the pursuit of the enemy and were left without horses. By noon a very lengthy line of march occupied the road from Charlotte to Salisbury. It consisted of the wretched remnant of the late southern army, a great number of distressed whig families, and the whole tribe of Catawba Indians (about three hundred in number, some fifty or sixty of whom were warriors, but indifferently armed). Among the rest were six soldiers who had left the hospitals with other convalescents; they had all suffered in Buford's unfortunate affair, and had but two sound arms among them—indeed, four of them had *not* one arm among them, and two only an arm apiece: each of them had one linen garment. Those officers and men who were recently wounded, and had resolution to undertake the fatigue, were differently transported—some in wagons, some in litters, and some on horseback. Their sufferings were indescribable. The distresses of the women and children who fled from Charlotte and its neighborhood—the nakedness of the Indians, and the number of their infants and aged persons—and the disorder of the whole line of march—conspired to render it a scene too picturesque and complicated for description. A just representation would exhibit an image of compound wretchedness; care, anxiety, pain, poverty, hurry, confusion, humiliation, and dejection, would be characteristic traits in the mortifying picture.

The inhabitants who had fled with their families soon began to disperse and take refuge among their friends in the interior of the country. The Catawbas had a district of country assigned them for hunting-grounds in North Carolina. Brigadier-General Smallwood continued the march of the regular infantry to Salisbury, and arrived the third day after. Armand's legion proceeded as they threatened when it was resolved to evacuate Charlotte: "If," said one of the officers, "you will make de retreat, we will retreat faster dan you!" They proceeded to Hillsborough. The fertility of the country between Charlotte and Salisbury, the hospitality and benevolence of the inhabitants, and the numbers of their habitations on the route, afforded in many instances that relief which was requisite to preserve life, besides a liberal supply of provisions for all this cavalcade.

It is not known whether, if the Americans had not evacuated Charlotte, Lord Cornwallis would not have made it an object to dispossess them; but as it was, his lordship contented himself with having defeated the southern army, driven it out of South Carolina, and cut up the only detachment respectable enough to afford a head to which the patriots of the country might assemble. His lordship certainly gave the world another instance in proof of the assertion that it is not every general, upon whom fortune bestows her favors, who knows how to avail himself of all the advantages which are presented to him. Victory is not always attended—perhaps never—with all the superiority it seems to bestow. The British army retired to Camden.

So unexpected an event gave the poor Americans time to breathe. General Smallwood halted his party at Salisbury, selected about one hundred and fifty effective men, and sent the remainder, perhaps fifty or sixty more, over the Yadkin river, with the wagons, women, &c. The effectives he officered according to his pleasure, and permitted the field officers, particularly those who had not formerly belonged to his brigade, to proceed to Hillsborough. Hall, Williams, and Howard, were of the number, who availed themselves at their leisure of this permission. At Salisbury, one hundred and twenty or thirty miles from the scene of the late action, Smallwood took time to dictate those letters which he addressed to Congress, and in which he intimated the great difficulties he had encountered and the exertions he had made to save a remnant of General Gates's army—letters which, with the aid of those he addressed to his friends in power, procured him, it was generally believed in the line, the rank of *major*-general in the army of the United States, and which probably prompted the resolution of Congress directing an inquiry into the conduct of General Gates. But many of the officers wrote to their friends from Salisbury, and being chagrined and mortified at not overtaking their commanding general in so long a retreat, expressed themselves with great disgust and freedom.

Major Anderson, who casually heard of the retreat of the detachment that had surprised Sumter, proceeded to Charlotte, where he found the militia inspirited by a change of circumstances, disposed to organize themselves, and form such corps as might protect the country from the incursions of the enemy, which might be expected from Camden. They requested the major to remain at Charlotte, and through him invited General Smallwood to return, importuning him, and even offering him the chief command of the militia of Mecklenburg—General Caswell, their countryman, having, as they alleged, abandoned them even before the expiration of the three days in which he had ordered them to assemble at Charlotte.

General Smallwood, however, declined the honor of this invitation, and sent orders to Major Anderson to join him without delay at Salisbury; and in order that these instructions might not be dispensed with on any pretence whatever, Lieutenant-Colonel Ford, the particular friend of Anderson, was charged with them and with directions to expedite the march of the party. The order was executed, and the mortified militia were left to depend upon their own exertions and their own fortitude, which, notwithstanding the discouragements they had met with, did not fail. They assembled, formed themselves into small partisan corps—and actually combated successfully the first detachments of the enemy that afterward came into their country. These are facts which entitle the patriots of Mecklenburg and Waxhaws to a whole page of eulogium in the best history that shall record the circumstances of the revolution.

The unfortunate General Gates, at Hillsborough, where the assembly of the state had convened, hearing from the officers who arrived there that the disasters of the army were not so completely ruinous as he had at first apprehended, applied himself assiduously to the legislature for the supplies necessary to re-equip the regular troops. But what supplies, or rather the quantum, that would be requisite, the general could not ascertain, having received no returns or reports of any kind from General Smallwood, who seemed to assume the command of the army.

In order therefore to obtain the requisite information, and to decide at once the doubt about command, General Gates wrote explicitly to General Smallwood, and ordered him to pass the Yadkin river with all the men under his command, and to proceed on the direct route to Hillsborough. This order had been anticipated: it was received by General Smallwood after he had passed the Yadkin and was on his march to Guilford Courthouse, on the route directed. At Guilford the troops were halted for refreshment; and, as there was a great plenty of provisions in the neighborhood, General Smallwood, without regarding the instructions he had received from General Gates, wrote to *the assembly of the state*, intimating that, with *their* approbation, he would continue there until other arrangements should be resolved on. The assembly properly declined interfering in matters which might involve a question of authority between two continental officers, and referred the proposition of General Smallwood to General Gates. General Gates did not entirely disapprove of the execution of the proposition, but in his letter to General Smallwood he required that certain returns, &c., should be forwarded to him without delay, and gave such explicit intimations that he was not disposed to relinquish his command of the southern army, as to induce General Smallwood to suspend for the present his hopes of succeeding thereto. He therefore marched immediately to Hillsborough, where he arrived with the tattered remains of the army early in the month of September. Thus ended the campaign of 1780.

A NARRATIVE OF EVENTS RELATIVE TO THE SOUTHERN ARMY, SUBSEQUENT TO THE ARRIVAL OF GENERAL GATES'S BROKEN BATTALIONS AT HILLSBOROUGH, 1780.

Hillsborough had been a place of rendezvous for all the militia raised in the interior of North Carolina, and a stage of refreshment for all the troops which had marched from the northward to succor Charleston or reinforce the southern army; consequently the resources of the country had been collected and generally applied. What remained did not afford an ample supply even for the fugitives of the late army, which were now collected in the town, and were cantoned, some in the houses of the inhabitants, and some in tents pitched near the courthouse, where the assembly of the state was convened. The assembly saw and regretted the wants of the troops, and did all that was then practicable for their relief. A comfortable supply of fresh meat, corn-meal, and wheat-flour was procured for the hospital, and the rest of the men were subsisted by provisions furnished by state commissaries in part and partly by the old expedient of collecting by detachments—an expedient which gave great umbrage to the country.

At this time Lord Cornwallis was with the principal part of his army at Camden, where his own wounded and those of the American army were very differently treated.

The worse than savage system of severity suggested by the malice of the king's minister, or conceived by the malignity of the king himself, which had been so fatally practised upon the prisoners in New York and Philadelphia, was now practised with equal barbarity on the prisoners taken in the southern department. Everywhere they were treated with cruel neglect or insolent severity. The difference of climates made some difference in consequences.

The same treatment, or rather worse, was suffered by the inhabitants of the country who had ever been in arms, or were even suspected of disloyalty. Some who were accused of having received protections and violated the conditions were hung *without any form of trial!* Prompt punishments for supposed crimes were inflicted at the will of superior officers in the different British garrisons, and every measure was adopted which the arrogance of power could devise, to subjugate the minds as well as the privileges of the people. The want of energy in the union of the United States and the imbecility of the states themselves gave great latitude to the effect of the British measures. Their emissaries were in all parts of the country, and were but too successful in the lower counties of North Carolina, where the inhabitants, except in and near the seaport towns, began to be generally disaffected to the American cause. Even in Chatham county a considerable body took arms and threatened to disperse the assembly of the state from Hillsborough. Indeed, so serious was the alarm upon this occasion, that to guard against a surprise of the town on a night when the insurgents were confidently expected, all the troops were kept under arms the whole night. As no arrangement had yet taken place, General Gates desired Colonel Williams to command them. The inhabitants were ordered to arm, and even the members of the assembly thought it incumbent on them to arm themselves also. The following fact may illustrate their character, as well for patriotism as soldiership:—

It was requested that a regular officer would lend his assistance in arranging the militia. The members of the assembly were collected near the courthouse (the seat of government), and were arming themselves when the officer arrived, who, taking them for the militia who stood in need of an adjutant, began the exercise of that office, and marshalled them in a manner which showed no respect for them as legislators. No exception, however, was taken to the conduct of the officer. The circumstance was mentioned afterward, only as one of those ludicrous incidents (and there were many) which occurred during the night of the alarm. Although the alarm proved false, it proved no less certain that the enterprise might have been effected by a few brave men, even on that very night. The hurry and confusion which it occa sioned discovered the expediency of re-establishing order among the troops, and every other man seemed to feel the obligation of giving his assistance as well to provide for present necessities as against future contingencies. Influenced by motives not to be disregarded, the government of North Carolina soon began to exert all its powers. The second class of the militia were ordered to assemble immediately; commissaries, quartermasters, and agents, with extensive powers, were appointed to procure every article requisite for another campaign; and, for want of funds (for the paper-money of the United States was now depreciated below calculation), these officers were authorized to take, on the account of government, all military stores, arms, provisions, clothing, &c., that were to be found, and to grant receipts or certificates for the same.

Notwithstanding that the disasters of the southern army, and a sense of common danger, had seemingly obliterated all recollection of former differences and animosities among the officers of the regular corps, it ought not to be dissembled that such were among the causes which, for a little time, postponed the new organization of the troops.

What cause General Gates had to apprehend being superseded in the command of the southern army, may be conjectured by those who have a knowledge of the facts; but what reason General Smallwood could have to hope to become his successor, none who are not grossly imposed on can possibly imagine.

The misunderstanding between these two officers was never, I believe, avowed; but, as Gates reassumed his command, Smallwood retired from it.

General Gist was not ambitious of the command of men so circumstanced; and, in fact, many other officers wished for an opportunity of returning home without a laurel or a scar.

A board of officers, convened by order of General Gates, determined that all the effective men should be formed into two battalions, constituting one regiment, to be completely officered, and provided for in the best possible manner that circumstances would admit. The sick and convalescent were to remain, but all the invalids were to be sent home; and the supernumerary officers were to repair to their respective states, to assist in the recruiting service.

The command of the newly-formed regiment was given to Colonel Williams and Lieutenant-Colonel Howard. Majors Anderson and Hardman commanded the battalions.

No sooner were these officers invested with command, than they began to restore order and discipline among the troops; and the colonel, who was inspector of the Maryland division of the army of the United States (comprehending the quota of Delaware also), demanded a general order, before any of the officers should depart, for the most correct returns that could be made under present circumstances, accounting as well for the men as for their arms, accoutrements, &c., &c. The latter part of the order could not be complied with in any satisfactory degree;

17

but after some time, the officers, by comparing notes and recollecting circumstances, rendered returns, from which the following abstracts were taken :—

Total of Maryland troops: Three colonels, four lieutenant-colonels, five majors, thirty-eight captains, fifty subalterns, twenty-four staff-officers, eighty-five non-commissioned officers, sixty-two musicians, and seven hundred and eighty-one rank and file.

The numbers which were killed, captured, and missing, since the last muster, could not with any accuracy be ascertained. The aggregate was—three lieutenant-colonels, two majors, fifteen captains, thirteen subalterns, two staff-officers, fifty-two non-commissioned officers, thirty-four musicians, and seven hundred and eleven rank and file. These, at least a very great majority of them, and all of them for aught I know, fell in the field, or into the hands of the enemy, on the fatal 16th of August. It is extremely probable that the number killed much exceeded the number taken prisoners.

The Delaware regiment being mustered, the returns stood thus: Four captains, seven subalterns, three staff-officers, nineteen non-commissioned officers, eleven musicians, and one hundred and forty-five rank and file, in actual service, &c., &c., &c. Eleven commissioned officers and thirty-six privates of the Delaware regiment fell into the hands of the enemy.

These details may not be unessential to those who have been concerned in the affairs of the late campaign, and may give satisfaction to those of my friends who may wish hereafter to have a true knowledge of circumstances.

The inhabitants of Hillsborough soon began to experience and complain of the inconvenience of having soldiers billeted among them; and the officers were equally sensible of the difficulty of restraining the licentiousness of the soldiers, when not immediately under their observation. Williams therefore drew his regiment out of town, distributing the few tents he had among the several companies. He encamped on a vacant farm, or rather in the woodland belonging to it, and covered his men with wigwams made of fence-rails, poles, and corn-tops, regularly disposed. The tents were chiefly occupied by the officers, but as they were all much worn, wigwams were soon preferred, on account of their being much warmer.

The usual camp guards and sentinels being posted, no person could come into or go out of camp without a permit. Parade duties were regularly attended, as well by officers as soldiers, and discipline not only began to be perfectly restored, but even gave an air of stability and confidence to the regiment, which all their rags could not disguise. In this encampment no circumstance of want or distress was admitted as an excuse for relaxing from the strictest discipline, to which the soldiers the more cheerfully submitted, as they saw their officers constantly occupied in procuring for them whatever was attainable in their situation.

Absolutely without pay, almost destitute of clothing, often with only a half ration, and never with a whole one (without substituting one article for another), not a soldier was heard to murmur after the third or fourth day of their being encamped. Instead of meeting and conferring in small, sullen squads, as they had formerly done, they filled up the intervals from duty with manly exercises and field-sports; in short, the officers had very soon the entire confidence of the men, who divested themselves of all unnecessary care, and devoted themselves to duty and pastime, within the limits assigned them.

The docility and contentment of the troops were the more extraordinary, as they were not unfrequently reminded (when permitted to go into the country) how differently the British troops were provided for.

The article of rum, the most desirable refreshment to soldiers, was mentioned among other inducements for them to desert; but so great was their fidelity to the cause, or so strong their attachment to their fellow sufferers and soldiers, that they not only rejected the most flattering propositions to go over to the enemy, but they absolutely brought some of the most bold and importunate incendiaries into camp, who were delivered to the civil authority, and some of them punished.

If any of my friends should inquire why I descend to particulars so minute and unimportant, I answer that I am not writing a history of the revolution, nor of the proceedings of government; and that it is *not* unimportant for any officer to observe every incident in the life and conduct of a soldier which may in any degree serve to illustrate his disposition. The general characteristic of a corps should never be mistaken, by the commanding officer especially. Misunderstandings often arise from it, and the consequences are usually what might be expected—unfavorable to both officers and men.

The legion commanded by Armand was, on the 8th of September, sent to forage and make cantonments in Warren county, whence Armand went to Philadelphia, and never returned.

General Gates did not conceal his opinion that he held cavalry in no estimation in the southern field. If he judged by the conduct of the legion, he ought to have confined his opinion to that corps particularly, for subsequent experience has evinced that no opinion could have been more erroneous.

Two brass field-pieces, which General Gates had left under a small guard at Buffalo ford, for want of horses, the first day of his march after taking the command, were brought to camp with a few iron pieces picked up at Hillsborough, and formed a little park in the centre of the ragged regiment of Maryland and Delaware troops, which constituted *the southern army* until the 16th of September, when Colonel Buford arrived from Virginia with the mangled remains of his unfortunate regiment, reinforced by about two hundred raw recruits, all of them in a ragged condition. Uniforms and other clothing were to be sent after them, but never arrived.

About the same time a small detachment of Virginia militia arrived, without even arms

On the 18th, the relics of Porterfield's corps, about fifty effective men, arrived under the command of Captain Drew, and joined Buford. Thus the remainder of those corps which had been recently cut to pieces, without being recruited or refurnished with clothing, camp equi page, &c., necessary for a campaign, were hastily assembled to form the head of an army to act against their conquerors.

The body of the proposed army was to consist of militia—the second class principally of those very militia who had so shamefully abandoned some of these same regulars at Camden but a few weeks before.

Confident hopes were, notwithstanding, entertained that the interior of the two Carolinas might be defended from the ravages of the enemy until Congress might gain time and find means to do something more effectual.

The officers and the men began to recover their usual spirits. Brigadier-General Smallwood, weary of waiting events at obscure quarters, and dissatisfied (as every officer of *real merit* naturally is) of rank without command in time of war, suggested that, as there were two nominal regiments and a company of artillery encamped, a nominal brigade might be formed, of which he claimed the command, and was gratified. Captain Anthony Singleton, of Virginia, commanded the artillery.

About this time, Colonel Morgan, of Virginia, whose heroic conduct under General Montgomery at Quebec, General Gates at Saratoga, and in other meritorious actions, will secure him an honorable page in the history of the war in the north, arrived at camp, without command, and with only two or three young gentlemen attending him.

The perfect security which Lord Cornwallis imagined resulted to his posts and to the communications between them, and the presumption that all the lower part of the country was in a state of absolute subjection and tranquillity, in consequence of his extraordinary not to say accidental success, induced him to send a small guard from Camden to convey one hundred and fifty of his prisoners, principally regulars, to Charleston.

Colonel Marion, of South Carolina, who has been mentioned in the previous part of these narratives, and who ought always to be mentioned with respect, had been stimulating his countrymen to act in concert with General Gates, until after the unfortunate 16th of August, when he and his followers were obliged to secrete themselves in the swamps and deserts which intersect a considerable part of the lower country. From one of these hiding-places Marion suddenly fell upon the British guard, surprised, and made the whole of them prisoners. He paroled the officers, and took a list of the privates to be exchanged. The American soldiers he sent off, with proper guides, to Wilmington, having first distributed among them the arms of their captors. A circumstance so honorable for a small squad of militia, particularly for their commanding officer, ought long to be remembered with admiration. Marion and his men retook to the swamps.

On the report in camp of this fortunate event, Lieutenant-Colonel Commandant Ford, who had not availed himself of the permission for supernumeraries to return home, went to Wilmington to meet the released captives, and to conduct them to camp; but as they had been subject to very little or no control after their releasement, being without any of their own officers, and doubting of the existence of any considerable body of their fellow-soldiers, many of them repaired home with all the expedition they could make. Colonel Ford did not recover more than about one half of the number released by Marion; and these, from their sufferings in captivity, their long and circuitous march from Camden to Wilmington, and thence by Cross creek to Hillsborough, and their want of almost all the necessaries of life, were very little fit for service.

While the American troops were collecting at Hillsborough, measures were taken by the state of North Carolina to expedite the embodying of the second class of their militia.

To intimidate the people from complying with the requisitions of government to collect forage and provisions, and probably with an expectation of striking terror through the country, Lord Cornwallis moved from Camden (in October) with a considerable body of troops, lightly equipped, which he led immediately to the town of Charlotte, and thence manœuvred about the country as far north as Phifer's mills. But, although his lordship could and would go where he pleased, he found himself much less at ease in this part of the country than in any other situation he had experienced. The militia of Mecklenberg and of Roan, the most inflexible whigs in the whole state, were continually in his presence. He could make no movement without being observed; no negligence could be committed on his part of which they did not take advantage. Major Davie, with his mounted volunteers, equipped as dragoons, sometimes intercepted his convoys of provisions, sometimes disturbed his pickets, and even once or twice insulted the van of his army on its march. These, however, were feeble and ineffectual resistances. His lordship could "go where he pleased."

This incursion of his lordship into the strongest part of the state stimulated the exertions of the legislature in measures to organize and equip their militia for the field. They began to rendezvous in considerable numbers at Salisbury. Smallwood was complimented with a request of the executive to take command of them, Caswell's confidence in the courage of his countrymen not being yet restored; and it was presumed that the militia would act with more subordination and perhaps with more bravery under a continental general than under one of their own neighbors. After making some conditions about horses for himself and his suite, the general accepted the honor.

At the same time it was contemplated to send forward as many of the regular troops as could be tolerably equipped for service; and it fortunately happened that at that time the state agents had forwarded to Hillsborough a small supply of coarse clothing and other articles convenient for the purpose.

General Gates ordered a committee to attend to the equitable distribution of these stores among the regular corps. But first, an appropriation was to be made for equipping four companies of light infantry to be drafted from the regiments, and destined to form a part of the corps to be sent in advance.

The execution of this part of the plan commenced on the 19th of October, the day the clothing arrived, and was very soon completed. The four companies of infantry were formed into one battalion, the command of which was obtained by Lieutenant-Colonel Howard.

About the 2d of November, Lieutenant-Colonels White and Washington came to camp with a very few effectives of the first and third regiments of dragoons, which had also been surprised, routed, defeated, and cut to pieces, the preceding spring. White had leave to go to Philadelphia, and Washington remained in command of the remnants of both corps, consisting of sixty or seventy effectives.

These corps joined the light infantry on their march toward Charlotte. A small corps of riflemen (say sixty), under Major Rose, had also joined the light infantry at Hillsborough. The gallant Colonel Morgan then took the command of a l the light troops, and proceeded with them toward Charlotte. He found the militia, under Smallwood, advanced as far as the Old Trading ford on the Yadkin river, seven miles from Salisbury, in safety. Lord Cornwallis, without any known adequate cause, thought proper to retire through Charlotte, cross the Wateree river, and encamp at Winnsborough. It is not probable that he was deceived by any exaggerated account of the newly-levied militia, nor is it probable that he had any fears from the relics of the corps which he had so recently cut to pieces. His lordship had been fatigued by the insolence of the volunteers, and chose to retire to a camp of repose.

Colonel Williams succeeded General Smallwood in the command of the brigade of continental troops. The diminution of its numbers, by the draft of four companies of light infantry, was in part restored by the arrival of recruits from Maryland and Virginia. These were constantly at the drill. A laboratory was erected, and employed in mending arms; and the residue of the clothing, &c., was distributed. Each man in the brigade was supplied with one new shirt, a short coat, a pair of woollen overalls, a pair of shoes, and a hat or a cap. The dividend of blankets was very inadequate to the occasion; they were apportioned to the companies: and every other practicable provision was made to prepare the brigade for the field. The officers exerted themselves, and the soldiers were emulous who should be the first in readiness to march. Even the convalescents were impatient of being left behind, so generally had the martial spirit revived in the soldiery.

The brigade marched on the second day of November, immediately after the light dragoons, with two brass field-pieces, some ammunition-wagons, and a small train of baggage. They followed the route of the light infantry to Charlotte, where they encamped.

The militia under Smallwood had apparently taken a permanent position at Providence, about fourteen miles south of Charlotte; and Morgan, now brigadier-general, was itinerant with his infantry about the Wateree.

Lord Cornwallis continued with the principal part of his forces at Winnsborough, and kept up the garrisons of Camden and Clermont.

Such were the relative situations of the two armies, when General GREENE arrived at Charlotte, on the 4th of December, 1780.

CHARLOTTE.—When General Gates had reviewed and contemplated his situation at Charlotte, he considered it the most eligible place to encamp for the winter with the principal part of his army. The light troops were to keep the field, and to act as an advance-guard. With this view, he ordered preparations to be made for building huts, and directed General Morgan to make a foraging excursion toward Camden. On the very day of General Greene's arrival, and after he had assumed the command of the army, Morgan reported that he had made a tour into the country, in the vicinity of Camden, but found the cattle were taken off, and so little grain or forage left, as to make it scarcely worth the fatigue of the troops; but that, fortunately, an event had taken place which made some compensation for their toil.

Mr. Rugely, proprietor of the farm called Clermont, had obtained the rank of lieutenant-colonel in the British army, and had obtained that of major for his son-in-law. These two officers, with about one hundred British troops and new levies, occupied a large log barn (the old council-chamber), which they fortified by a slight entrenchment and a line of abattis, so as to render it impregnable to small-arms. This post was on the left of Morgan's route, as he returned from foraging, but too near to Camden for him to risk anything like a siege or blockade. It was suggested that the cavalry might go and reconnoitre it. Washington, pleased with the idea, approached so near as to ascertain that the enemy had discovered him and were intimidated. He humorously ordered his men to plant the trunk of an old pine-tree, in the manner of a field-piece, pointing toward the garrison; at the same time, dismounting some of his men to appear as infantry, and displaying his cavalry to the best advantage, he sent a corporal of dragoons to summon the commanding officer to an immediate surrender. The order was executed in so firm a manner, that Colonel Rugely did not hesitate to comply instantly; and the whole garrison marched out prisoners-of-war.

The corporal was made a sergeant of dragoons; the old fort was set on fire; and Washington retired with his prisoners without exchanging a shot.

Soldiers, like sailors, have always a little superstition about them. Although neither General Gates nor General Greene could be considered as having any agency in this little successful affair, it was regarded by some, and even mentioned, as a presage of the future good fortune which the army would derive from the genius of the latter. But I have superseded my old friend rather abruptly, and with almost as little ceremony as it was directed by Congress. As I approach the close of this narrative, I assume the epistolary style, in which I intend to make all my future remarks, as they may thus be more easily transcribed for communication.

The letters which were addressed to Congress, respecting the overthrow of his whole army, were so vague and unsatisfactory, and others which were written were so disingenuous, that it was conceived by Congress absolutely requisite to have a full inquiry into the circumstances of the campaign and the conduct of the commanding officer.

General Washington was requested to nominate an officer to supersede General Gates; and it was resolved that a court of inquiry should be held, of which Major-General the Baron Steuben was appointed president. General Greene, whom General Washington distinguished by an election to the command of the southern army, arrived at headquarters, as before observed, on the 4th of December, 1780, with full powers.

A manly resignation marked the conduct of General Gates on the arrival of his successor, whom he received at headquarters with that liberal and gentlemanly air which was habitual to him.

General Greene observed a plain, candid, respectful manner, neither betraying compassion nor the want of it; nothing like the pride of official consequence even *seemed.* In short, the officers who were present had an elegant lesson of propriety exhibited on a most delicate and interesting occasion.

General Greene was announced to the army as commanding officer by General Gates; and the same day General Greene addressed the army, in which address he paid General Gates the compliment of confirming all his standing orders.

The detention of the baron Steuben in Virginia, and no major-general being present or authorized to serve in his stead, made it impracticable to hold the court of inquiry at this time or place. General Gates therefore, with the approbation of General Greene, repaired to Philadelphia, in order to meet the charges and to counteract the calumnies against him.

I can not conclude this narrative without remarking that a soldier's fame is always precarious during his life. If General Gates had fallen at the commencement of the action of Camden, who would not have acceded to the opinion that the disasters of the day were owing principally to that circumstance? The laurels of Saratoga would have been ever green on his tomb, and history would have exulted in the merits of the hero!

What difference, in point of real merit, would there have been (or could there be) between falling by an early, accidental shot, or submitting to the irresistible impulse of the militia, who went like a torrent from the field, forcing almost everything before them? And yet, what a difference in the public opinion! Instead of praises, panegyric, and monumental honors, he was censured, calumniated, and even condemned, unheard.

The severity of this treatment was aggravated by a recent event, which was carefully kept from his knowledge while in camp, but which too soon overwhelmed him in distress. His only son, an elegant young man, well educated, and just entering into active scenes of life, was suddenly cut off by the stroke of death.

None but an unfortunate soldier, and a father left childless, could assimilate his feelings to those of this unhappy gentleman; yet many sympathized with him, remembered his former public services, wished for the return of tranquillity to his afflicted mind, and hoped even for a restoration of his honors.

General Greene took great pains to collect the best information relative to the circumstances of the late campaign; and his communications to influential characters finally determined Congress to rescind their resolution respecting General Gates, and to restore him to his command in the northern army.

www.ingramcontent.com/pod-product-compliance
Lightning Source LLC
LaVergne TN
LVHW020117110826
845151LV00001B/183

* 9 7 8 1 4 2 5 5 4 2 4 9 8 *